# Ethnicity and Inequality in Hawai‘i

Jonathan Y. Okamura

TEMPLE UNIVERSITY PRESS
1601 North Broad Street
Philadelphia PA 19122
www.temple.edu/tempress


Published 2008
Printed in the United States of America

∞ The paper used in this publication meets the requirements of the American National Standard for Information Sciences—Permanence of Paper for Printed Library Materials, ANSI Z39.48-1992

Library of Congress Cataloging-in-Publication Data
Okamura, Jonathan Y.
Ethnicity and inequality in Hawai'i / Jonathan Y. Okamura.
p. cm.—(Asian American history and culture)
Includes bibliographical references and index.
ISBN-13: 978-1-59213-755-8 (cloth : alk. paper)
ISBN-13: 978-1-59213-756-5 (pbk. : alk. paper)
1. Ethnology—Hawaii. 2. Ethnic groups—Hawaii. 3. Minorities—Hawaii. 4. Hawaii—Ethnic relations. 5. Hawaii—Social conditions. I. Title.
DU624.6.O53 2008
305.8009969—dc22
2007041300

4 6 8 9 7 5 3

052010P

For M. G. Smith

# Contents

# Preface

I have long wanted to write this book. As a high school student, after my family had moved in 1964 to what would eventually become Silicon Valley, California, I naively offered to write an essay on ethnic inequality in Hawai'i for *Life* magazine. I recall being very disappointed that such a major magazine did not even reply to my letter, especially since my mother had been a faithful subscriber for more than a decade. Forty years, a high school diploma, and two degrees in anthropology later, I am probably better qualified to address the problem of ethnic inequality that not surprisingly is still with us in Hawai'i. Thus, I am primarily concerned herein with how ethnic inequality is maintained in the islands; beyond that research issue, I am personally concerned with how ethnic inequality can be eliminated or at least significantly reduced. I would like to believe that *Ethnicity and Inequality in Hawai'i* provides a means for addressing these two issues, not only as an academic book but also as a work that can contribute to community discussion and action toward fostering a more equal Hawai'i, particularly for those who remain subjugated and marginalized.

I need to acknowledge the contributions of a number of individuals who have enabled me in different ways to complete the writing of this book. I am especially grateful to Michael Omi who urged and encouraged me for nearly a decade to write a book on ethnic relations in Hawai'i. I particularly appreciate his very critical comments, thought-provoking questions, and suggestions for major revisions of my manuscript that he made in his capacity as one of the editors of the Asian American History and Culture series of Temple University Press. I am also thankful for the useful comments and suggested revisions made by the other (anonymous) reviewer. I was especially fortunate to be able to work with Janet Francendese, editor in chief of Temple University Press, who has been a delight from the very beginning. I am very thankful to her for facilitating a prompt review of my manuscript by the reviewers and the Temple University Press faculty board.

I extend my grateful appreciation to a number of friends who critically read chapter drafts, made comments and discussed them with me. They include several of my fellow Ethnic Studies faculty members at the University of Hawai'i (UH) at Manoa: Ibrahim Aoude, Monisha Das Gupta, Noel Kent, and Ty Tengan. Other friends who did the same are Rick Baldoz, Joyce Chinen, Mary Yu Danico, Rod Labrador, Franklin Ng, and John Rosa. I fortunately was able to draw upon their considerable expertise and knowledge of ethnicity and ethnic relations in Hawai'i and of other subjects as well. In addition to Noel Kent's and Ibrahim Aoude's suggestions regarding this work, I have also benefited from years of ongoing discussions with them on many of the topics discussed in this book. I also would like to acknowledge several other friends of mine at UH Manoa who, while not contributing directly to my writing this book, have nonetheless assisted in its completion through their support of my work in general over the years. They include Leonard Andaya, Candace Fujikane, Christine Quemuel, Karen Umemoto, and Geoff White.

Portions of a few chapters were presented at national conferences, including the Association for Asian American Studies (AAAS) annual conferences in 2005 and 2007 and the Filipino American National Historical Society biennial conference in 2006. I am especially grateful to August Espiritu for the very helpful comments he made regarding my paper while serving as the discussant of a panel I organized for the 2005 AAAS conference.

As for research assistance, I thank Karen Oki and Pancho Delos Santos for diligently gathering newspaper articles on the arrest and execution of Filipinos from microfilm records. I also benefited from the discussions I had with a few of my graduate students who were doing research on topics similar to some of those addressed in this book. They include Juri Ishikawa, who wrote a fine master's thesis on *yonsei* (fourth-generation) Japanese American women in Hawai'i; Yukari Akamine, who is doing dissertation research in sociology on Okinawan identity; and Brandon Ledward, who completed a highly informative PhD thesis in anthropology on *hapahaole* Hawaiians (those with European ancestry and phenotypic traits).

Finally, I express my appreciation to my wife, Cynthia, for allowing me the time and space to work on this book. I also thank our daughter, Mika, who graduated from college in 2007 with a double major in anthropology and

Asian American studies (neither at my urging), for providing me with insights on yonsei youth culture.

This book is dedicated to the late Prof. M. G. Smith who was my graduate supervisor in the Department of Anthropology at University College London when I went there in 1972. Prof. Smith's work on pluralism and the plural society was one of the main reasons that I went to London to study social anthropology. I was extremely fortunate to have had weekly tutorial sessions with him as the major part of my training in social anthropology. The theories and concepts developed in his books—such as *The Plural Society in the British West Indies* (1965a), *Stratification in Grenada* (1965b), *Pluralism in Africa* (1969, coedited with Leo Kuper), *Corporations and Society* (1975), and *Culture, Race and Class in the Commonwealth Caribbean* (1984)—have been major theoretical influences on my thinking about issues pertaining to race, ethnicity, and stratification and are clearly reflected in the arguments and analyses presented in this book. Beyond the considerable influence of his prodigious scholarship on mine, I greatly appreciate the personal support and encouragement he extended to me over the years.

# 1
# Introduction

At a 2005 University of Hawaiʻi (UH) Board of Regents meeting in Honolulu, I presented testimony in opposition to proposed tuition increases throughout the UH system. My argument was based on knowledge of how disastrous the consequences had been for Hawaiʻi students, especially ethnic minorities, when tuition was raised substantially in 1996 and 1997. In the three minutes I was allowed to speak before the Regents, I pointed out that after those tuition hikes, enrollment in the UH system plummeted from 50,000 to 45,000 students within three years. At our flagship UH Manoa campus, it declined from 19,800 to 17,000 students and took eight years to recover to the previous level. While all ethnic groups in Hawaiʻi were adversely impacted by the tuition increases, underrepresented minorities—such as Filipino Americans and Native Hawaiians, the two largest groups in the public school system—suffered much greater losses. I emphasized to the Regents that Filipino American enrollment in the UH system had decreased from 7,500 to 6,000 students within three years and was still more than 1,000 students lower than in 1995.

Spring commencement ceremonies at UH Manoa had been held the previous Sunday, so I told the Regents about an interview I had seen on the evening news with a Native Hawaiian female graduate and her parents. Surrounded by many of her relatives and friends, the lei-bedecked young woman said she was the first member of her family to attend college and that she planned to continue on to graduate school. Her parents spoke about how proud they were of her and how they wished she would be a role model for her younger siblings who would be encouraged by her example also to attend college. They mentioned how "expensive" they found it to send their daughter to UH Manoa, and I noted that this was the case even though as a Native Hawaiian student she had access to federal financial assistance provided by the Native Hawaiian Higher Education Act. If this family found the tuition costly now, I asked, how much more expensive would it be for them with annual increases of $816 for six consecutive years?

My allotted time was rapidly expiring, so I concluded my testimony by asking the Regents to review their own policy on "Nondiscrimination and Affirmative Action" before voting on the tuition increase. Since I would not have been surprised if most of them had never read or even heard of this policy, I quoted it as stating: "The University of Hawai'i is an equal opportunity/affirmative action institution and is committed to a policy of nondiscrimination on the bases of race, sex, age, religion, color . . ." I told the Regents that if they approved the tuition increases, they would be contradicting their own policy to provide equal access to the university, since massive tuition hikes would inevitably result in significantly decreased minority student admission and enrollment.[1]

My arguments, and those of others who expressed their opposition to raising tuition, fell on deaf ears and minds that were very likely already decided. I was not very surprised when, after nearly three hours of testimony, the Regents voted unanimously in favor of the proposed higher tuition. In their comments during a short discussion before voting, most of them noted their concern for the financial stability of the university and maintained that the tuition increases would generate funds needed to replace stagnating appropriations from the state government. Although many of the Regents are corporate executives or have business backgrounds, none of them asked the UH vice president, who presented the administration's tuition proposal, the basic question of whether students would continue to enroll at their current level if tuition was raised substantially.[2] Or in terms of operating a business, the Regents probably did not ask themselves if customers would continue to buy a product if its price increased 140 percent in six years.

The decision of the UH Board of Regents to approve a hefty tuition hike is yet another example of how and why ethnic inequality is maintained in Hawai'i. As a publicly supported institution, the University of Hawai'i should be one of the primary means by which socioeconomically disadvantaged minorities—such as Native Hawaiians, Filipino Americans, and Samoans—can advance themselves. Already substantially underrepresented in the UH system and together constituting a majority of public school students, these groups were further excluded after tuition was raised beginning in fall 2006.

As discussed in Chapter 4, "Educational Inequality and Ethnicity," I consider policy decisions such as that by the UH Board of Regents to be manifestations of institutional discrimination against ethnic minorities insofar as these groups are subject to unequal or unfair treatment through these policies. It might be argued that all Hawai'i residents must pay the higher tuition if they wish to attend UH, so how can the Regents' decision to increase tuition be considered discriminatory, especially if we assume that they did not intend to discriminate against any ethnic group? The reason is that not all ethnic groups have the financial means to meet the higher cost of tuition; consequently, ethnic minorities are impacted much more adversely compared to the more socioeconomically privileged groups such as Chinese Americans, Whites, and Japanese Americans. These groups have the financial resources to pay the increased tuition or to send their children to universities in the continental United States and thus to maintain their dominant social status in Hawai'i.

In this book, I discuss other ways by which ethnic inequality and hierarchy are perpetuated in Hawai'i. While ethnic relations clearly have improved since World War II, they have not progressed sufficiently for a substantial proportion of Hawaii's people who continue to be denied the privileges, benefits, and resources that are enjoyed by the more socioeconomically advantaged ethnic groups. I do not disagree that ethnic inequality in Hawai'i has become less severe during the past sixty years and that opportunities (for example, in higher education) have been created for ethnic minorities that were extremely restricted—and, for some groups, virtually nonexistent—prior to the war. However, ethnic inequality has not been sufficiently reduced and, since the 1970s, has become further entrenched due to the state's overdependence on tourism and the ongoing globalization of Hawaii's economy. Socioeconomic mobility into the middle class that was very possible during the two decades after World War II for Chinese Americans, Japanese Americans, and Korean Americans, all of whom started life in Hawai'i on the plantations, has become much more difficult for other ethnic minorities to attain.

My purpose in writing this book is both personal and academic. Personally, I am concerned about social equality and social justice for aggrieved ethnic minorities in Hawai'i. Their continuing subjugation is not being adequately addressed by government, the private sector, and the larger society and, in fact, is being obscured by academic analyses, journalistic descriptions, and cultural representations that glorify Hawai'i as a unique model of ethnic amity and equality. As someone whose family has had the good fortune to live in Hawai'i since 1885, I am personally committed to fostering equality, justice, and opportunity for all the people who consider the islands their home. While clearly an academic work, *Ethnicity and Inequality in Hawai'i* also expresses my personal advocacy and concern for a qualitatively better society in Hawai'i where ethnicity is not a restrictive barrier to individual dreams and collective goals.

My scholarly reason for writing this book is to provide an analysis of how ethnic inequality is maintained in Hawai'i. I argue that ethnicity, as the dominant organizing principle of social relations in Hawai'i society, structures inequality among ethnic groups in various institutional domains, such as education and the economy. Following sociologists Melvin L. Oliver and Thomas M. Shapiro in *Black Wealth/White Wealth* (2006: 23), I view inequality in its "material aspects" as consisting of "disparities in life chances and command over economic resources," such as income and education, among ethnic groups. Through their concept of the "sedimentation of racial inequality," Oliver and Shapiro (5) emphasize how disparities, particularly in wealth between African Americans and Whites, have accumulated over time and thus persisted "generation after generation." As the authors observe, "The cumulative effect of such a process has been to sediment blacks at the bottom of the social hierarchy," while "[w]hites in general . . . were able to amass assets and use their secure economic status to pass their wealth from generation to generation" (53). Similarly, the effects of ethnic inequality in Hawai'i are also cumulative and transmitted from one generation to the next, although with markedly different consequences for dominant and subordinate groups.[3] In addition to differences in wealth, ethnic inequality is evident in the lack of collective social mobility by minority groups and thus the persistence of the socioeconomic status hierarchy among ethnic groups in Hawai'i since the 1970s. Besides operating as a structural principle, ethnicity contributes to the maintenance of ethnic inequality by serving as a cultural representation of ethnic groups; these representations include the ethnic identities that are ascribed to groups, such as through denigrating stereotypes.

I discuss ethnic identity construction as a potential means that ethnic groups can employ to alleviate their unequal social status in Hawai'i. Some groups, particularly those that are politically or economically disadvantaged such as Native Hawaiians, create and articulate distinct identities for themselves in order to advance their political or economic interests. In contrast, other ethnic minorities—such as Filipino Americans and Samoans—encounter great difficulty in employing ethnic identity formation as a way to promote their collective concerns because of the stigmatizing stereotypes and other representations that tend to dominate their identity in Hawai'i. Furthermore, the privileged ethnic groups—such as Japanese Americans and Chinese Americans—do not have to resort to constructing particular ethnic identities for themselves since they have other means and resources to maintain their dominant economic and political status in society.

With regard to theoretical perspectives that inform my analysis of ethnic inequality in Hawai'i, race theorist Howard Winant in *The New Politics of Race* (2004: ix) contends that, "Race is situated at the crossroads of identity and social structure, where difference frames inequality." Winant's provocative argument derives from his and race relations scholar Michael Omi's concept of racial project insofar as such projects perform the "ideological work" of establishing links between representation (of which identity is a major form) and structure (Omi and Winant 1994: 56). The second part of Winant's 2004 argument is also based on the distinction and linkage between representation and structure, since difference can be culturally represented and inequality is socially structured. Along these lines, Omi and Winant (1994: 57) have maintained that "race continues to signify difference and structure inequality." If ethnicity is substituted for race, this latter assertion has much relevance for my argument concerning the relation between ethnicity and inequality in Hawai'i. Ethnicity certainly signifies difference in Hawai'i, particularly cultural differences that are evident in the diverse and changing ethnic identities of island groups that can be considered cultural representations, either by the ethnic groups themselves (as asserted identities) or by other groups (as assigned identities). Ethnicity also structures inequality in regulating differential access to resources, rewards, and privileges among ethnic groups.

Adapting Winant's argument (2004: ix) to the Hawai'i situation, I contend that ethnicity is situated at the intersection of ethnic identity and social structure where ethnic difference frames inequality. Ethnicity is operative at this conjuncture since it serves as both cultural representation and structural principle. As a form of cultural representation, ethnicity—particularly ethnic identity—signifies difference among ethnic groups that hold unequal status in the social structure of Hawai'i society. In this sense, ethnic difference demarcates or frames inequality; that is, socioeconomic inequality in Hawai'i is understood predominantly as ethnic inequality because ethnicity is the primary structural principle of social relations. In a society in which race or class is the dominant organizing principle, racial or class difference frames the inequality among its constituent groups (that is, races or classes) and socioeconomic inequality is viewed as either racial or class inequality.

The intersection of ethnic identity and social structure reinforces each other, and thus ethnic inequality, by enhancing the framing of inequality based on ethnic difference. However, this conjunction has differential consequences for different ethnic groups, depending on their relative social status in society. It serves to maintain the socioeconomically advantaged groups in their privileged position, while sustaining the subjugation of the socioeconomically subordinate groups. Ethnic identity construction provides a means for the latter ethnic groups to contest their disadvantaged social status by seeking to disrupt the intersection of ethnic identity and social structure by representing themselves with identities of their own making. Ethnic identity formation thus can be employed by at least some groups to subvert the maintenance of ethnic inequality in society.

My analyses concerning the nature of ethnicity and ethnic relations differ substantially from those of other scholars who contend that Hawai'i is truly the "Aloha State," distinguished by its egalitarian, tolerant, and harmonious ethnic relations. Such arguments only perpetuate the ethnic status order and thus the power and privilege of the dominant groups—Chinese Americans, Whites, and Japanese Americans—and conversely the subjugation of Native Hawaiians, Filipino Americans, Samoans, and other ethnic minorities. In advancing my understanding of ethnic inequality in Hawai'i, one of the major obstacles I have encountered is the prevalent view of the islands as a virtual paradise of ethnic relations and as a multicultural model for other racially and ethnically diverse societies. But before discussing the "Hawai'i multicultural model," I need to explain my emphasis on ethnicity rather than race in analyzing inequality in Hawai'i.

## Why Ethnicity, Not Race?

My concern is with ethnicity and ethnic relations in Hawai'i rather than with race and race relations. In focusing on ethnicity, I do not argue for the declining significance of race in the United States, nor do I support the ethnicity paradigm that seeks to reduce race to an element of ethnicity (see Omi and Winant 1994: 20). Instead, I emphasize that in Hawai'i, ethnicity, as opposed to race (or class), is the primary structural principle of social relations. This is because the groups that comprise island society—for example, Filipino Americans, Samoans, Whites, and Puerto Ricans—are socially constructed as ethnic rather than racial groups. In other words, people in Hawai'i attribute greater social significance to the presumed cultural differences that distinguish groups from one another than to their phenotypic differences such as skin color. As ethnic groups, they are believed to differ culturally in terms of their respective values, practices, beliefs, and customs, although these differences have diminished markedly over the generations.[4] Clearly, much of the traditional culture, particularly language, that was practiced by Native Hawaiians or brought by immigrant groups during the period of plantation labor recruitment (1852–1946) has been lost by their descendants, and assimilation into "local" and a generalized American culture has occurred.

In contrast, phenotypic differences, including skin and hair color, are not considered by Hawaii's people to be as socially significant as cultural differences in distinguishing groups from each other.[5] This is probably because there is a considerable overlap in skin color and hair color among most of the non-White ethnic groups that makes using such physical indicators problematic as defining criteria, even if those phenotypic differences are subjectively perceived rather than objectively defined. Even Haoles or Whites, the largest "racial" group in Hawai'i, are believed to differ from non-White groups primarily because of cultural differences more than because of their skin color.

This understanding is evident in the long-term distinction made between Haoles and locals insofar as the former are perceived as nonlocal to some extent because they do not practice local culture, and particularly because they do not speak "pidgin" or Hawai'i Creole English.

Another reason for the comparative nonsignificance of race in Hawai'i is that its constituent groups—Japanese Americans (25 percent), Filipino Americans (23 percent), Native Hawaiians (20 percent), and Chinese Americans (15 percent)—are major segments of island society compared to their counterparts in the continental United States (Hawai'i Department of Business and Economic Development and Tourism 2003b). In California, these four groups constitute 1.2, 3.2, 0.2, and 3.5 percent, respectively, of the population (Lai and Arguelles 2003: 124). In Hawai'i, the much larger proportion of the state population that is represented by Japanese Americans, Filipino Americans, and Chinese Americans is the primary reason why Asian American is not commonly used as a racial category. As major political and economic groups with differing interests, power, and resources, they have less of a need and desire than their continental counterparts to establish alliances with each other specifically as Asian Americans. This argument is not to deny that historically these ethnic groups did form coalitions among themselves (and with other ethnic groups), such as in the rise to power of the Democratic Party in the 1950s, but they did not do so consciously as people of Asian descent. Similarly, the substantial percentage of Hawaii's population that is represented by Native Hawaiians (20 percent) and to some extent by Samoans is also a factor that explains why those and other groups are not racialized collectively as Pacific Islanders and are viewed as culturally distinct.

My contention that ethnicity rather than race is the dominant organizing principle of social relations in Hawai'i is also supported by my discussion and analysis of socioeconomic and educational inequality (Chapters 3 and 4) which demonstrate that ethnicity structures unequal access to opportunities and benefits. Ethnic inequality, rather than racial inequality, thus prevails in Hawai'i, as evidenced by the widely differing social status of ethnic groups that ostensibly belong to the same racial category, such as Japanese Americans and Filipino Americans. Furthermore, other ethnic groups—such as Chinese Americans and Whites—share a similarly high socioeconomic status, despite belonging to different racial groups.

## Multiculturalism and the Hawai'i Multicultural Model

Both academics and the general public primarily perceive ethnic relations in Hawai'i as distinguished by their tolerance, equality, and harmony. This long-standing, widespread view was first advanced in the 1920s by Romanzo C.

Adams, the first scholar of island race relations, in his arguments concerning the "unorthodox race doctrine" of Hawai'i that was based on "mores of racial equality" (1936: 56). Adams also characterized Hawai'i as a "racial melting pot" because of its high intermarriage rate that he accounted for thusly: "Because there is no denial of political rights and economic or educational privilege on grounds of race, because racial equality is symbolized, the social code permits of marriage across race lines" (1937: 62).

I have long wondered how Adams, who had lived in Hawai'i since 1919 and thus presumably was aware of the highly unequal social status held by the different "races," nevertheless maintained that political, economic, and educational status was not allocated according to race. In his zeal to establish racial equality, despite its nonexistence, Adams privileged intermarriage as the most significant dimension of Hawai'i race relations because, in comparison to the rest of the United States, it was by far the most distinctive feature. While a majority of states had passed antimiscegenation laws, no such laws or strong public opinion against interracial marriage existed in Hawai'i. Furthermore, like other sociologists during the pre–World War II period, Adams was a committed assimilationist, which is evident from the very first paragraph of his *The Peoples of Hawaii* (1933: 5): "There is abundant evidence that the peoples of Hawaii are in process of becoming one people. After a time the terms now commonly used to designate the various groups according to the country of birth or ancestry will be forgotten. There will be no Portuguese, no Chinese, no Japanese—only American." Like his proclamations of racial equality, Adams obviously was very much mistaken that ethnic groups would eventually lose their distinct identities.

During the post–World War II period, the sanguine view of race relations in Hawai'i continued to be advanced by the two leading race relations scholars at the University of Hawai'i, Andrew W. Lind and Bernhard L. Hormann. In books such as *Hawaii: The Last of the Magic Isles*, Lind (1969: 9) followed Adams in emphasizing the egalitarian nature of race relations: "The important and distinctive fact about Hawaiian race relations is, of course, the existence of a code of equalitarian relations which is deeply rooted in and has developed out of customary conduct of a similar nature, and the code does then exercise a coercive influence upon all who might be disposed to violate it." Hormann (1952: 142), who had lived in Hawai'i since the age of nine, also paid sociological homage to Adams in his perspective of island race relations: "The continued absence of open violence therefore bespeaks of a certain restraint, a tolerance which has become traditional in the islands. Dr. Romanzo Adams called this Hawaii's 'unorthodox race doctrine.' The general acceptance of racial tolerance, friendliness, mutual cooperation, and intermingling as a 'principle' transforms it into a continuous force in the direction of further unification."

During the poststatehood period (1959), Lind and Hormann were joined by other academics who offered similar viewpoints concerning the positive nature of race relations in the islands, despite the obviously changing structure of those relations and the significantly changed political economy. Perhaps one of the earliest arguments that Hawai'i could serve as an exemplary model for other racially divided societies throughout the world was advanced by Lawrence Fuchs in his classic social history, *Hawaii Pono* (1961: 449): "Hawaii illustrates the nation's revolutionary message of equality of opportunity for all, regardless of background, color, or religion. This is the promise of Hawaii, a promise for the entire nation and indeed, the world, that peoples of different races and creeds can live together, enriching each other, in harmony and democracy." Given the brutal violence encountered by the leaders and participants in the civil rights movement as they courageously challenged racial segregation in the South beginning in the mid-1950s, the "promise of Hawaii" may indeed have seemed like a "revolutionary message of equality of opportunity." However, that promise has yet to be fulfilled for most of Hawaii's people, let alone the nation and the rest of the world.

Under the influence of the multiculturalism discourses beginning in the 1980s, the "Hawai'i multicultural model" emerged; that is, the notion that Hawai'i represents a model for emulation by other ethnically and racially diverse societies in managing their conflicts and other diversity-related problems. Journalist Susan Yim (1992a: B1, B3) proposed: "If America's mushrooming minority populations are to live together in harmony, perhaps they should take a close look at our multicultural test tube." In his edited book, *Multicultural Hawai'i: The Fabric of a Multiethnic Society*, former UH political scientist Michael Haas (1998: 306) contended that "scholars who either decry multiculturalism or advance multiculturalism in theoretical terms usually do so without drawing upon the wisdom of an actual model," and that "those on the mainland who favor or oppose multiculturalism must now take the Hawai'i model into account."[6]

Another advocate of Hawai'i as a multicultural model for other societies is former ethnic studies professor Ronald Takaki, who was born and raised in the islands. In an essay, "Look to Hawaii for Answers on Race" (1998: 5), he maintained that: "In the coming century, the rest of the nation will experience expanding ethnic diversity. Will we be able to work it out? To paraphrase Rodney King, 'Can we all get along?' A century ago, immigrant plantation workers decided that their answer was 'yes.' More and more Americans on the mainland must now confront that same question. Hopefully, we will be guided by Hawaii's plantation past." For Takaki, the "plantation past" was notable for, among other things, the "power of inter-group cooperation" between Japanese and Filipino workers in the 1920 strike, although that strike was unsuccessful. He also noted how in the plantation camps, "families were sharing their various ethnic foods" with one another and that over time "a common language" (Hawai'i Creole English) developed as part of a larger cultural and social process of the "blending of languages, of cultures and of interests" among immigrant groups (Takaki 1998: 5). Like other proponents of the Hawai'i multicultural model, Takaki has a very selective view of Hawai'i history and tends to ignore the many prevalent examples of intergroup conflict, such as the blatant racism of both Whites and non-Whites against Filipino Americans and Japanese Americans prior to World War II. His emphasis on the role of "immigrant plantation workers" in the emergence of "Hawaii's multiculturalism" completely erases the historical experiences and contributions of Native Hawaiians as the indigenous people whose lands were seized for the development of the plantation industry.

If, as Takaki hopes, we can be "guided by Hawaii's plantation past," the primary "lesson our country can draw from it" would be not to institutionalize the racism and discrimination against immigrants and Native Hawaiians that was such a dominant condition of that historical period and certainly not to romanticize that era lest we forget what its history really indicates. It also must be emphasized that eliminating racism and discrimination toward the establishment of racial equality requires far more than just getting along with others. In other words, what is needed goes well beyond individual members of society accepting others, intermarrying with them, and sharing a common culture.

Besides academics, journalists in Hawai'i are also regular contributors to what Lisa Lowe (1996: 85) has referred to more generally as "the production of multiculturalism." Former editor of the *Honolulu Advertiser* John Griffin (2004: B1, B4) wrote an essay, "Hawai'i's Ethnic Rainbow," that focused on the intermarriage dimension of the multicultural model. He noted "Hawai'i's special situation" with more than 20 percent of its residents being of multiracial descent, compared to only 2.4 percent for the nation as a whole, and with about half of its marriages ethnically or racially "mixed." Continuing to privilege island ethnic relations, Griffin maintained that "Hawai'i may be so far ahead of most other places in the nation that we are considered more of a unique society than an example." Nonetheless, he "remains glad our racial-ethnic front is, on balance, such a positive example."

Griffin's commentary (and that of others by journalists with similar views) is significant not so much about what he contends because his ideas concerning multiculturalism in Hawai'i have been stated previously. Its publication in the news media, however, enables the essay to be read by potentially hundreds of thousands of island residents and countless others throughout the world on the Internet, far more than will ever read any of my articles expressing contrary arguments published in an academic journal or book. By including oft-repeated tropes of Hawai'i as the "ethnic rainbow," "positive example," and "melting pot," the essay confirms and reinforces readers' beliefs of the "special" and "unique" nature of island ethnic relations in which "cultural variations are a positive factor." It is not even necessary to read the article to get its general message of ethnic harmony and tolerance since its title and the accompanying photograph—numerous and closely seated Hawai'i residents of differing ethnicity in the shape of a rainbow—are common symbols regularly used to convey that idea.[7]

Based on arguments by advocates of the Hawai'i multicultural model, I have discussed elsewhere (Okamura 1998a: 267) that its principal dimensions include: (1) a tradition of tolerance and peaceful coexistence; (2) harmonious ethnic relations evident in cordial relationships and a high rate of intermarriage; (3) equality of opportunity and status; and (4) a shared local culture and identity. Of these four dimensions, the most valid is the first, concerning tolerant ethnic relations, because Hawaii's people do believe and endorse as a behavioral norm that they should treat others of differing ethnicity than their own with tolerance and cordiality. There is much to be valued in having such a norm of interethnic relations that is certainly not the case in other ethnically or racially divided communities, for example, Los Angeles during the 1992 race riot. If there is anything exceptional about island ethnic relations, it may very well be this normative emphasis on getting along with and accepting others. However, this cultural norm, popularized as the "aloha spirit," is more significant in interpersonal relationships than in ethnic group relations. Its emphasis in face-to-face interactions, and because it can be experienced directly in those interactions, may well obscure the many ways that ethnic groups relate to one another in unfair and intolerant ways, such as the differential distribution of higher education, employment, and wealth among them.

The analytical distinction made by Christine Inglis (1996) among three perspectives of multiculturalism is very useful in understanding how the concept has been applied by its Hawai'i advocates in developing their multicultural model.[8] The "demographic and descriptive usage" of multiculturalism is primarily concerned with the "way in which the cultural differences within [a multicultural society] are produced, received or reproduced" (cited in Wieviorka 1998: 883). This "sociological approach" views multiculturalism as "the problem, rather than the response" and thus "the starting point for proposing political orientations." In contrast, the "ideology and norms usage" of multiculturalism refers to a "political philosophy approach" that "question[s] in what way [multiculturalism] is desirable or undesirable, what it contributes, and what it costs society, in the light of criteria which may be moral or ethical, but also economic." From this perspective, multiculturalism is a "possible response" instead of a problem to be addressed. Lastly, in the "programme and policy usage," multiculturalism is a "principle of political action which materially underpins the institutions, the basic law of a state . . . with the intention of articulating the right of individuals and groups to maintain a specific culture," together with the possibility for individuals to participate fully in civic, economic, and legal affairs (cited in Wieviorka 1998: 883).

The second of Inglis's three usages of multiculturalism, regarding ideology and norms, is most commonly employed by supporters of the Hawai'i multicultural model since they certainly view multiculturalism as a response, if not "the answer" as they claim, rather than a problem to be solved.[9] Model proponents perceive cultural diversity in the islands as highly desirable given that it has contributed to the blending and sharing of the cultures of Native Hawaiians and the immigrant plantation groups that have resulted in a common local culture and identity shared by Hawaii's people. They further claim that the islands have not experienced the same racial and ethnic conflict as other societies because of the normative emphasis on tolerance and harmony, evident in the high intermarriage rate, and because of ideological support for equal opportunity. From an ethical perspective, model advocates maintain that multiculturalism has been for the ultimate good of Hawai'i and its people—including ethnic minorities—since it has brought positive benefits for all, such as socioeconomic mobility. Furthermore, these supporters contend that Hawaii's multiculturalism can serve as a response not only for the state but also for other racially or ethnically divided societies in which multiculturalism is perceived as a problem to be solved, as in the demographic and descriptive usage. Differentiating among Inglis's three usages of multiculturalism enables one to comprehend the grandiose, if not false, claims made by proponents of the Hawai'i multicultural model that it constitutes a solution for other societies, no matter how racially, ethnically, or otherwise different they may be from Hawai'i.

A general problem with multicultural approaches is their emphasis on culture and cultural differences, rather than race and racial differences, to distinguish groups in a common society. If the differences among such groups are viewed as primarily due to their respective cultures and since culture can be learned, multicultural perspectives, much like assimilation theory, can minimize the difficulty that racialized minorities encounter in seeking to participate equally in society. Lowe (1996: 86) observes how, in its zeal for equal inclusion, multiculturalism obscures the power and status differences among ethnic and racial groups: "Multiculturalism levels the important differences and contradictions within and among racial and ethnic minority groups according to the discourse of pluralism, which asserts that American culture is a democratic terrain to which every variety of constituency has equal access and in which all are represented, while simultaneously masking the existence of exclusions." In this regard, Stuart Hall (2000: 211) has noted how particularly "commercial" multiculturalism "celebrate[s] difference without making a difference" in resolving disparities in power and privilege among racial and ethnic groups.

Insofar as it reduces the salience of racial barriers and racial differences, multiculturalism can be viewed as a form of "postracialism," evident in assertions that America has gone beyond race and is a "postracial" society. As observed by Winant (2004: xviii–xix): "Contemporary racial hegemony fosters the widespread claim—articulated at both the 'highbrow' and 'grassroots' cultural levels—that the world has entered a stage of 'postracialism' after all the conflicts and reforms of recent years. As if to say, 'At last! At last! We have progressed beyond those backward and benighted notions of race!' " By proclaiming that the United States is a "color-blind" society, postracialism serves to obscure persisting racial hierarchy and inequality rather than provide a means to address those problems.

Given the supposed declining significance of race in American society, multiculturalism also can be understood as part of the larger sociological movement to maintain the "ethnicity paradigm" as the dominant theoretical approach in the sociology of race (see Omi and Winant 1994: 14). This initiative is evident in arguments that seek to eliminate the analytical distinction between racial and ethnic group and, by extension, race and ethnicity. In *Postethnic America*, historian David Hollinger (2000: 39) advanced the term "ethno-racial bloc" to refer to groups commonly considered races because, among other reasons, it "acknowledges that the groups traditionally called racial exist on a blurred continuum with those traditionally called ethnic." In society at large, there is undoubtedly a considerable blurring of the difference between races and ethnic groups, but social scientists and historians should not contribute further to this confusion by abandoning the analytical distinction between these two concepts. Hollinger himself acknowledges the greater significance of race than ethnicity in structuring inequality in the United States: "When we caution ourselves not to ignore race by conflating race and ethnicity, we generally mean to remind ourselves of the sharpest inequalities of treatment within the American nation-state" (38). These "sharpest inequalities" suffered by aggrieved races, as races and not as ethnic groups, provide the rationale for maintaining the conceptual difference between racial and ethnic group and between race and ethnicity.[10]

From another perspective, Cornell and Hartmann (1998: 32) contend that "[d]efinitionally, . . . there is nothing that says that a race cannot be an ethnic group, or vice versa." As an example of such definitional boundary crossing, they note one of the most distinctive races in American history—African Americans (33):

> American Blacks also fit both definitions [of race and ethnic group]. They are held by others and often by themselves to be members of a distinct race, identified primarily by skin color and other bodily features. At the same time, they also have become an ethnic group, a

> self-conscious population that defines itself in part in terms of common descent (Africa as homeland), a distinctive history (slavery in particular), and a broad set of cultural symbols (from language to expressive culture).

This argument highlights the "They All Look Alike" problem of the ethnicity approach to race identified by Omi and Winant (1994: 22). This perspective considers African Americans as a single ethnic group while ignoring the significant ethnic differences among them based on culture, national origin, and language, for example, between Haitian immigrants and Black Americans descended from slaves taken to the South. Cornell and Hartmann's reduction of race to ethnicity can be applied to other groups that are generally viewed as races in the United States, such as Latinos and Asian Americans. If the latter constitute an ethnic group, then should Korean Americans, Vietnamese Americans, and Asian Indians be considered ethnic categories instead of ethnic groups? Do all Asian Americans, including post-1965 immigrants, really share a "distinctive history" and a "broad set of cultural symbols," including language and religion?

If racial groups can be considered simultaneously as races and ethnic groups, there would seem to be no sociological reason for maintaining an analytical distinction between these two concepts. However, as social anthropologist M. G. Smith (1982: 10) observed more than twenty years ago in his critique of the *Harvard Encyclopedia of American Ethnic Groups* (Thernstrom, Orlov, and Handlin 1980), the latter "clearly prefers to equate race with ethnicity and so to eliminate those fundamental differences within America between its major racial stocks on one hand and the multitudes of ethnic groups on the other which have exercised and continue to exercise such profound influences on the development and structure of the society from its earliest beginnings." Obscuring or eliminating the differences between racial and ethnic groups is very related to the initiative to advance ethnicity as of greater social significance than race in U.S. society. If, in fact, that is the case, then societal institutions and America in general can be made to seem more open to and inclusive of "ethnic" minorities, including African Americans, than as limiting their access and participation through racial barriers that are far more difficult to overcome than ethnic barriers. As Winant (2004: 43) states, "Such an approach reduce[s] race to ethnicity and almost entirely neglect[s] the continuing organization of social inequality and oppression along racial lines." African American studies scholar Michael Eric Dyson (2004 40–41) refers to this reductionist approach as "the liberal theory of race" that "conceives of race as merely a part of one's broader ethnic identity," which is supposedly "more crucial than race in explaining the condition of black people." However, Dyson contends that this theory "cannot explain why blacks have failed to 'assimilate'" like ethnic minorities because it does not acknowledge the "unique structural character of racism [and] historical content of racial oppression—slavery, Jim Crow laws, structural unemployment, gentrification of black living space, [and] deeply ingrained institutional racism."

In arguing against the assertions of the Hawai'i multicultural model, I have maintained that it is, in Omi and Winant's (1994: 56) terms, a "racial project," since it provides an overly positive representation and interpretation (but not an explanation) of ethnic relations (Okamura 2000: 125). As a representation, the model emphasizes the amicable and tolerant nature of island ethnic relations, while ignoring or obscuring the highly unequal structure of these relations that contradict what the model claims them to be.[11] While Omi and Winant (1994: 56) contend that a racial project also consists of an "effort to reorganize and redistribute resources along particular racial lines," the Hawai'i model instead serves to maintain the ethnic status quo and thus the political and economic dominance of Chinese Americans, Haoles, and Japanese Americans. Thus, it is not surprising that the leading advocates of the model are representatives of these ethnic groups. In their emphasis on societal inclusiveness and cultural diversity, model proponents do not acknowledge the salience of power and status disparities among ethnic groups. I am especially concerned with the dimension of the multicultural model that contends equality of opportunity is available to all ethnic groups in Hawai'i, although I also discuss in the following chapters the significance of intermarriage and of local identity and culture for ethnic relations.

In *Interracial Justice: Conflict and Reconciliation in Post-Civil Rights America*, law professor Eric Yamamoto (1999: 77) also challenges the "race relations model" of Hawai'i. He argues that "it falsely essentializes the complex interplay of location, institutions, cultures, and people, glossing over myriad subtle and overt racial conflicts" and "unduly valorizes Hawai'i, in effect saying 'be like Hawai'i,' without carefully teasing out the complexities of race relations and explaining the relevance of one locale's experiences to another's." Hawai'i will always appear superficially to have "better" ethnic relations than most major cities in the continental United States where collective racial violence has occurred with much greater frequency. Furthermore, in valorizing island ethnic relations and claiming that other societies can look to Hawai'i for *the* answer—as though there is only one solution to problems of racial inequality and conflict throughout the world—the notion that ethnic inequality may be a persisting problem in Hawai'i does not get raised. In other words, if Hawai'i ain't broken ethnically, why fix it?

Another major factor in the perpetuation of ethnic inequality is that the great majority of island residents supports the Hawai'i multicultural model or the general belief in the positive nature of island ethnic relations. A statewide survey in 1996, published in the *Honolulu Advertiser*, found that 83 percent of its 800 respondents thought that islanders from different ethnic groups "get along better than in other places" and 87 percent agreed that the aloha spirit is "important in how people live" (cited in Pratt 2000: 244). As a racial project, the multicultural model is disseminated widely through various means, including the news media, the public school system, and popular culture. Government and community leaders exhort residents to express the aloha spirit in their daily interactions with one another, including driving on the freeway. Schoolteachers provide a simplistic version of Hawai'i history that emphasizes the cultural contributions of Native Hawaiians and the immigrant plantation groups, such as food and games, but that omits the racism and discrimination that long excluded them from fully participating in society. While local comedians and disc jockeys dispense jokes that ridicule the language, culture, and practices of ethnic groups, particularly Filipino Americans, they maintain that such "ethnic humor" is directed at all groups, and therefore no one should take offense. They remind us that we are fortunate to live in a society where we can all laugh at ourselves—as if that is really what is occurring when we are actually laughing at others who are the targets of the jokes.

## Why Hawai'i?

What can a book on ethnicity and ethnic relations in Hawai'i contribute to comparative scholarship on race and ethnicity in the United States and elsewhere? Hawaii's relatively small population of 1.2 million includes limited percentages of African Americans and Latinos and a plurality proportion of Asian Americans, and it is physically separated from the continental United States—differentiating it as a setting of race and ethnic relations from the rest of the nation. However, until the 1960s, Hawai'i was certainly viewed as a significant if not major site in the comparative study of race, a veritable "laboratory of race relations." Some of the leading race relations scholars, such as Robert Park, Herbert G. Blumer, and E. B. Reuter, took sabbatical leaves to conduct research or taught as visiting professors at the University of Hawai'i. Attracted by its research opportunities, Park and other Chicago sociologists went to Hawai'i "as if it was a pilgrimage site" (Yu 2001: 82).

Through their research and publications on Hawai'i, Adams, Lind, Hormann, Clarence Glick, and others established the UH Department of Sociology as a highly regarded center for the study of race and race relations. In 1954, during the academic heyday of the department, Honolulu was the setting of an international "Conference on Race Relations in World Perspective," attended by forty eminent researchers invited from throughout the world, such as Blumer, E. Franklin Frazier, J. S. Furnivall, and Everett C. Hughes (Lind 1955). Through the 1960s, Hawai'i was often included in comparative studies on race relations and discussed, together with Brazil, as an example of a society with especially tolerant and egalitarian race relations (see Banton 1998: 130). In *Caste, Class and Race*, Oliver Cromwell Cox (1948) described "The Ruling-Class Situation" in various racial settings: "The small white ruling class, already limited in its power to segregate, now finds it practically impossible to identify any one group for racial discrimination. 'Equality among all peoples' tends to become the social philosophy. Instances of this are found in the island of Trinidad and in Hawaii especially."

Since the 1970s, however, the Hawai'i experience has not been included as prominently in theoretical and comparative discussions of race and ethnicity in the United States. If Hawai'i is discussed, it is generally by academics who are based in the islands or were raised there, for example, Ronald Takaki in *A Different Mirror: A History of Multicultural America* (1993) and Eric Yamamoto in *Interracial Justice* (1999).[12]

What accounts, then, for this omission of the Hawai'i situation from comparative scholarship on race and ethnicity in the United States? I believe it is due to the historical and contemporary exaggerated, if not false, claims about the egalitarian, harmonious, and tolerant nature of island ethnic relations. These arguments have resulted in the view of the Hawai'i experience as exceptional and unique and thus not comparable to other more problematic sites of race relations. Why include the Hawai'i case if, as some scholars maintain, its ethnic relations are not a problem? Or is such a conclusion itself an indication of the questionable research and analyses being conducted on race and ethnicity issues in the state?

Nonetheless, I maintain that a study of ethnicity and ethnic relations in Hawai'i can contribute to the comparative analysis of race and ethnicity, particularly in Asian American studies. Hawai'i consists of a variety of Asian American groups—including Japanese Americans, Okinawan Americans, Filipino Americans, Chinese Americans, Korean Americans, and Vietnamese Americans—that constitute major or at least significant segments of island society. It thus provides a research setting that demonstrates the complexity of their differential experiences and relations with one another that cannot be explained by reference to an overall "Asian American experience." Furthermore, in Hawai'i some Asian American groups are major political and economic constituents of island society, unlike the situation for the most part in the continental United States. A few of them, such as Japanese Americans and Chinese Americans, hold dominant socioeconomic and political status together with Whites, while others, including Filipino Americans, continue to occupy subordinate positions that they attribute to the discrimination they encounter from the former groups. A study focused on the ethnic relations and ethnic identity of Asian American and other ethnic groups can highlight the social and cultural differences among them and the significance of ethnicity as an organizing principle in maintaining those differences.

In Asian American studies, the term "Asian Pacific American" (APA) is commonly and inappropriately employed (Okamura 2003: 186–187), and there are several Asian Pacific American studies programs at universities in various parts of the country. With its majority population of Asian Americans and Pacific Islanders, Hawai'i provides a more valid site for research and analysis on their respective status and experiences, especially their relations with one another. In marked contrast to the continental United States, Pacific Islanders—including Native Hawaiians, Samoans, Tongans, Chamorros, and Marshallese—comprise one-fourth of the state population. Research on these and Asian American groups in the islands can lead to far more significant insights and analyses than those based on the presumed "APA experience" that follows from the unwarranted assumption that the highly differential experiences of Asian American and Pacific Islander groups can easily be generalized. Furthermore, a study of these groups in Hawai'i can result in problematizing the Asian Pacific American racial category and questioning its analytical significance. The Hawaiian sovereignty movement that represents Native Hawaiians as the indigenous people of Hawai'i is a clear example of why the historical and contemporary experiences and status of Pacific Islanders cannot readily be assimilated into an overall Asian Pacific American categorical construct.

Rather than viewing the Hawai'i case of race and ethnicity as exceptional, in some ways it is very comparable to the situation in the continental United States. Despite being one of the most geographically separated places in the world, Hawai'i also experienced the post–World War II "break" in the long-standing "global racial system" as discussed by Winant (2001: 133–134; 2004: xiii). He attributes this "global shift" toward racial equality and justice throughout the world to the convergence of various political movements, including those against colonialism, apartheid, and fascism and the U.S. civil rights movement. In Hawai'i, the movement against racial exclusion and inequality was led by the International Longshoremen's and Warehousemen's Union, which organized plantation workers into their first multiracial labor union in 1945, and by the Democratic Party, which gained control of the Territorial Legislature in 1954 for the first time in the islands' history. Furthermore, Winant's (2004: xiii) description of the eventual consequences of the postwar break on the global racial order also applies to some extent to Hawai'i: "[D]espite the real amelioration of the most degrading features of the old world racial system, the centuries-old and deeply entrenched system of racial inequality and injustice was not eliminated."

## Outline of the Book

My contention that ethnicity is situated at the intersection of ethnic identity and social structure where ethnic difference frames inequality is developed through the organization of the chapters in this book. Chapter 2 provides demographic information on Hawaii's ethnic groups and on some of their internal social and cultural differences. Chapters 3 and 4 review the scope and nature of ethnic inequality in Hawai'i through an analysis of the educational and larger socioeconomic status orders in which ethnicity is the primary structural principle. Chapters 5, 6, and 7 are concerned with ethnic identity construction (or its relative absence) among several groups, including Native Hawaiians, Okinawan Americans, Japanese Americans, and Filipino Americans. These three chapters demonstrate how ethnic identity can be viewed as a cultural representation of groups, either by the groups themselves or by others through denigrating stereotypes assigned to an ethnic group.

Chapter 2, "Changing Ethnic Differences," seeks to demonstrate the increasing social and cultural complexity of ethnic identity and ethnic relations in Hawai'i as a result of various ongoing social processes. These processes include the relatively high intermarriage rate among island residents and their consequent multiethnicity and multiraciality, immigration from Asia and the Pacific, and out-migration to and in-migration from the continental United States, all of which contribute to social and cultural changes in ethnic relations and identities, cultural norms and values, and political beliefs.

Chapter 3, "Socioeconomic Inequality and Ethnicity," analyzes the role of ethnicity as the dominant organizing principle of the socioeconomic status system. Based on 2000 U.S. census data, it compares the occupational status and income rank of eight major ethnic groups in Hawai'i. The chapter shows that the stratification order is "racialized" insofar as ethnicity regulates the highly unequal distribution of socioeconomic rewards, privileges, and resources among ethnic groups.

Toward further analysis of the persistence of ethnic inequality in Hawai'i, Chapter 4, "Educational Inequality and Ethnicity," discusses the significance of ethnicity as a structural principle in the Hawai'i public education system at both the kindergarten through high school (K–12) and postsecondary levels. It contends that ethnic minorities—including Filipino Americans, Native Hawaiians, and Samoans—are subject to institutional discrimination in the public school system, particularly through its long-term underfunding. Thus, rather than serving as a means of socioeconomic mobility for ethnic minority groups, public education is a site of institutionalized inequality that maintains the ethnic stratification order of unequal Hawai'i.

Chapter 5, "Constructing Ethnic Identities, Constructing Differences," discusses three examples of identity formation by groups in Hawai'i: Native Hawaiians, 1.5-generation Korean Americans, and locals. In applying the constructionist approach to these case studies, I argue that these groups have created and expressed distinct identities for themselves in order to foster their social, political, or economic interests, including contesting their unequal status in Hawai'i.

In contrast to those groups that actively engage in identity construction, Chapter 6, "Japanese Americans: Toward Symbolic Identity," reviews Japanese Americans as an ethnic group that does not have to articulate a particular ethnic identity for themselves to advance their collective concerns because they already hold relatively high political and economic status and have other means (such as financial resources) to maintain that status. Although I do not discuss Chinese Americans and Whites, they are two other ethnic groups that do not have to create and assert a specific identity to ensure their dominant social position. Chapter 6 also discusses how Okinawan Americans or *Uchinanchu* (overseas Okinawans) construct a distinct ethnic identity to differentiate themselves from Japanese Americans given the fluid boundary between these two groups.

Chapter 7, "Filipino Americans: Model Minority or Dog Eaters?" is concerned with Filipino Americans as a subordinate ethnic minority that clearly could benefit from using identity formation (as well as other strategies) as a collective means to advance themselves socioeconomically and politically. However, the primary obstacle they encounter is the widespread prevalence of racist stereotypes that restrict their ability to construct a positive ethnic identity and contribute to their subjugated status.

Chapter 8 concludes the book by bringing together some of the major results and generalizations from the previous chapters toward an overall analysis of how ethnic inequality is perpetuated in Hawai'i. It also discusses possible strategies for reducing, if not eliminating, ethnic inequality by fostering collective socioeconomic mobility among disadvantaged ethnic minorities. These strategies focus on mitigating the cultural and structural barriers that restrict minority advancement—such as racist stereotyping and institutional discrimination—and on providing these groups with greater educational and employment access and opportunities.

# 2

# Changing Ethnic Differences

This chapter is concerned with various social and demographic processes that contribute to the increasing complexity of ethnicity and ethnic relations in Hawaiʻi. It seeks to demonstrate that, as a result of these processes, ethnic identity and ethnic relations are far more problematic and complex than might be assumed from the islands' reputation as a veritable "racial paradise" and multicultural model for other racially and ethnically divided societies. The social processes discussed include: intermarriage and the resulting multiraciality and multiethnicity of Hawaii's people; immigration from abroad and in-migration from the continental United States; and out-migration, including what has been termed the "brain drain" of well educated young people to the continent. Together, these processes result in an ever more culturally and socially diverse society consisting of ethnic groups that through intermarriage produce a substantial racially and ethnically mixed population. Immigration leads to ethnic groups, such as Filipino Americans, that are internally culturally diverse with recent immigrants maintaining to some extent their homeland cultures and practices, while their American-born counterparts follow the local culture of Hawaiʻi. In-migration results in ethnic groups, such as Whites, that include a significantly large segment of recent newcomers with different cultural beliefs and values than those prevalent in the islands. Lastly, out-migration leads to many ethnic groups losing members and their cultural knowledge and social ties to Hawaiʻi to the continental

United States. I begin with a discussion of Hawaii's population by ethnicity based on 2000 U.S. census data.

## Ethnic Composition of Hawai'i

According to the 2000 U.S. census, Hawai'i has a population of 1,211,537 that includes a wide diversity of ethnic groups, although not as many as other ethnically and racially diverse states such as California (see Table 2.1).[1] Like California, no ethnic group in Hawai'i constitutes a numerical majority; this has been the case since the late 1880s as a result of the decimation of the Native Hawaiian population following Western contact in 1778 and the recruitment of Asian and European plantation laborers beginning in the mid-nineteenth century (Lind 1980: 34). Also like California, Hawai'i has relatively large White and Asian American populations but smaller African American and Native American communities. Both academics and the general public commonly describe Hawai'i as consisting of a number of ethnic groups, such as Native Hawaiians, Chinese Americans, Japanese Americans, Filipino Americans, and "Caucasians." While not necessarily false, this description implies that those and other ethnic groups are ethnically unmixed and mutually exclusive units that reproduce themselves as such; thus, each group is said to represent a specific percentage of the state population. However, decades of substantial intermarriage have resulted in considerable racial and ethnic mixtures within all of those groups that are obscured by categorical terms such as "Filipino American."

The 2000 census addressed this issue by allowing respondents for the first time to indicate membership in more than one racial category rather than restricting them to a single group, even though they may have been of multiracial or multiethnic descent. The resulting distribution of Hawaii's population into numerous racial and ethnic categories, including combinations of two or more racial groups (for example, Asian American and White), provides a more accurate representation of the state population given the high rate of intermarriage during the past century. Previous censuses that divided Hawaii's people into a finite number of what appeared to be mutually exclusive ethnic groups ignored the large proportion of members of most groups who are of mixed ancestry. On the other hand, the sociological value of the census limiting respondents to only one ethnic or racial category was that it provided some indication of the primary ethnic identity that respondents chose for themselves; that is, the principal ethnic identity that an individual asserts for him or herself in most social situations of daily life.

Given the option of asserting multiple racial membership in 2000, more than one-fifth (21.4 percent) of Hawai'i residents reported that they belong to two or more races, a figure nearly nine times greater than that for the United

**TABLE 2.1 POPULATION OF HAWAI'I BY ETHNICITY, 2000**

| | Ethnic Group Alone | | Ethnic Group Alone or in Any Combination | |
|---|---|---|---|---|
| GROUP | NUMBER | PERCENT | NUMBER | PERCENT |
| White | 294,102 | 24.3 | 476,162 | 39.3 |
| Japanese American | 201,764 | 16.7 | 296,674 | 24.5 |
| Filipino American | 170,635 | 14.1 | 275,728 | 22.8 |
| Native Hawaiian | 80,137 | 6.6 | 239,655 | 19.8 |
| Chinese American | 56,600 | 4.7 | 170,803 | 14.1 |
| Korean American | 23,537 | 1.9 | 41,352 | 3.4 |
| African American | 22,003 | 1.8 | 33,343 | 2.8 |
| Samoan | 16,166 | 1.3 | 28,184 | 2.3 |
| Vietnamese American | 7,867 | 0.6 | 10,040 | 0.8 |
| Tongan | 3,993 | 0.3 | 5,988 | 0.5 |
| American Indian and Alaska Native | 3,535 | 0.3 | 24,882 | 2.1 |
| Laotian American | 1,842 | 0.2 | 2,437 | 0.2 |
| Guamanian or Chamorro | 1,663 | 0.1 | 4,221 | 0.3 |
| Asian Indian | 1,441 | 0.1 | 3,145 | 0.3 |
| Thai American | 1,259 | 0.1 | 2,284 | 0.2 |

Note: For "Ethnic Group Alone," the percentages do not add up to 100 because groups less than 1,000 are not included. For "Ethnic Group Alone or in Any Combination," "Number" refers to responses rather than individuals; therefore, the percentages add up to more than 100. There were about 1.57 million responses for the 1.21 million ethnically unmixed and mixed persons in Hawai'i in 2000.

Source: "Ranking of Races: 2000," table 1.35, *The State of Hawaii Data Book 2004*.

States as a whole (2.4 percent). Furthermore, of the 259,343 persons in the state who claimed multiracial descent, about one-third (32.4 percent) indicated membership in three or more races. Note that those multiracial percentages do not include persons of multiethnic ancestry (for example, Filipino and Japanese), and I estimate below that the combined multiracial and multiethnic population represents about 40 percent of Hawaii's people.

An issue to consider when respondents indicate membership in more than one ethnic or racial category on a census or other survey form (perhaps because they thought they had to) is that such an assertion does not necessarily constitute a claim to a particular ethnic identity. In their daily lives, such individuals may assert a primary ethnic or racial identity that emphasizes belonging to only one of those groups that may not necessarily represent the largest component of their ancestry. In short, ethnic and racial identities are socially constructed by both individuals and groups rather than being accurate representations of ancestral background.

Another new feature of the 2000 census was the introduction of the racial category "Native Hawaiian and Other Pacific Islander." This new category resulted from some Native Hawaiians who wanted to have their group transferred from the census category of Asian American and Pacific Islander to the category of American Indians and Alaska Natives (Espiritu and Omi 2000). Their reasoning was that Native Hawaiians as an indigenous people have more in common with the latter groups than with Asian Americans who are historically and contemporaneously immigrants to the United States. After several years of debate, the Office of Management and Budget, which has responsibility for developing racial and ethnic categories used by the federal government, resolved the issue by creating the new racial category that combined Native Hawaiians with Pacific Islanders.

As for Hawaii's population by ethnicity, much to the surprise of many Hawai'i residents, the largest ethnic group is Whites or Haoles, based on the Hawaiian term *haole* for foreigner. They have been the largest group since the 1960s as a result of considerable in-migration from the continental United States following statehood in 1959. As evident in Table 2.1, in 2000 the percentage of Hawai'i residents who said they were White (ethnic group alone or in any combination) was the highest (39.3 percent) among all ethnic groups, while those who reported being White only were 24.3 percent.[2] The former figure thus includes a significant number of persons who also claimed to belong to one or more other racial or ethnic groups. While group population figures from previous U.S. censuses cannot be directly compared with those in the 2000 census because of the multiple racial membership option, in 1990 one-third (33.4 percent) of Hawai'i residents indicated that they were White (Hawai'i Department of Business and Economic Development and Tourism 1993). The number of Whites very likely did increase during the 1990s, particularly as a result of in-migration from the continental United States to the neighbor islands (see below). Given this ongoing movement, Whites should maintain their position as the largest ethnic group in the state in the near future.

The White population of Hawai'i is quite diverse socially and culturally, including: the descendants of those who arrived before or during World War II; those who came after the war or statehood and their offspring born in Hawai'i; and others who have arrived since the 1980s. In addition, a substantial portion of the White community consists of U.S. military personnel and their dependents, a segment that regularly changes in composition as these individuals are transferred to new assignments after a few years and are replaced by others. These different categories among Whites are evident in the use of distinguishing terms by themselves and non-Whites, such as "local Haole," "mainland Haole," and "military Haole."

While they certainly were not all White, armed forces personnel stationed in Hawai'i in 2000 totaled about 39,000, with their civilian dependents numbering another 43,000 (Hawai'i Department of Business and Economic Development and Tourism 2003). If 70 percent of those personnel and their families are estimated to be White, they would number about 55,000 persons or about 12 percent of the total White population of Hawai'i. The great majority of military personnel and their dependents are concentrated on or very near military bases on O'ahu, with only about 500 of the former and a little more than 1,000 of the latter stationed on the neighbor islands. In addition to their employment status, this residential concentration and their regular movement in and out of the islands enhance the social distinctiveness, if not social segregation, of the military component of the White population, as indicated by the term "military Haoles" to differentiate them.

An ethnic group that is classified as White by the U.S. census is Portuguese Americans, although many of them would not claim to be White or Haole. Unlike most Europeans, Portuguese immigrated to Hawai'i as plantation laborers between 1878 and 1887 and from 1906 to 1913 (Nordyke 1989: 44–45). Beginning with the 1940 census, Portuguese Americans were included with Whites—or "Other Caucasians" as they were officially referred to in Hawai'i at that time—and were no longer distinguished in a separate ethnic category (Lind 1980: 34).[3] The previous 1930 census reported 27,588 Portuguese, and their population had been increasing since the turn of the century. While they have certainly intermarried with other ethnic groups and, as a result, probably fewer persons of Portuguese descent would claim that as their sole ethnic identity, many others continue to assert Portuguese American as their primary ethnic identity. Thus, there is no reason to assume that they have been completely assimilated into the White population. The 2000 census indicated that 48,527 persons reported being of Portuguese ancestry, although they undoubtedly were not all Portuguese only (Hawai'i Department of Business and Economic Development and Tourism 2002). Nonetheless, they represent more than 10 percent of the total White population of Hawai'i.

Many Portuguese Americans continue to distinguish themselves from Haoles—despite the socioeconomic advantages of being considered White—because of the very significant class, status, and cultural distinctions between these two ethnic groups that have persisted over time. These differences have resulted in many Portuguese Americans not wanting to be perceived as Haole. Furthermore, the fact that many Portuguese Americans continue to assert this as their ethnic identity, although they are racially White, is another indication that the constituent groups in Hawai'i society are socially constructed as ethnic rather than racial groups.

Table 2.1 indicates that the second largest ethnic group is Japanese Americans (296,674, alone or in any combination) who represent one-fourth (24.5 percent) of Hawaii's population. More than two-thirds of them (201,764) said they are Japanese alone; thus, the one-third of Japanese Americans who are of mixed ancestry is a tremendous increase from the 2.2 percent who stated they were such in 1950 when the U.S. Census Bureau included additional questions on racial mixture in Hawai'i (Lind 1980: 28). This much higher proportion is not surprising given the increasing outmarriage rate of Japanese Americans since the 1970s among the *sansei* (third) and *yonsei* (fourth) generations. While they were the largest ethnic group in Hawai'i for more than sixty years (1900–1960s), including a high of 43 percent in 1920, the Japanese American proportion of the state population has been declining since the 1960s. This trend is very likely to continue in the near future due to the low birthrate of Japanese American women and their delayed marriage age, limited immigration from Japan, and the "brain drain" out-migration of fourth-generation Japanese Americans to the continental United States.

The Japanese American ethnic category obscures the considerable number of Okinawan Americans or *Uchinanchu* in Hawai'i for whom the census does not have a separate ethnic classification.[4] Okinawa became a prefecture of Japan in 1879, and Okinawans were recruited to Hawai'i as plantation laborers beginning in 1900. In 1924 when immigration from Japan to the United States ended, the 16,536 Okinawan Americans were about 16 percent of the Hawai'i Japanese American population and were the fourth largest prefectural group. One estimate of the Okinawan American population in Hawai'i is 45,000 (Okinawan Centennial Celebration Committee 2000: 71) and is probably based on those of Okinawan ancestry, including multiracial/ethnic persons. However, this estimate incorrectly assumes that everyone who is of Okinawan descent claims that as their ethnic identity. Many fourth-generation Okinawan Americans, especially if they are Okinawan and Japanese, may prefer Japanese American as their primary ethnic identity. Thus, a precise figure for those who claim Okinawan American as their ethnic identity is not that easily determined, but it would certainly be less than the total number of persons with Okinawan ancestry. Certainly not just among Okinawan Americans but also with other ethnic and racial groups in Hawai'i and elsewhere, ancestry does not necessarily equate with ethnic identity.

As the largest immigrating group to Hawai'i, Filipino Americans rank third in population (275,728, alone or in any combination) and are 22.8 percent of state residents. Many Filipino Americans have Hawaiian ancestry and are more likely to assert being Native Hawaiian than Filipino as their primary identity. This tendency is a factor that explains the dramatic gain of more than 107,000 in the number of persons who reported being Filipino American between 1990 (168,682) and 2000. That is, when limited to a single ethnic category, many Filipino Americans who are of Hawaiian ancestry chose to indicate they are Native Hawaiian because of the greater pride they may have in being of Hawaiian rather than Filipino descent. The Filipino American community consists of two principal segments: those born in Hawai'i (or the continental United States) and those who emigrated from the Philippines to Hawai'i, especially after 1965 when U.S. immigration laws were liberalized to allow for the reunification of families. The distinction between what are referred to as "local" and "immigrant" Filipinos is much more than demographic and is reflected in social divisions and cultural and socioeconomic differences between these two components of the Filipino American community. The immigrants themselves include Ilokanos, Visayans, and Tagalogs who speak different languages and come from widely separated regions in the Philippines. Given ongoing immigration and their relatively higher birthrate, Filipino Americans very likely will exceed Japanese Americans in population by the 2010 census and emerge as the second-largest ethnic group in Hawai'i.

In 2000, 239,655 persons reported that they were Native Hawaiian (alone or in any combination), thus comprising 19.8 percent of the state population. Some 80,137 persons claimed to be Native Hawaiian only, much less than the 138,742 in 1990 who said they were Native Hawaiian when the single ethnic/racial group restriction prevailed. Under the influence of the Hawaiian sovereignty movement and its construction of a unique identity for Native Hawaiians as the indigenous people of Hawai'i, it might have been expected that more of them would have opted to claim Native Hawaiian as their sole group membership. Furthermore, according to a state Department of Health survey, only about 9,000 "unmixed" Hawaiians were still living in Hawai'i in 1992 (Hawai'i Department of Business and Economic Development and Tourism 1997),[5] so that the great majority of those who indicated they are only Native Hawaiian could be viewed as making a political statement concerning the significance of their ancestry to them. Nonetheless, among the other 160,000 persons who stated they are of Hawaiian ancestry, a substantial number may assert a primarily Native Hawaiian identity in their everyday lives.

Chinese Americans (170,803, alone or in any combination) constituted 14.1 percent of Hawai'i residents in 2000 with 56,600 reporting they are multiracial or multiethnic. In 1990, 68,804 persons stated that they were Chinese American, and the difference of 102,000 more in 2000 can be attributed particularly to Native Hawaiians of Chinese descent who indicated membership in the former group in 1990 when they could opt for only one ethnic/racial category. Substantial intermarriage occurs between Chinese Americans and other ethnic groups, such as Japanese Americans and Whites, and some of their offspring may have contributed to the greater number of Chinese Americans in 2000. Some of the increase in the Chinese American population also is due to immigration, especially from China during the 1990s. In addition, a significant percentage of Vietnamese immigrants are ethnically Chinese, and some of them operate family-owned businesses in Chinatown in downtown Honolulu.

Korean Americans are a relatively small but recognizable ethnic group in Hawai'i at 41,352 (alone or in any combination) and 3.4 percent of the state population. They also are comprised of two communities: the first consists of the descendants of the initial group of 6,500 immigrants who arrived between 1903 and 1905 to work on the sugar plantations and who were later joined by 1,000 picture brides between 1910 and 1920; the second includes post-1965 immigrants and their offspring. This latter group is substantially more numerous and is augmented by continuing immigration, although it has declined considerably since the 1990s as a result of the economic development of Korea. Korean immigrants have established a commercial and residential "Koreatown" near the Ala Moana Center in Honolulu that includes grocery stores, restaurants and cafes, beauty and nail salons, and other family-operated businesses (Pang 2005: A6–A7).

As evident in Table 2.1, other Asian American groups that are much more numerous in the continental United States are less represented in Hawai'i. In descending order, they include Vietnamese Americans, Asian Indians, Laotian Americans, and Cambodian Americans. To some extent, the smaller numbers of these ethnic groups reflect their much later immigration as political refugees beginning in 1975 with the Communist liberation of Vietnam, Laos, and Cambodia. However, about 650 "Hindus," who were very likely Sikhs from the Punjab region in northwest India, were recruited to work on the plantations in 1908, but most of them left later for the West Coast.

At 87,699, Latinos or Hispanics (alone or in any combination) comprise a significant percentage (7.2 percent) of Hawaii's population, although many islanders would be surprised to learn there are supposedly many more of them than full Chinese Americans. One reason for this relative invisibility of Latinos is that many of them, including their dependents, are with the U.S. military and thus, like Whites, they are a somewhat segregated and transient community. Of the various Latino groups, only Puerto Ricans have had a historical presence in the islands since they arrived as plantation laborers in 1900. While about 8,000 Spanish labor recruits were brought to Hawai'i between 1907 and 1913, most of them soon left the plantations for California.[6] Mexican Americans are present in the military as well as among recent immigrants who work as tourism, construction, and agricultural workers on the neighbor islands of Maui and Hawai'i. Their increasing presence is evident in the approximately 1,100 Spanish-speaking students enrolled in English for Second Language Learners programs in the public schools who outnumber Cantonese and Korean speakers (Martin 2005e).

A very sizable 37,163 persons, or more than 40 percent of the total Latino population of Hawai'i, opted for the "Other Spanish/Hispanic/Latino" census category, thus making them the largest Latino group. Since there is a very limited Spanish, Cuban, Salvadoran, and Guatemalan presence in Hawai'i, the only explanation I have for this considerable number of persons is that it is primarily the result of Filipino Americans claiming to have Spanish ancestry. This tendency is a very common phenomenon in Hawai'i, particularly among young Filipino Americans because of the denigration of their ethnic identity, an issue discussed in Chapter 7.

African Americans totaled 33,343 (alone or in any combination) in 2000 or 2.8 percent of the state population, with about two-thirds indicating they are African American only (22,003). A plurality of Blacks are associated with the U.S. military in Hawai'i, either as active personnel or their spouses and dependents, and they comprise about 15 percent of both groups or more than 12,000 persons. This segment of the African American community can be considered a population in flux with regular movements to and from the continental United States. The Black historical presence in Hawai'i dates back to the early nineteenth century and includes a small number of Africans from the Cape Verde Islands who arrived on whaling ships beginning in 1820 and found work as cooks, barbers, and musicians (Nordyke 1989: 71). After Hawai'i became a U.S. territory in 1900, two hundred African Americans were recruited as plantation laborers in 1901 from Alabama, and from Louisiana where they may have been sugarcane growers (Lind 1980: 37).

After Native Hawaiians, the next largest Pacific Islander group is Samoans (28,184, alone or in any combination), who are much fewer in number than Latinos but far more widely known among Hawai'i residents because of negative stereotyping. The first significant movement of Samoans to Hawai'i consisted of several hundred who had joined the U.S. military during World War II and were relocated to Hawai'i in 1951 following the closure of a navy base in the U.S. territory of American Samoa (Franco 1987: 3). Samoans from American Samoa can freely enter the United States as American nationals. Their experiences in Hawai'i, such as social and cultural adjustment and employment and housing discrimination, are very similar to those of Asian and Pacific Islander immigrants. Increasing numbers of Micronesians from the former U.S. Trust Territory of the Pacific, especially Marshallese and Chuukese, have been arriving in Hawai'i since the 1990s and, like American Samoans, they can enter the United States without restriction. Other smaller groups of Pacific Islanders include Tongans and Chamorros from Guam and the Northern Mariana Islands.

Another racial group with a relatively small representation in Hawai'i are American Indians and Alaska Natives (3,535), several hundred of whom are affiliated with the military. The more than 21,000 persons who reported in 2000 to be multiracial Native American or Alaska Native can be partially attributed to the nearly 6,000 Whites who claimed to be of American Indian ancestry, although they may not necessarily be able to trace descent to a specific ancestor. Otherwise, it is difficult to account for the tremendous gain of nearly 19,000 American Indians and Alaska Natives in Hawai'i since 1990 when they numbered 5,099. The Native American community is sufficiently large that it can organize four annual powwows—including two in Honolulu and one each on Kaua'i and Hawai'i Island—that feature drummers and dancers from different tribal groups.

Another source of data on the ethnic composition of Hawaii's population is provided by the Hawai'i Department of Health through a sample survey of state residents conducted by telephone annually in recent years. In 2000 the sample consisted of 17,183 randomly selected persons and excluded those in institutions or military barracks and the very small populations on Ni'ihau island and in Kalawao, Moloka'i (the former exile community of Kalaupapa for persons with Hansen's disease). Thus, it is not surprising that the survey had a lower figure for Hawaii's population (1,156,014) than that of the U.S. census, although it did have a higher number for Native Hawaiians (254,910) (Hawai'i Department of Business and Economic Development and Tourism 2001). With its emphasis on ethnicity rather than race, the survey uses classification principles and ethnic categories that are considered to be more relevant to the Hawai'i situation than those employed by the U.S. Census Bureau.

A basic distinction made in the categories of the Department of Health survey is among "Unmixed (except Hawaiian)," "Mixed (except Hawaiian)," and "Hawaiian/part Hawaiian." Any respondent who reports having a Hawaiian ancestor is placed in the latter category, whether or not they claim to be Hawaiian. Anyone who says they have non-Hawaiian ancestors from two or more ethnic groups is assigned to the amorphous "Mixed" category, although they may assert membership in only one of those groups in their daily life. Respondents who indicate belonging to only one non-Hawaiian ethnic group are classified as "Unmixed" and placed in one of a number of ethnic categories, including Caucasian, Japanese, Chinese, Filipino, Korean, and Samoan/Tongan. Note that the Caucasian group is considered to be unmixed, although many Whites in Hawai'i and elsewhere in the United States are descended from several European ancestry groups such as Germans, Irish, or English. The survey does provide a useful estimate of roughly 480,000 for the total ethnically mixed population of Hawai'i if its non-Hawaiian mixed figure (230,410) is added to 250,000 as the approximate number of Hawaiians of mixed descent. The former figure constitutes almost 40 percent of Hawaii's total population, thus making persons of mixed ancestry the largest category in the state.

## Intermarriage and Multiethnicity/ Multiraciality

Interracial and interethnic marriage is a long-term historical process in Hawai'i that was established as a common practice by the early nineteenth century, if not earlier, between Native Hawaiian women and European and American men. Since the early 1900s, when data on such marriages began to be maintained, Hawai'i has had a much higher outmarriage rate than the continental United States. Furthermore, there were never any laws or strong public opinion against intermarriage in Hawai'i, while numerous states had antimiscegenation laws that were finally ruled unconstitutional in 1967 in the *Loving v. Virginia* decision of the U.S. Supreme Court. With notable exceptions, for many island ethnic groups, there was limited social stigma attached to outmarrying such that its prevalence increased progressively over the decades. Hawaii's overall intermarriage rate appears to have peaked in the early 1980s and stabilized since then at almost half of the marriages involving at least one state resident. In marked contrast, during the 1980s, the interracial marriage rate in the United States was considerably lower: White (<3 percent), African American (4 percent), Asian American (25 percent), and Latino (29 percent) (cited in Fu and Heaton 1997: 57).

Intermarriage, of course, is the primary factor in the substantially large ethnically and racially mixed population of Hawai'i. Outmarriage has also been advanced as both cause and effect of the supposedly tolerant and harmonious ethnic relations in the islands. It is argued to be the cause of such positive relations insofar as intermarriage brings together people from diverse ethnic groups such that they become more familiar with and appreciative of different cultural practices, values, and beliefs. Outmarriage also is viewed as creating cross-cutting ties of alliance between different ethnic groups and therefore lessening the possibility of conflict between them. On the other hand, intermarriage is said to be a major effect or outcome of Hawaii's prevalent ethnic harmony and acceptance that encourages people from differing groups to marry one another since societal constraints are very limited. Whether viewed as cause or effect, Hawaii's relatively high outmarriage rate can be understood as the result of certain demographic factors rather than primarily due to tolerant and harmonious ethnic relations.

In *Interracial Marriage in Hawaii,* sociologists Xuanning Fu and Tim B. Heaton (1997) have conducted the most recent comprehensive study of intergroup marriage in Hawai'i. They focused on the twelve-year period from 1983 to 1994 with data obtained from marriage certificates at the state Department of Health. The sample for their study consisted of 117,428 marriages registered in Hawai'i during that period in which at least one of the spouses was a Hawai'i state resident. This methodological qualification is necessary to eliminate "honeymoon weddings" in which nonresident couples travel to Hawai'i for a combined wedding and honeymoon since their inclusion would seriously distort the pertinent data.[7]

The overall outmarriage rate for Hawai'i between 1983 and 1994 was 46 percent and varied among the major ethnic groups from a high of 72 percent for Korean American brides to a low of 20 percent for African American women (Fu and Heaton 1997: 93). Both sexes of all the major ethnic groups participate in intermarriage at roughly the Hawai'i rate with the notable exception of Whites, particularly females, who generally have not outmarried at or above the overall standard. The rates for various groups are (women first):

African American (20 percent, 56 percent), Chinese American (65 percent, 61 percent), Filipino American (56 percent, 44 percent), Japanese American (51 percent, 44 percent), Native Hawaiian (58 percent, 54 percent), Korean American (72 percent, 42 percent), and White (27 percent, 37 percent).

Using frequency of intermarriage as an indicator of social distance, Fu and Heaton (1997: 117) did a cluster analysis of the social distance among the fourteen ethnic groups in their study. They thereby identified three intermarrying clusters of groups: (1) Chinese Americans, Japanese Americans, Korean Americans, and other Asian Americans; (2) Whites, Native Hawaiians, Filipino Americans, and Portuguese Americans; and (3) African Americans, Samoans, Latinos, Native Americans, and other Pacific Islanders. Ethnic groups within each cluster have a shorter social distance from each other than from the groups in the other two clusters as measured by frequency of intermarriage (158). The second cluster is located between the other two in terms of the social distance among them; in other words, ethnic groups in the second cluster intermarry with groups in the first and third clusters more frequently than groups in these two clusters intermarry with each other. The first cluster of "East Asian" American ethnic groups holds relatively high socioeconomic status in Hawai'i, although Korean Americans, particularly women, rank somewhat below Chinese Americans and Japanese Americans (see Chapter 3). The second cluster, with the exception of Whites, consists of socioeconomically disadvantaged ethnic groups, as does the third cluster, except for African Americans. This last cluster includes ethnic groups that are among the smallest in population. Besides ethnicity, class—as determined by income, occupational and educational status (see Chapter 3)—is also a significant factor in the outmarriage patterns among ethnic groups; for example, middle-class and higher-status Whites are more likely to intermarry with members of the East Asian American groups than with representatives of the second cluster of Native Hawaiians and Filipino Americans.

Demographic factors continue to contribute to Hawaii's high outmarriage rate, as they did in the past when the very limited number of Chinese and Filipino women led men from those groups to seek the companionship of other women, especially Native Hawaiians. As Fu and Heaton (1997: 157) conclude: "The demographic structure of the marriage market underlines high rates of outmarriage in Hawaii. High ethnic heterogeneity concentrated in a small geographic area, lack of a racial [numerical] majority, and presence of several small groups impose constraints on mate selection and lead to high exogamy in a comparatively closed marriage market." The authors also note that, if the effects of group size are controlled for, Hawai'i residents are about seven times more likely to marry within their own ethnic group than to outmarry, despite the substantial ethnic diversity of the population and the considerable tolerance for intermarriage (109). The very high outmarriage rate of Korean American females and very low rate of African American women can be attributed to demography, especially the relatively small size of their respective ethnic groups in Hawai'i. In the 1960s and 1970s when Korean Americans were less than 2 percent of the population, the intermarriage rate of Korean American women exceeded 80 percent (Lind 1980: 114), perhaps due to the maturing of the third-generation descendants of the original immigrants of the early 1900s.

The comparatively low intermarriage rate of African American women can be accounted for by the fewer females than males in a small population, although prejudice against them might also be a factor. A similarly unbalanced gender ratio prevailed among Filipino women prior to World War II and Chinese women before the 1920s that resulted in limited outmarrying because of their great desirability among men of their respective ethnic groups. The much lower outmarriage rate of White women compared to that of other women in Hawai'i is explained by both demographic and social factors. Belonging to the largest ethnic group in the state, White females have less difficulty finding spouses from their own group. Between 1983 and 1994, both White grooms (46,400) and brides (40,000) had by far the largest number of marriages in Hawai'i (Fu and Heaton 1997: 101). Socially, a probable significant factor in the low intermarrying rate of White women is pressure from family and community for them not to outmarry, especially in the past with the absence of antimiscegenation laws in Hawai'i.

In *Assimilation in American Life*, Milton Gordon (1964: 71, 80) maintained there is an "indissoluble connection, in the time order indicated, between structural assimilation [immediately preceding] and marital assimilation," the latter characterized by "large-scale intermarriage," as in Hawai'i. He argued that structural assimilation, distinguished by "large-scale entrance of the minority group into the social cliques, clubs, and institutions of the core society at the primary group level[,] inevitably will lead to a substantial amount of intermarriage." However, before the 1960s in Hawai'i, high rates of intermarriage (33 percent, Lind 1980: 114) had occurred before structural assimilation, if the "core society" of Hawai'i at that time is understood to have been dominated politically, economically, and culturally by Whites. Gordon (1964: 80) also contended that: "If marital assimilation, an inevitable by-product of structural assimilation, takes place fully, the minority group loses its ethnic identity in the larger host or core society, and identificational assimilation takes place." While almost half of Hawai'i marriages are outmarriages, it might be argued nonetheless that this comparatively high proportion does not constitute "full" marital assimilation. At any rate, even with high percentages of intermarriage since before World War II, minority and other groups in Hawai'i have not lost—and do not appear to be losing—their ethnic identity, and they have not developed a "sense of peoplehood based exclusively on [the] host society," the condition that denotes identificational assimilation (71). Thus, in

Hawai'i, marital assimilation preceded structural assimilation rather than being its "inevitable" result.

The inevitable consequence of Hawaii's high intermarriage rate is a high proportion of multiethnic/racial persons being born in the islands. An estimated 60 percent of the babies born in the 2000s in Hawai'i are of multiethnic or multiracial descent; this is due to higher birthrates among some of the larger groups, such as Native Hawaiians and Filipino Americans, who also intermarry at comparatively high rates (Yim 1992b: B3). Given the high outmarriage rate since before World War II (23 percent in the 1930s), there has been a substantial multiethnic/racial population since that time that has increased to about 40 percent of island residents.

Thus, studies of intermarriage in Hawai'i that provide specific outmarrying rates for different ethnic groups are based on a methodological fiction; that is, they presume that the intermarrying groups are ethnically unmixed, which is hardly the case after nearly a century of outmarriage among the major ethnic groups. This fiction is evident in the study by Fu and Heaton (1997: 70) which points out that when marriage certificate data are recorded by the Hawai'i Department of Health, only one ethnic group for each groom or bride is specified. If more than one ethnic group is listed by an individual on the marriage certificate, the department's coding rules include: (1) if Hawaiian is one of the groups listed, the person is coded as part Hawaiian; (2) if a non-White and a White ethnic group are indicated, the former is recorded; and (3) if more than one non-White ethnic group is reported, the first one is used. Clearly, single ethnic group membership is being assigned to multiracial/ethnic individuals, but the larger methodological issue is that intermarrying groups are themselves the products of generations of outmarriage rather than being supposedly unmixed ethnic units.

## Immigration and In-migration

Hawai'i was receiving an annual average of less than 6,000 immigrants during 1999–2003; this figure had declined since the 1970s and 1980s when it was more than 7,000 (Hawai'i Department of Business and Economic Development and Tourism 2005). In the 2000s, immigrants are generally not considered a significant burden on public resources or as a competitive threat to local residents seeking work, given the extremely low unemployment rate of less than 3 percent. Even during the recession in Hawai'i for most of the 1990s, no noticeable anti-immigrant or anti-immigration sentiments emerged that can be attributed to the limited number of annual immigrants and to the kinds of jobs they commonly obtain in less-desirable service and agricultural work. Immigrants, including Filipinos, Koreans, and Japanese, are well known to provide a considerable proportion of service and sales workers in the highly fluctuating tourist industry, and Filipinos are the largest group employed in the declining sugar industry.

However, strong anti-immigration attitudes and actions were evident in the early 1970s, soon after several thousand predominantly Asian immigrants began arriving in Hawai'i each year following passage of the 1965 Immigration Act. In addition, between 1970 and 1975, an annual average of 20,000 in-migrants from the continental United States (excluding military) were moving to the state (Hawaii Department of Planning and Economic Development 1976 cited in Matsuoka, Lum, and Ome 1998: 1). The state Commission on Population and the Hawaiian Future reported its major findings from a 1972 survey of Hawai'i residents: (1) population growth was a major public concern that the state government was responsible for addressing; (2) migration (including from the continental United States) to Hawai'i needed to be controlled in some way; and (3) a public campaign should be initiated to discourage immigration to Hawai'i (Office of the Governor, State of Hawai'i 1977 cited in Matsuoka, Lum, and Ome 1998: 1). Both the governor and the state legislature responded to these concerns by seeking to limit the number of immigrants and in-migrants settling in Hawai'i, for example, by enacting legislation that established restrictive eligibility criteria for welfare assistance. Rather than being welcomed with aloha, immigrants and continental newcomers were viewed as external threats to the islands because of their substantially increased presence (Okamura 1980). Furthermore, the 1970s were marked by violent clashes between local and immigrant students in the public schools—especially between Philippine-born and Hawai'i-born Filipinos—that emerged after the arrival of immigrants in growing numbers (Okamura 1983).

The Philippines has continued to provide Hawai'i with a majority of newcomers every year since the 1965 Immigration Act was passed. The annual number of Filipino immigrants has ranged from a high of 6,426 in 1970 to a low of 2,472 in 1999 and averaged about 3,000 in the early 2000s (Hawai'i Department of Business and Economic Development and Tourism 2005). A substantial majority of Filipino plantation laborers recruited between 1906 and 1946 were Ilokanos from the northern Philippines; due to the family reunification provisions of U.S. immigration law, they consequently dominated Philippine immigration to Hawai'i. But since the 1980s, Visayans from the central Philippines and Tagalogs from Manila and its surrounding provinces have significantly increased their representation among Filipino immigrants and the Filipino American community.

Chinese are the second-largest immigrating group with more than 600 arrivals each year—including from the People's Republic of China (PRC), Hong Kong, and Taiwan—with most of them from the PRC (Hawai'i Department of Business and Economic Development and Tourism 2005). Closely following them are Japanese with about 500 immigrants per year; among Asian immigrants to the United States, they are one of the least-immigrating groups because of the higher standard of living in Japan. Korean immigrants to Hawai'i have declined substantially (as is the case nationally) from an annual average of more than 1,000 in the 1980s to less than 300 due to the economic development of Korea. They are followed by Vietnamese with about 200 annually and by Canadians and Mexicans with about 100 each per year (Hawai'i Department of Business and Economic Development and Tourism 2005).

Given these differing numbers of annual immigrants, ethnic groups also differ significantly in their proportion of foreign born: Chinese American (16 percent), Filipino American (36 percent), Japanese American (7 percent), Korean American (42 percent), Vietnamese American (68 percent), and White (5 percent).[8] These data for each group include racially or ethnically mixed persons but, if they were limited to those who are unmixed, it is very likely that the percentage of foreign born would be higher since most immigrants would not be of mixed ancestry. In short, ongoing immigration results in Chinese Americans, Filipino Americans, Korean Americans, and Vietnamese Americans having significantly large Hawai'i-born and foreign-born segments within their respective communities. This situation contributes to the social and cultural diversity of these ethnic groups, including differing ethnic identities expressed by these segments.

## *In-migration*

According to the 2000 census, during the decade of the 1990s, substantial population increases occurred on Hawaii's neighbor islands: Maui (28 percent, including Moloka'i and Lana'i), Hawai'i Island (24 percent), and Kaua'i (14 percent) (Omandam 2001). In contrast, O'ahu, which has 72 percent of the state population, had a much lower population gain (5 percent). In terms of absolute numbers, the neighbor islands together gained more than 59,000 new residents, while O'ahu grew by about 40,000, despite most of the jobs, higher education institutions, and economic opportunities in general being located on that island. It might be argued that the neighbor island growth was primarily due to Hawai'i residents moving from one island to another, particularly from O'ahu to the other islands. However, according to the U.S. Census Bureau, from 1995 to 2000 the net population gain from the other islands to Maui County (736) and Hawai'i Island (553) was not especially large, while Kaua'i had a net population loss (1,068) from island-to-island migration (Hurley 2003: A25). These figures emphasize the significance of in-migration from the continental United States for the population increases on the neighbor islands, especially on Kaua'i. According to the U.S. Census Bureau, in the early 2000s, neighbor island population growth continued at a higher rate than on O'ahu very likely because of the improving state economy: Maui (5.9 percent), Hawai'i (6.6 percent), Kaua'i (3.9 percent), and O'ahu (3.0 percent) (Gima 2004: A3).

Due to the option of indicating more than one race in the 2000 census, population data by race and ethnicity are not comparable to those for 1990. However, the general consensus in Hawai'i is that the White population on the neighbor islands grew significantly during the 1990s, and that most of this growth was due to the arrival of newcomers from the continental United States. In 2000, one-fifth (20.4 percent) of Whites (alone or in any combination) in Hawai'i (five years and older) had been living in another state in 1995, although some of them had moved to Hawai'i because of their association with the U.S. military. However, as noted above, there were a little more than 1,500 military personnel and their dependents residing on the neighbor islands in 2000, so those new White residents were predominantly civilians. Also, the percentage of Whites on Maui (34 percent), Hawai'i Island (32 percent), and Kaua'i (30 percent) is much higher than on O'ahu (24 percent) (Hawai'i Department of Business and Economic Development and Tourism 2003b).

Another indication of the considerable in-migration of Whites to Hawai'i is that nearly half of them (48 percent, including multiracial Whites) were born in another state, a figure that is much higher than that for the state as a whole (23 percent). The comparable percentage for racially unmixed Whites would very likely be much higher because a greater proportion of multiracial Whites were born in Hawai'i. This relatively high percentage of Whites born elsewhere contributes to the perception that as an ethnic group they are not local, despite their long historical presence in Hawai'i for more than 200 years.

As a notable example of newcomer-driven population growth, Kihei, Maui, where Whites are the largest ethnic group, grew by more than 50 percent during the 1990s as a result of new housing developments and emerged as the tenth-largest city or town in Hawai'i. Its recent experience is very similar to that of other Hawai'i communities described by Matsuoka, Lum, and Ome (1998: 34):

> [Haole] newcomers settle in newly established, ethnically homogeneous enclaves that provide them with a safety zone for continuing their social practices. It is a settlement pattern, that on the surface, resembles that of other foreign immigrant groups. The critical difference being that newcomers from the continent often have investment capital and are of a higher socioeconomic status than other residents within a jurisdiction. This suggests that, despite their brief length of residency, they assume greater economic and political power than locals and immigrants from the Philippines.

This greater economic power was evident in the ability of Whites to migrate to Hawai'i, and especially the neighbor islands, during the recession years of the 1990s when the unemployment rate (6 percent) exceeded that on the continental United States. Their move was likely made because of a previous offer of employment, particularly in a managerial or professional position in the tourist industry that tends to dominate the neighbor island economy. As noted by Matsuoka, Lum, and Ome (1998: 29): "there is a tendency for over-representation of continental-Caucasians in top management positions within these [mainland-based] corporations. . . . With Hawai'i's primary industry being tourism and its support industries, many Westbound intended residents were likely to be working in the tourist industry." Despite their higher socioeconomic status, in-migrants from the continental United States lack an understanding of Hawaii's multiethnic history and often have had limited social relationships with Asian Americans and Pacific Islanders, the groups that together are a majority in the state.

## Out-migration to the Continental United States

At the same time that White newcomers from the continental United States were moving to Hawai'i, local residents were leaving the islands, especially for the western states. The U.S. Census Bureau estimated that nearly 100,000 residents left Hawai'i between 1990 and 1999 for the American continent (Kakesako 2000a: A1). Undoubtedly, some of this movement included armed forces personnel transferring to other assignments and their dependents. Thus, according to the U.S. Census Bureau, between 1995 and 2000, San Diego County, California, where the U.S. Navy 3rd Fleet is based, ranked first among counties as the destination for Hawai'i residents leaving the city and county of Honolulu (O'ahu, 7,800) and also was first among counties that provided new residents to O'ahu (5,100) (Hurley 2003: A31). However, Clark County, Nevada, where Las Vegas is located and that has no large military base, was the second-ranked destination for departing O'ahu residents (7,700). This finding is no surprise to Hawai'i residents who are well aware of the migration of their relatives, friends, and islanders in general to Las Vegas during the 1990s. They are attracted by the lower cost of living, especially housing, in Las Vegas, sometimes referred to as the "ninth island" of Hawai'i because of the many former state residents who live there and the estimated 40,000 islanders who travel there each month. Other counties that lack a significant military connection to Hawai'i and ranked high among the destinations of departing O'ahu residents were Los Angeles County (6,200) and Phoenix's Maricopa County (3,000) (Hurley 2003: A31).

It is not especially difficult to determine why so many islanders decided to leave their home and relatives. The continental out-migration occurred during the economic slump in Hawai'i of the 1990s, a decade during most of which the national economy was booming. In contrast, Hawai'i lost 7,500 jobs between 1992 and 1996, including 2,000 in agriculture due to plantation closures and 3,000 in construction in 1996 alone (Matsuoka, Lum, and Ome 1998: 4). This movement of Hawai'i residents to the continental United States became so pronounced during the 1990s that one segment of it has been termed the "brain drain," referring to the out-migration of the state's "best and brightest" high school and college graduates who annually depart in search of better educational and employment opportunities.

The college graduates in the brain drain are leaving the islands or deciding not to return after completing their degrees at universities in the continental United States because of the difficulty they face in finding financially rewarding and professionally challenging jobs in Hawaii's tourism-dominated economy. Besides more lucrative employment, these economic migrants are attracted to the continent because of its lower cost of living (except for the San Francisco Bay area) and greater opportunities for professional advancement. Until more companies have been established that can offer competitive salaries, Hawai'i will continue to lose its bright young people, such as Angie Nishimoto, a graduate of one of the academically better public high schools. After receiving a master's degree in computer science and electrical engineering from the Massachusetts Institute of Technology, she accepted a $57,000 a year position with a high-tech firm in California rather than return home (Perez 1999: A1). The substantial volume of this out-migration of top high school and college graduates is a significant factor in the increase in the median age of island residents from 32 to 36 years between 1990 and 2000. As a result of this demographic shift, according to a U.S. Census Bureau researcher, "Hawai'i is aging faster than any other state" (cited in Kakesako 2000a: A8).

Due to the considerable financial cost, Hawai'i students who attend college in the continental United States tend to be from the more socioeconomically advantaged ethnic groups, that is, Chinese Americans, Whites, and Japanese Americans. These students together comprise the largest group of students at the academically better public high schools and a substantial majority at the more exclusive private high schools. While only about 5 percent of the graduates of Waipahu High School—which serves predominantly Filipino American, Native Hawaiian, and Samoan students—enroll annually in universities in the continental United States, 87 percent of the 1998 graduates of Punahou School (one of the top private high schools) left Hawai'i to attend college (Leong 1999: A8).

The phenomenon of college graduates not returning to Hawai'i after earning their degrees occurs especially among graduates of the academically highly selective private high schools such as 'Iolani and Punahou, which was established in the mid-nineteenth century for the children of missionary families.

One of those Punahou alumni who graduated with a bachelor's degree in the 1990s was Kirk Taniguchi who later earned a graduate degree from Columbia University's business school (Barrett and Creamer 1996: A2). Having obtained a position as a securities analyst with Merrill Lynch & Co. on Wall Street, he explained why he decided to remain in New York: "I did not return to Hawaii because I did not see the same type of opportunities that were available on the mainland. While my rent in New York City is ridiculously high, I can afford to live here since my compensation is also higher. If I were to live in Hawaii, I would expect to face much lower levels of compensation, with a cost of living comparable to New York City."

The pernicious circular effects of the brain drain on the Hawai'i economy have been noted by University of Hawai'i financial economics professor Nicholas Ordway: "[It] probably reinforces a single-industry state, i.e. tourism, which doesn't depend on that many well-educated individuals. It is probably making Hawai'i less attractive to high-tech industries" (cited in Leong 1999: A8). The brain drain thus further reduces employment options in the islands both for those in it and for those remaining behind because it lessens the likelihood of the development of knowledge-intensive industries. One positive benefit of the brain drain for the local economy is that it serves as a safety valve that reduces pressure on the job market. Unemployment would be much higher if greater numbers of those in the brain drain chose to return to Hawai'i for work. Thus, the state unemployment rate is artificially low (less than 3 percent in the mid-2000s) because so many young people have moved away or not returned knowing that they would face limited job prospects even with a college degree.

Matsuoka, Lum, and Ome (1998: 38–39) emphasize that a possibly more significant consequence of the out-migration of the local populace than the brain drain is the "cultural drain" of islanders who are knowledgeable and appreciative of Hawaii's local culture and its ethnic groups and their cultural traditions and values. Their concern is that the ongoing brain drain and in-migration of Whites from the American continent are together "headed in a direction that favors cultural homogenization and diminishing diversity" in Hawai'i. Matsuoka (1999: A6) correctly predicted in 1999 that the combined effects of out-migration and the annual arrival of several thousand Whites from the continental United States and immigrants from abroad would result in a minority population of Hawai'i-born residents by 2004. This was the first time since the late 1890s that island-born residents were in the minority (see Lind 1980: 92). Most residents therefore lack the long-standing social and cultural ties to and appreciation of the land, peoples, and cultures of the islands that are such distinctive features of Hawaii's people. Such a situation may not seem especially significant in states, such as California, that receive tens of thousands of immigrants and in-migrants from other states each year. However, in the social and demographic context of Hawai'i, which has a much smaller population with long-term historical and familial ties to the islands, having a majority population not born in the state does raise concerns about possible cultural and other social conflicts.

In addition to the brain drain of highly educated young people, another ongoing out-migration of Hawai'i residents to the continental United States can be attributed to the economic decline of the 1990s. This migration actually began in the late 1980s, prior to the recession, when—fueled by massive Japanese investment and expanding tourist and construction industries—the local economy was booming. However, the economic boom resulted in extremely high housing costs, with the median price of a single-family home nearly $500,000 in 1990, and in Honolulu emerging as the second most expensive metropolitan center in the United States. Many young families who felt priced out of the housing market and believed that more lucrative employment opportunities lay across the Pacific decided to move, especially to western states such as California, Nevada, Arizona, and Washington, where the cost of living was much less than in Hawai'i. This difference in the cost of living between Hawai'i and the West Coast, the so-called "paradise tax," was estimated to be as high as 38 percent in the early 1990s. In the mid-2000s, island residents continue to migrate to the continental United States, particularly because of an overheated housing market that has driven the median price of a single-family home in Hawai'i to new highs in excess of $600,000.

## Conclusion

This chapter has discussed various ongoing social and cultural processes that heighten the complexity of ethnic identity and ethnic relations in Hawai'i by enhancing the differences among and within groups. I have sought to demonstrate how these processes contribute to changing and diverse ethnic identities and complex ethnic relations as a prelude to their further discussion and analysis. These ongoing social and demographic processes—such as Hawaii's high intermarriage rate, immigration from Asia and the Pacific, and in-migration from the continental United States—result in a growing multiethnic population and an increasing number of ethnic groups that are themselves internally culturally diverse. Hawaii's ethnic groups consist of constituent segments with their own distinct ethnic identities, such as local and immigrant Filipinos and local and "mainland" Haoles, that can create difficulties for an ethnic group seeking to construct a common ethnic identity for itself. These internal segments and their diverse ethnic identities are a significant aspect of the complex nature of ethnic relations in Hawai'i. In later chapters, I discuss the construction and expression of their respective ethnic identities by various groups and the assignment of identities to other groups through denigrating cultural representations of them.

# 3

# Socioeconomic Inequality and Ethnicity

This chapter is concerned with determining the relation between socioeconomic status and ethnicity in Hawai'i; that is, ascertaining the significance of ethnicity as an organizing principle in the allocation of socioeconomic status. I review 2000 U.S. census data on occupational status and income level as objective indicators of socioeconomic status of eight major ethnic groups in Hawai'i. These groups include African Americans, Chinese Americans, Filipino Americans, Native Hawaiians, Japanese Americans, Korean Americans, Samoans, and Whites. I argue that considered together, occupational status, income level, and educational achievement (also viewed as an indicator of socioeconomic status; see Chapter 4) demonstrate the institutionalized scope and nature of ethnic inequality in Hawai'i. This chapter also discusses the results from my ongoing longitudinal study of ethnic stratification in island society based on U.S. census data since 1970 that clearly establish the lack of collective social mobility among ethnic minorities since that decade and thus the persistence of ethnic inequality.

As noted in Chapter 2, the U.S. Census Bureau initiated a major change in 2000 by allowing respondents for the first time to indicate membership in more than one racial category. This change has significant implications for the comparability of data from previous censuses to those in 2000, since the number of federally recognized racial categories has increased exponentially from four to sixty-three, including various combinations of those four major racial groups.[1] For this chapter on ethnic stratification, I have chosen to use the census data tabulated for ethnic or racial "group alone or in combination with one or more other races." The alternative is to use the census data for "group alone," meaning information from respondents who claimed membership in only one racial or ethnic category. The primary disadvantage of using those data is that they exclude the substantial proportion of Hawai'i residents (21.4 percent) who are multiracial and who were included in previous census surveys because they had no choice but to indicate belonging to only one ethnic or racial group. Admittedly, there are also disadvantages in using the ethnic or racial group alone or in combination data that are primarily due to multiple counting. A census respondent who indicated that she is Korean American and White has her, for example, income data, tabulated twice, once as a Korean American (with "unmixed" Koreans) in combination with being White, and once as a White (with "unmixed" Whites) in combination with being Korean American. I have decided to use the group alone or in combination data because they are more inclusive in scope and do not exclude from consideration a large number of Hawai'i residents.

In strict terms, the 2000 census results for racial and ethnic groups are not directly comparable to those from previous censuses because the procedures for claiming group membership have changed. Thus, it would not be valid to compare, for example, the occupational status of a given ethnic group in 2000 with that in 1990 and state that the group had "increased" or "decreased" its status. However, with regard to the overall occupational ranking of ethnic groups, a valid comparison can be made between the relative position in 2000 of a group with its relative rank in previous decades. For example, a group could be said to hold a subordinate status in relation to the other ethnic groups in 2000 as it did in 1990.

The following sections discuss and compare the occupational status and median income of eight major ethnic groups in Hawai'i toward an analysis of the salience of ethnicity as a regulating principle of the socioeconomic status system. I argue that the stratification order is "racialized" and that ethnicity structures the highly unequal distribution of socioeconomic benefits and rewards among island ethnic groups.

## Occupational Status

Table 3.1 presents 2000 census data on the distribution by gender of the seven major occupational categories used by the U.S. Census Bureau within each of the eight major ethnic groups in Hawai'i.[2] The upper three categories consist of white-collar occupations, while the lower four groupings include blue-collar jobs that generally provide less in wages and benefits to workers and involve less-desirable working conditions, although not necessarily in all cases.

**TABLE 3.1 OCCUPATIONAL DISTRIBUTION WITHIN ETHNIC GROUPS IN HAWAI'I, 2000 (PERCENT)**

| OCCUPATIONAL CATEGORY | Hawai'i | | African American | | Chinese American | | Filipino American | | Japanese American | | Native Hawaiian | | Korean American | | Samoan | | White | |
|---|---|---|---|---|---|---|---|---|---|---|---|---|---|---|---|---|---|---|
| | M | F | M | F | M | F | M | F | M | F | M | F | M | F | M | F | M | F |
| Management/ Business | 13.8 | 12.0 | 13.7 | 9.7 | 12.8 | 12.7 | <u>6.7</u> | 7.8 | 16.9 | 13.9 | <u>9.1</u> | 10.3 | 14.7 | 12.1 | <u>6.7</u> | <u>5.4</u> | 15.4 | 12.7 |
| Professional | 16.6 | 22.2 | 19.1 | 24.0 | 16.4 | 19.3 | <u>8.4</u> | <u>13.6</u> | 18.6 | 24.4 | <u>9.5</u> | <u>16.9</u> | 14.7 | <u>13.5</u> | <u>7.7</u> | <u>14.0</u> | 19.9 | *27.3* |
| Sales and Office | 17.5 | 39.3 | 19.4 | 38.1 | 19.2 | 43.1 | 15.4 | 39.3 | 21.1 | 45.3 | 14.6 | 44.0 | *22.9* | 42.4 | 15.7 | 45.0 | 16.7 | 36.8 |
| Construction/ Maintenance | 16.1 | 0.6 | <u>10.2</u> | 1.6 | 15.0 | 0.5 | 17.6 | 0.5 | 16.2 | 0.5 | *20.5* | 1.0 | 15.4 | 0.3 | 15.8 | 1.0 | 16.5 | 0.6 |
| Production/ Transportation | 13.4 | 4.2 | 15.6 | <u>3.1</u> | 14.0 | 4.3 | *17.5* | *6.5* | 10.8 | <u>2.5</u> | *18.8* | *5.1* | 11.5 | 3.4 | *24.0* | *6.5* | 12.3 | <u>2.9</u> |
| Service | 20.9 | 20.9 | 21.2 | 23.5 | 21.6 | 19.6 | 31.4 | *30.3* | <u>15.2</u> | <u>13.0</u> | *25.3* | 22.1 | 19.9 | *27.9* | *29.3* | *28.0* | 17.8 | 19.2 |
| Farming/ Fishing | 1.7 | 0.8 | 0.9 | 0.0 | 1.0 | 0.4 | 2.9 | 2.0 | 1.1 | 0.4 | 2.2 | 0.5 | 0.9 | 0.4 | 0.9 | 0.2 | 1.4 | 0.5 |

Note: Italicized numbers indicate overrepresentation in an occupational category compared to Hawai'i workers, while underlining denotes underrepresentation.

Source: "Sex by Occupation for the Employed Civilian Population 16 Years and Over," table PCT86, from Summary File 4 of the 2000 U.S. Census, http://factfinder.census.gov/servlet/DatasetMainPageServlet?.

While information on "Farming/Fishing" occupations has been included in the table, I do not comment further on this category because very few men (4,800) and women (2,100) are employed in this declining area that had more than 15,000 workers in 1990. The data in the table are limited to employed civilians, sixteen years and older, so the substantial military segment among Whites and African Americans is not included. Between 1990 and 2000 there was an increase of about 10,000 employed women in Hawai'i, while the comparable figure for men declined by more than 1,000. This decrease in employed males was due to the higher unemployment rate of men compared to that of women in 2000 and possibly the greater number of men than women in the "brain drain" out-migration to the continental United States during the 1990s.

The column for "Hawai'i" provides data on the percentage distribution of male and female workers among the major occupational categories. It thus represents an overall "average" of occupational distribution for Hawai'i workers that can be compared with figures for specific ethnic groups. For example, if the respective percentages of women and men from an ethnic group employed as "Professionals" are greater than that for Hawai'i females (22.2 percent) and males (16.6 percent), this may be an indication of the higher occupational status of that ethnic group compared to others.

As a composite picture of occupational distribution among island workers, the data in the Hawai'i column also provide information on the nature of the state economy. One obvious feature is the high percentage of both men and women employed in "Service" occupations, which is not very surprising for an economy dominated by tourism for several decades. Since 1990, service work has become the largest occupational category for men and continues as the second largest area for women (Okamura 1998c: 190). There was an increase of almost 14,000 males and 6,000 females employed in service occupations between 1990 and 2000, which is noteworthy insofar as the tourist industry and Hawaii's economy in general were in recession for much of that decade. Another distinctive characteristic of the state economy is its small manufacturing sector evident in the limited number of production workers (13,000 men, 6,000 women). Comparisons between 1990 and 2000 for other occupational categories are not as directly possible because the Census Bureau changed its classification of workers; for example, technical workers were included with professionals in 2000, but they were included with "sales and administrative support" workers in 1990.

Gender differences in occupational status are evident from the percentage data in the Hawai'i column. "Sales and Office" work continues to be the largest category of employment for women with nearly 103,000 in that one field, including more than 60 percent in office occupations. Nonetheless, women are well represented in the highest-status occupational categories in management, business, and financial operations ("Management/Business") and in professional and related occupations ("Professional") where they outnumber men by more than 5,000 workers. In contrast, men continue to dominate blue-collar work in construction, extraction, and maintenance occupations ("Construction/Maintenance") and in production, transportation, and material moving work ("Production/Transportation"). Like tourism, the construction industry suffered major job losses during the 1990s recession in Hawai'i but began a substantial recovery in the early 2000s. Another gender feature of Hawaii's economy is its relatively high labor force participation rate of females (59 percent), particularly among Filipino Americans (64 percent) and Chinese Americans (61 percent). This rate contributes to women trailing men in the labor force by less than 20,000 workers, and the gap has continued to decrease.

The other columns in Table 3.1 provide percentage data on occupational distribution by gender within the same eight major ethnic groups in Hawai'i that were included in my analysis of the 1990 census data on socioeconomic status (Okamura 1998c). If occupational status was being distributed equally, the percentages for each ethnic group would be roughly similar to those for Hawai'i workers as a whole. Obviously, that is not the case; thus, the data in the table provide a means for determining the scope and nature of inequality in the allocation of occupational status among ethnic groups and the significance of ethnicity in structuring that unequal distribution.

The relative occupational status of an ethnic group can be determined by comparing its percentages in the various occupational categories with those for Hawai'i as a whole. In my three previous analyses (1982, 1990, 1998c) of ethnic stratification in Hawai'i, I used a 20 percent margin of difference (either above or below) with the percentages for Hawai'i men and women to ascertain if an ethnic group is represented at parity, is overrepresented, or is underrepresented in a given occupational category. For example, as evident in Table 3.1, although the percentage of Chinese American men (12.8 percent) in Management/Business occupations is lower than that for Hawai'i males (13.8 percent), they can be considered to be represented at parity because their 1.0 percentage point difference is within the 20 percent margin of difference for parity representation (2.8 percentage points). In contrast, Filipino American males (6.7 percent) are underrepresented in the Management/Business field since their percentage point difference (7.1) with the Hawai'i figure for men exceeds the 20 percent margin of difference for parity. Japanese American men (16.9 percent) provide an example of overrepresentation in Management/Business because their percentage point difference (3.1) is greater than the 2.8 percentage point margin of difference for parity. In general, an ethnic group can be considered to have a relatively high occupational status if it is employed at or above parity in most of the white-collar occupational categories, and if it is represented below parity in most of the blue-collar categories. Conversely, an ethnic group with a relatively low occupational status is overrepresented in most of the blue-collar fields and underrepresented in most of the white-collar classifications.

As can be seen in Table 3.1, in the Management/Business occupational category, only Japanese American men are overly represented. Both male and female African Americans, Chinese Americans, Korean Americans, and Whites, and female Japanese Americans and Native Hawaiians are employed at parity. Japanese American men and women in management/business include top executives, accountants and auditors, and financial managers. Chinese American men in the same field are employed as financial specialists and top executives, while women are accountants and auditors and top executives. White males and females in management/business also include top executives and financial specialists. In contrast to those groups, Filipino American and Samoan men and women, and Native Hawaiian men are substantially underrepresented as managers and business specialists.

In the professions, only White women are employed above parity, including as schoolteachers, registered nurses, and top executives. Both sexes of African Americans, Chinese Americans, and Japanese Americans, and White and Korean American males have parity representation. White men in the professions work as schoolteachers, computer specialists, lawyers, physicians and surgeons. Japanese American male professionals include engineers, computer specialists, and schoolteachers, while females are schoolteachers, registered nurses, counselors and social workers. Chinese American women professionals are employed in the same latter three fields, while men work as computer specialists, engineers, and lawyers. Underrepresented professionals include Samoan, Filipino American, and Native Hawaiian men and women, and female Korean Americans.

Sales and Office work is the largest single occupational category for women in all of our ethnic groups. This was also the case in 1990 and thus reflects the continued channeling of women into such white-collar occupations. However, for some immigrant groups—such as Filipinos, Koreans, and Samoans—higher percentages of females employed in sales and office work instead of service jobs are an indication of occupational mobility rather than restriction. Among women, all of the groups have parity employment in sales and office occupations. The same is true for men, except for Japanese Americans and Korean Americans who are overrepresented.

In the blue-collar occupational categories, we find greater representation by Native Hawaiians, Filipino Americans, and Samoans. In Construction/Maintenance work, some of the occupations—such as carpenters, electricians, painters, and plumbers—are considered skilled craftwork, and wages therefore can be higher than for some white-collar positions. All of the ethnic groups are employed at parity in this area, with the exception of Native Hawaiians who are overly represented and African Americans who are underrepresented.

Production/Transportation workers—including food processing workers, truck drivers, and apparel workers (for example, seamstresses)—can be considered semiskilled laborers. Represented above parity in this category are both male and female Samoans, Filipino Americans, and Native Hawaiians. Filipino American and Native Hawaiian men work particularly as truck drivers and laborers. Nearly one-fourth of Samoan males are employed in production/transportation, especially in the same above jobs. Many Filipino immigrant women work as seamstresses, in some cases sewing Hawaiian-style garments for tourists such as matching *muu'muu* dresses and aloha shirts. The other ethnic groups are represented either at or below parity (Japanese American and White females)

At the lowest end of the occupational scale in Service work, both sexes of Filipino Americans and Samoans, Korean American women, and Native Hawaiian men are employed above parity and, with the exception of the latter group, they are considerably overrepresented. Service work is the largest occupational category for male Filipino Americans, Chinese Americans, Samoans, and Native Hawaiians that can be attributed to the substantial proportion of immigrants among the three former ethnic groups, many of whom are employed in the tourist sector. Filipino American women and men are overly represented in service occupations due to the considerable number of post-1965 immigrants who work in the tourist industry as hotel maids, building and grounds maintenance workers, and food service workers, although many of them also are employed in service jobs outside tourism. About one-half of male Samoans in service occupations are "protective service workers" (for example, security guards) and janitors, and Samoan females work as food preparers and maintenance workers. While Korean American women are represented above parity in service work, their percentage is much less than it was in 1980 (42 percent) (Okamura 1990: 3). The relatively high proportion of Korean females in service work is due to the employment of immigrants as cooks and waitresses in Korean restaurants and as "personal appearance" workers such as manicurists. Immigrants also account for the parity representation of Chinese Americans in service jobs, such as cooks, food preparation workers, and maintenance workers.

Some Native Hawaiian men are employed in more financially remunerative service positions such as law enforcement officers and firefighters. However, considerably more of them work as security guards, building and grounds cleaners, cooks and food service workers with many in the tourist industry. While Japanese Americans are underrepresented in service occupations, the significant percentages of males and females in service work is partially due to immigrant employment as cooks, waitresses, and food preparation workers in Japanese restaurants that cater to tourists from Japan and elsewhere.

The data reviewed above can be used to represent the occupational status hierarchy among ethnic groups in Hawai'i. Japanese Americans and Whites hold higher status in the occupational scale given the overrepresentation of men of the former group in management/business and in sales and office work, and of White women in the professions. In addition to their parity employment in the other white-collar occupational categories, these two groups are represented below or at parity in blue-collar work. In 1990 Japanese Americans and Whites also held relatively high occupational rank (Okamura 1998c: 195).

In the intermediate range of the occupational status order are African Americans, Chinese Americans, and Korean Americans. They have parity representation in white-collar occupations, except for the underrepresentation of Korean American women in the professions and the overrepresentation of Korean American men in sales and office work. Both sexes of these three ethnic groups are not overly employed in blue-collar work with the exception of female Korean Americans as service workers. Chinese Americans are the only ethnic group in which both males and females are represented at parity in all six occupational categories. In 1980 and 1990, African Americans and Korean Americans also had intermediate rank in the occupational status hierarchy (Okamura 1990: 7; 1998c: 195).

At the lower end of the occupational status scale are Samoans, Filipino Americans, and Native Hawaiians. Men and women of these ethnic groups are excessively employed in production/transportation and in service work, except for Native Hawaiian females in the latter. With the same group as the exception in management/business, Filipino American, Native Hawaiian, and Samoan men and women are underrepresented as managers/business specialists and as professionals. Both sexes of the same three ethnic groups have parity employment as sales and office workers and as construction/maintenance workers, except for Hawaiian males who are overly represented as the latter. In 1980 and 1990, Native Hawaiians, Samoans, and Filipino Americans had similarly low occupational status (Okamura 1990: 7; 1998c: 195).

The apparent intermediate rank of Chinese Americans in the occupational status hierarchy warrants discussion because I do not believe it reflects their actual employment position in Hawai'i. Chinese Americans held high occupational ranking in 1990 given the overrepresentation of men as professionals and male and female parity representation in the other white-collar work categories (Okamura 1998c: 191). With the notable exception of service work, Chinese American men were underrepresented in the other blue-collar occupational categories, while women were employed at parity. But because the census data from 1990 and 2000 for ethnic groups are not readily comparable, it cannot be argued that Chinese Americans experienced a "decline" in their occupational status during the 1990s, only that they have a lower position in 2000 in contrast to their higher status in 1990.

The reason for this difference in the 1990 and 2000 relative occupational status of Chinese Americans is uncertain, but it is unlikely that it can be attributed to an actual decline in their significant socioeconomic resources such as income, educational attainment, wealth, and property. Given their relatively high socioeconomic status, it is also improbable that Chinese Americans, except for recent immigrants, were subject to institutionalized discriminatory practices in employment and education. The difference in the 1990 and 2000 occupational status of Chinese Americans may very well be due to the change in determining ethnic group membership since many Native Hawaiians could have indicated their Chinese ancestry in the 2000 census. Native Hawaiians as a group have a significantly lower employment status than Chinese Americans. Therefore, if a sufficient number of Native Hawaiians were included with Chinese Americans as a "group alone or in combination," this may have resulted in the lower occupational rank of Chinese Americans.[3] Thus, the intermediate occupational status of Chinese Americans can be understood as resulting from the 2000 census data on Chinese Americans alone or in combination with other races rather than reflecting the employment status of those who claim Chinese American as their primary ethnic identity.

## Family and Individual Income

As can be seen in Table 3.2, the median income ranking of families, females, and males by ethnic group in Hawai'i is roughly comparable with that for occupational status.[4] For family income, Japanese Americans and Chinese Americans are the only groups above the Hawai'i median ($56,961), although Whites are very near to it. All the other ethnic groups are below the state median. With the exception of the reversed positions of Whites and Filipino Americans, the same income ranking of groups obtained in 1990 when Japanese Americans and Chinese American were again the only two groups above the Hawai'i median (Okamura 1998c: 196).

A factor contributing to the higher income status of Chinese American families is their relatively high female labor force participation rate (61 percent). This factor also accounts for the higher income rank of Filipino American families than might be expected from their low occupational and educational status. The income ranking of White families below the Hawai'i median is surprising given that group's high occupational status, but this can be attributed to the significant proportion of lower-paid military personnel in their population. The same factor accounts for the comparatively low-income status of African American families, despite their intermediate occupational position. The lesser earnings of Native Hawaiian and Samoan families correspond to their low occupational and educational status. In the case of Korean Americans, the considerably lesser income of women compared to men con-

**TABLE 3.2 MEDIAN INCOME OF ETHNIC GROUPS IN HAWAI'I, 1999 (DOLLARS)**

| ETHNIC GROUP | FAMILY | MALE | FEMALE |
|---|---|---|---|
| Japanese American | 69,214 | 44,034 | 33,962 |
| Chinese American | 57,312 | 39,759 | 29,255 |
| White | 55,543 | 37,332 | 30,990 |
| Filipino American | 53,942 | 30,213 | 24,795 |
| Native Hawaiian | 49,282 | 35,049 | 26,654 |
| Korean American | 46,613 | 39,089 | 27,605 |
| African American | 42,097 | 29,062 | 25,943 |
| Samoan | 33,040 | 28,633 | 23,349 |

Note: Ethnic group includes the group alone or in any combination. Male and female median income is for full-time workers, fifteen years and older, who worked year-round in 1999.

Source: "Median Family Income in 1999 (Dollars)," table PCT113, http://factfinder.census.gov/servlet/DatasetMainPageServlet? and "Median Income in 1999 (Dollars) by Sex by Work Experience in 1999 for the Population 15 Years and Over with Income," table PCT133, http://factfinder.census.gov/servlet/DatasetMainPageServlet?. Both tables are from Summary File 4 of the 2000 U.S. census.

tributes to the relatively low-income rank of their families, despite their intermediate occupational position.

Concerning median male income, Japanese Americans, Chinese Americans, Korean Americans, and Whites (in descending order) have earnings above the Hawai'i median ($36,808), while the other ethnic groups are all below this figure. This situation also prevailed in 1990 (Okamura 1998c: 196). The income hierarchy among men approximates their ranking by occupational status (see Table 3.1) in which these same four ethnic groups generally hold higher positions in Management/Business and as Professionals. Conversely, the lower income status of Filipino American, Native Hawaiian, and Samoan males is consistent with their overrepresentation in Production/Transportation and Service work. To some extent, the higher income rank of Japanese American men can be attributed to their relatively older median age (forty years) compared to the Hawai'i male median (thirty-five years) insofar as earnings generally increase with age. The higher income status of Chinese American men is significant given the increasing percentage of service workers among them as a result of ongoing immigration from China and Hong Kong since the 1990s.

Regarding median female income, only Japanese Americans and Whites are above the median for Hawai'i ($29,831), although Chinese Americans are slightly below that level. The other ethnic groups all have earnings less than the Hawai'i median, which also was the case in 1990. The female income ranking is very comparable to that for their occupational status (see Table 3.1) with Chinese American, Japanese American, and White women well represented in Management/Business and Professional positions, while Samoan, Native Hawaiian, and Filipino American females are especially employed in Service and Production/Transportation work. Like their male counterparts, the older median age of Japanese American women (forty-three years) in comparison to Hawai'i females (thirty-eight years) contributes to their higher earnings. Due to their overrepresentation in service work, Korean American women do not have the same relatively high-income status as their male counterparts. Similarly, the lower income position of Chinese American women compared to men is probably due to the increased presence of immigrant service workers in their labor force.[5] The income data also indicate that women continue to be paid lower salaries than men, despite having similar occupational status and educational attainment, particularly those in white-collar positions.

A study by the U.S. Bureau of Labor Statistics that analyzed wages in 2004 by state and occupation reported that Hawaii's average annual wage of $36,300 ranked nineteenth nationally and was below the national average of $37,000 (Schaefers 2005: A1).[6] As noted above, a major factor in the lower income received by island workers is the large number of them employed in service occupations, particularly in the tourist industry. The lesser number of higher-paying professional, management/business, and other white-collar positions is another factor that limits the opportunities for socioeconomic mobility by members of ethnic minorities, particularly those with college degrees.

The three objective indicators of socioeconomic status—occupational status, family and individual income, and educational attainment—considered together provide an overall hierarchical ranking of ethnic groups in Hawai'i. Facilitating this composite ethnic hierarchy is the substantial degree of correspondence among the three rankings based on occupational, income, and educational status. This congruence is a clear indication of the significance of ethnicity as the primary organizing principle of the socioeconomic status system and of how it serves to integrate the distribution of occupation, income, and education in Hawai'i society. In the absence of ethnicity as the dominant regulating principle, there would be less consistency among the three status rankings and more of a general distribution of individuals from different ethnic groups at different levels of the socioeconomic status order. In other words, Hawaii's stratification system would be based primarily on class or individual achievement as the organizing principles rather than ethnicity.

As made evident above, the ethnic stratification order in Hawai'i continues to be dominated by Chinese Americans, Whites, and Japanese Americans; this has been the case since 1990 when the latter group joined the two former groups (Okamura 1998c). These three ethnic groups have the highest occupational status given their overrepresentation or parity representation in the upper-level employment categories. This high occupational status is reflected in family income (except for Whites), female income (except for Chinese Americans), and male income that are above the Hawai'i median. Providing for their higher occupational and income rank is the high educational attainment of Chinese Americans, Japanese Americans, and Whites, all of whom have bachelor's degree or higher completion rates above the state median (see Chapter 4). This high degree of educational achievement and college enrollment ensures that these three groups will be able to maintain their dominant socioeconomic position for another generation.

Holding intermediate status in the ethnic stratification system are African Americans and Korean Americans as they did in 1980 and 1990. Both groups occupy the general middle range of the occupational, income, and educational status hierarchies. African American men and women are represented at parity in nearly every occupational category, although they rank low in terms of income because of the military segment of their population. While Korean American men have income above the Hawai'i median, their female counterparts are below the median for women. Similarly, in terms of college completion, the percentage for Korean American males is above the state median, while females are below the median for Hawai'i women.

The lower end of the ethnic stratification order is occupied by Native Hawaiians, Samoans, and Filipino Americans, as was the case from 1970, if not earlier, to 1990 (Okamura 1982, 1990 and 1998c). These groups continue to have the lowest occupational, income, and educational status of the ethnic groups included in my analyses. They continue to be excessively represented in the lower-level occupations, while represented below parity in the higher employment categories. As a result, their income is below the Hawai'i median for families, men, and women. The low occupational and income rank of Samoans, Native Hawaiians, and Filipino Americans is clearly related to their low level of educational attainment. They persist in having bachelor's degree or higher completion rates far below the Hawai'i median, and the college or graduate school enrollment percentages of Samoans and Native Hawaiians are considerably lower than the state median (see Chapter 4). Their continuing subordinate socioeconomic status reflects the cumulative effects of ethnic inequality transmitted from one generation to the next among these three groups.

The consequences of the limited educational achievement of Filipino Americans, Native Hawaiians, and Samoans extend well beyond the decade of the 2000s because it means that they will continue to occupy the lower levels of the ethnic stratification order in Hawai'i. Higher education (as opposed to work experience) has increasingly become the principal means for entry into the more financially rewarding occupations that also provide better employment, health insurance, and retirement benefits. The continued restricted access of these three groups to postsecondary education can only result in their continued socioeconomic subordination in Hawai'i. Other ethnic minorities not considered in my census analyses—such as Puerto Ricans, other Pacific Islanders (for example, Tongans, Chamorros), and Southeast Asians (for example, Vietnamese Americans, Laotian Americans, Cambodian Americans)—are very likely in the same socioeconomically disadvantaged position as the three main minority groups discussed in this chapter. For example, with regard to occupational status, service work is the largest employment category among both male Puerto Ricans (26.9 percent) and Vietnamese Americans (29.4 percent), while female Puerto Ricans (29.2 percent) and Vietnamese Americans (31.4 percent) are also greatly represented in the same area. At the opposite end of the occupational status hierarchy, both men and women from these two groups are minimally employed as professionals (females first): Puerto Ricans (15.7 percent, 9.6 percent) and Vietnamese Americans (11.6 percent, 8.4 percent). Not surprisingly, then, in terms of median family income, both Puerto Ricans ($36,505) and Vietnamese Americans ($28,697) rank among the lowest of our ethnic minorities with earnings much less than the state median ($56,961). As for the percentage with a bachelor's degree or higher among those twenty-five years and older, Puerto Ricans (8.6 percent) and Vietnamese Americans (11.8 percent) again are among the lowest of our minority groups and well below the Hawai'i median (26 percent). These and other data on differential occupational, income, and educational status among the ethnic groups discussed in this chapter clearly demonstrate that ethnic inequality will persist for another generation, if not longer, and is the cumulative result of previous inequality in Hawai'i.

## "Racialized" Stratification Order

I have been conducting a longitudinal study of the socioeconomic status system of Hawai'i based on U.S. census data on occupational status, educational attainment, and income level by ethnicity for 1970, 1980, and 1990 (Okamura 1982, 1990, and 1998c, respectively). This chapter is the latest analysis of the ethnic stratification order using 2000 census data. The study includes the major ethnic groups in Hawai'i: African Americans, Chinese Americans, Filipino Americans, Native Hawaiians, Japanese Americans, Korean Americans, Whites, and Samoans. In my analyses of the socioeconomic data, I have sought to identify the organizing principles of the stratification system in Hawai'i that regulate or structure the distribution of socioeconomic status among ethnic groups rather than merely to present an overall hierarchical ranking of those groups. Accordingly, I follow the analytical distinction advanced by social anthropologist M. G. Smith (1975: 272) between stratification as an unequal empirical distribution of resources and privileges and as a "set of specific principles" that organize that distribution: "Inequalities in the distribution of social assets, opportunities and values are thus central to stratification; but the concrete empirical distribution of these inequalities presupposes some principle or principles to regulate, integrate and order the differentiation. Analytically, then, the stratification can be reduced to a set of specific principles that generate and organize the prevailing distribution of resources and opportunities."

The previous results from my longitudinal study include that, since the end of the economic boom and the emergence of tourism as the dominant industry in the 1960s, the ethnic stratification order in Hawai'i has remained relatively constant with groups holding the same relative positions since 1970. The one notable exception to this overall pattern is the upward mobility of Japanese Americans from an intermediate position in 1980 to a higher socioeconomic status in 1990 shared with Chinese Americans and Whites. However, for Native Hawaiians, Filipino Americans, and Samoans, this relative constancy in the stratification system denotes a significant lack of opportunity for upward mobility available to them. Based on these findings, I have argued that ethnicity is the primary organizing principle of the socioeconomic status system, and therefore ethnic inequality, rather than equality of opportunity, is institutionalized and entrenched as a fundamental condition of the social stratification order (Okamura 1998c: 186–187). The analyses presented here and in Chapter 4 regarding educational attainment are consistent with the results from my prior analyses and thus confirm the continued institutionalization of ethnic inequality. As stated in Chapter 1, ethnic difference frames inequality in Hawai'i as evident in the highly unequal status of ethnic groups in the stratification order. Indeed, ethnic inequality has become more pronounced since 1970 and provides little indication that it may diminish in the near future.

Clearly, the stratification system in Hawai'i is highly "racialized," and ethnic groups are subject to "differential racialization" given that socioeconomic rewards and resources, such as employment, income, and education, are very unequally distributed among them.[7] In elaborating on the concept of differential racialization, Michael Omi (1994: 207) observed that:

> The problems encountered by a rich entrepreneur from Hong Kong and a recently arrived Hmong refugee are obviously distinct. The sites and types of discriminatory acts each is likely to encounter, and the range of available responses to them, differ by class location. . . . [A] differential racialization has developed between and within different Asian American communities with important consequences for individual identity, collective consciousness, and political organization.

In Hawai'i, a differential racialization has developed among and within different ethnic groups with differing consequences for socioeconomic status, political power, and identity formation. As Eric Yamamoto (1999: 117) has noted: "The concept of differential racialization . . . acknowledges that historical and contemporary influences racialize different racial groups and subgroups differently, . . . thereby creating different racial statuses and power for subgroups. . . . Differential racialization of groups creates differing racial meanings for racial groups and subgroups." Those meanings influence not only "collective consciousness" and "political organization" but also access to socioeconomic resources and opportunities insofar as racial and ethnic groups are differentially subject to "discriminatory acts."

Since I have argued for the greater significance of ethnicity rather than race as a structural principle of social relations in Hawai'i, I need to clarify that by a racialized stratification order, I am still contending that ethnicity is the preeminent principle in the allocation of socioeconomic status insofar as "ethnic" (rather than racial) significance and meaning are extended to the social practice (or process) of status distribution. By differential racialization, I am referring to the very different consequences and significance that ethnicity (rather than race) has for different ethnic groups in Hawai'i in structuring social relations, particularly unequal relations, among them. For the socioeconomically dominant groups—including Whites, Japanese Americans, and Chinese Americans—ethnicity as the primary regulating principle of the stratification system works to their considerable advantage in providing them greater access to socioeconomic benefits and privileges, such as well-paying professional positions and private schooling and a college education in the continental United States for their children. In contrast, for the socioeconomically subordinate groups—including Native Hawaiians, Filipino Americans, Samoans, other Pacific Islanders, Puerto Ricans, and Southeast Asians—ethnicity as the dominant organizing principle serves to restrict their access to socioeconomic opportunities and rewards. Consequently, most of them are relegated to low-wage and low-mobility jobs that cannot provide for the collective upward advancement of themselves and their children. By excluding ethnic minorities from equal opportunity in education and employment, ethnicity as a structural principle enforces the socioeconomic status hierarchy among ethnic groups and thus maintains ethnic inequality in Hawai'i.

Focusing on ethnicity as the primary regulating principle of the socioeconomic status order can make the operations of that system appear more abstract than necessary. Ultimately, the reason that ethnicity provides greater benefits and opportunities for Chinese Americans, Whites, and Japanese Americans is because these groups, or at least a sufficient number of their members, control the stratification order by occupying positions of authority and power. From their positions in various institutional sectors of society, such as government, education, economy, and law, they are able to make decisions and take actions that benefit members of their own ethnic groups to a greater extent than members of other groups.[8] These decisions and actions include appropriating state funds for public education, implementing equal opportunity and affirmative action policies, awarding state and county government contracts, and hiring employees in a private company or government unit.

Having greater control of decisions such as these enables members of the dominant ethnic groups to ensure that ethnicity, rather than other structural principles such as equal opportunity, has greater salience in socioeconomic status allocation.

At a much lower level of society, Japanese Americans, Chinese Americans, and Whites also make decisions and take actions as parents that positively affect the future life chances of their children and, indirectly, the ethnic groups to which they belong. Given the considerable financial resources they control in the form of income, real estate, investments, savings, and other forms of accumulated wealth, families from the privileged ethnic groups are able to reproduce themselves socially in the same or higher socioeconomic status through what ethnic studies scholar George Lipsitz (1998: vii) has referred to as "inter-generational transfers of inherited wealth." Parents can invest in the education and future socioeconomic security of their children by sending them from kindergarten to a college-preparatory private school that can provide entry to a prestigious college or university in the continental United States. Eventually, these parents pass on their accumulated financial resources to their children who have become highly educated, professionally employed, and substantially remunerated adults, thus enabling them to maintain themselves and their own children in a superior socioeconomic position "from generation to generation," much like the accumulation and transferal of White wealth discussed by Oliver and Shapiro (2006).

Since the 1970s, ethnic relations in Hawai'i have become increasingly structured by the economic and political power and status wielded by Chinese Americans, Whites, and Japanese Americans over other ethnic groups.[9] In occupying their privileged position, these groups intermarry with one another, send their children to the same exclusive private schools, reside in the same affluent neighborhoods, and socialize with each other at the same private clubs. As a result, Hawai'i is becoming even more unequal by developing into a two-tier stratified society, the lower level of which is occupied by Filipino Americans, Native Hawaiians, Samoans, and other numerically small ethnic minorities, such as other Pacific Islanders, Southeast Asians, and Puerto Ricans.[10]

## Maintenance of Ethnic Inequality

Beyond the workings of ethnicity as the primary organizing principle in the allocation of socioeconomic status in Hawai'i, two additional factors maintain ethnic inequality by limiting collective socioeconomic mobility by ethnic minorities. First, Hawaii's economy is overdependent on tourism, creating a labor market dominated by service and sales jobs that do not constitute viable avenues for upward advancement. Second, ongoing institutional discrimination, together with the nonimplementation of equal opportunity and affirmative action policies, restricts the access of ethnic minorities to higher education and higher status employment.

Regarding the economy, there is no question that tourism has dominated Hawaii's economy since the 1960s as the major industry.[11] At more than $12.2 billion per year, "visitor-related expenditures" in the tourist industry comprise almost one-fourth of the gross state product of about $51 billion, and tourism generates the same proportion of state and county tax revenues ($1.2 billion).[12] Nearly one-third (31 percent) of the jobs in Hawai'i are created directly or indirectly by the tourist industry, primarily in service and sales work. More than 180,000 Hawai'i workers depend for their livelihood directly or indirectly on the state of the "visitor" industry and whether or not those "guests" decide to visit the islands for a short vacation.

Despite being a private industry, tourism receives substantial government support through funding provided to the Hawai'i Tourism Authority (HTA), the state agency with primary responsibility for marketing the islands throughout the world. The agency was established in 1998 as one of the major recommendations of the Economic Revitalization Task Force organized by the governor to develop initiatives to deliver Hawai'i from its economic doldrums of the 1990s.[13] In 1999, the HTA budget was more than doubled to $61 million per year and to $71 million in 2002, but this massive additional funding did not result in an increase in tourist arrivals (Mak 2004: 157). The tourist industry is also financially supported by other state government units, including the School of Travel Industry Management at the University of Hawai'i (UH) Manoa that trains future management personnel. Several UH community colleges offer "hospitality and tourism education" and "culinary arts" vocational education programs that teach students how to become hotel staff and food service workers. As a private, for-profit activity, tourism arguably should be self-sufficient and not depend on Hawai'i taxpayers for financial assistance.[14] The state government justifies its support of the tourist industry with taxpayer dollars by emphasizing the large number of Hawai'i residents and their families whose livelihood derives from tourism and the significant contributions that it makes to tax revenues. But these arguments ultimately demonstrate that the state needs to lessen its overdependence on tourism because it has become such a huge single factor in the overall quality of life of Hawaii's people and not merely in the economy.

Growing opposition to the dominant role of the tourist industry in Hawai'i is evident from a 2005 statewide survey of 1,352 island residents sponsored by the Hawai'i Tourism Authority (Schaefers 2006: A1). For the first time, a majority (55 percent) of the survey respondents agreed with the statement "This island is being run for tourists at the expense of local people," although such concurrence has been increasing steadily since 1988 (when the response was 44 percent). Attitudes toward the tourist industry varied widely by ethnic group with Filipino Americans (56 percent) most likely to agree that tourism has been "mostly good" for them and their families, which is not surprising given the significant percentage of this group employed in the industry. In contrast, Native Hawaiians (31 percent) were least likely to view tourism as being beneficial for them (Schaefers 2006: A11).

Not surprisingly, the downturn in tourism beginning in 1991 had dire consequences for Hawaii's economy and people, not just in terms of fewer available jobs but also in less tax revenues for funding government services and programs. The prolonged recession endured by island residents during most of the 1990s clearly can be attributed to the tourism slump that was the direct result of a series of unforeseen events: the 1990–1991 U.S. recession, the Gulf War, the extended recession in Japan, and the 1997–1998 Asian financial crisis. Given the overall economic impact of tourism, a large majority of Hawaii's people are affected by how well or not the industry is doing, although not to the same extent. Ethnic minorities whose livelihoods are directly dependent on the number of arriving tourists, such as Filipino and Samoan immigrants and Native Hawaiians, are far more likely to be hurt financially by a downslide in tourism than are the socioeconomically privileged ethnic groups.

By the mid-1990s, the U.S. economy was booming, especially in California, with a thirty-year low in the nation's unemployment rate, the stock market hitting all-time highs, and bulging tax revenues that significantly reduced the federal debt. The robust national economy should have meant that Americans had the extra savings to spend on their dream vacation in the islands that would help resuscitate the struggling local economy. Nonetheless, Hawaii's economy remained in the doldrums for most of the latter half of the 1990s, unable to mount a recovery. According to a U.S. Commerce Department report, between 1992 and 1999, the state economy shrunk an average of 0.3 percent annually, while the nation's economy expanded at an annual average rate of 4 percent ("Hawaii's Economy Dead Last in 1990s," *Honolulu Star-Bulletin* 2001: A1). During this period, Hawai'i had the worst economic performance in the entire nation and was rated by several observers, including *U.S. News and World Report*, as the state with the worst economy based on various objective indicators such as the number of new jobs created and gross state product growth ("Isle Economy Is Rated Worst," *Honolulu Star-Bulletin* 1992: D1; Lynch 1996: D1).[15] An economy consistently rated among the worst in the nation can hardly be expected to provide viable means for reducing ethnic inequality.

While Hawaii's economy showed signs of being rejuvenated by 2000, the terrorist attacks on September 11, 2001 on the World Trade Center and the Pentagon, although taking place thousands of miles across the Pacific Ocean and the continental United States, were another major setback on the long road to economic recovery. The attacks had disastrous consequences for the state economy with fear of flying becoming a new factor in the downturn of tourism. As a highly volatile industry, tourism is extremely sensitive to economic and political fluctuations in the global economy and international geopolitics that occur with regularity in places very distant from the islands' beaches, such as Iraq, Thailand, Japan, and Afghanistan. The Hawai'i economy struggles mightily under such overly dependent and ever-fluctuating economic and political conditions to provide significant and long-term opportunities for socioeconomic mobility so that ethnic minority groups, and not just individuals, can advance themselves.

In the mid-2000s, the tourist industry and, consequently, Hawaii's economy were doing exceedingly well for the first time in about fifteen years. A record high of 7.4 million tourists arrived in 2005 (Schaefers 2006: C1), although the seven million milestone was nearly reached during the last economic boom period in the early 1990s. Hotel room occupancy approached its highest levels since 1986 with projected continuing increases of arrivals from both the continental United States and Japan (Godvin 2005). As a result of robust tourist and construction industries (due to a general construction boom and massive federal spending on military facilities), the state economy was once again thriving. Hawaii's unemployment rate was 2.4 percent in spring 2006 (3 percent is considered "full employment"), the lowest in the nation since 2004 and a little more than half the national rate of 4.7 percent ("Hawaii Jobless Rate Drops to 2.4 Percent," *Honolulu Star-Bulletin* 2006: C1). Carl Bonham, executive director of the University of Hawai'i Economic Research Organization, commented on the expanding local economy: "We're simply adding jobs faster than the labor force is growing. What is causing that is an extremely vibrant economy. There's virtually no sector of the economy that isn't adding jobs. Employers are finding it difficult to find qualified workers in a whole variety of fields. . . . We're firing on all cylinders" (quoted in Segal 2005).

While certainly more desirable than the recession of the 1990s, the economic upsurge in tourism, jobs, and tax revenues masks the differential negative impact it can have on the lives of Hawaii's people. Before home prices in Hawai'i started their meteoric ascent in the mid-2000s, with the median price of a single-family home on O'ahu at more than $600,000, the 2000 census indicated wide disparities among ethnic groups in family home ownership: Japanese Americans (73 percent), Chinese Americans (63 percent), Filipino Americans (58 percent), Native Hawaiians (52 percent), Whites (49 percent), and Korean Americans (46 percent). The relatively low percentage for Whites can be attributed to their large number of military families who are provided with housing as a benefit. The home ownership gap undoubtedly has widened even further as a result of six consecutive years of rising home prices since 1999, much to the disadvantage of ethnic minorities. Home ownership has long-term socioeconomic benefits for families, such as using the equity developed over time to finance the children's college education or enabling the children to become home owners themselves. Lesser access to home ownership among Hawaii's ethnic minorities contributes to the perpetuation of their socioeconomic subordination by restricting them from its considerable financial advantages and benefits. Thus, there is no necessary reason to assume that the robust economy of the mid-2000s, given its reliance on tourism, will significantly reduce ethnic inequality, although no doubt a certain number of individuals from minority groups will benefit.

The other major factor that contributes to the maintenance of ethnic inequality in Hawai'i is institutional discrimination. Through policies, practices, and laws, such unequal treatment denies ethnic minorities the same opportunities and privileges enjoyed by the dominant ethnic groups, particularly in education and employment. As discussed in Chapter 4, the annual practice of the state government to underfund the public school system by a substantial amount subjects their majority clientele of ethnic minority students to discrimination by denying them an adequate education. In the UH system, the policy decisions of the Board of Regents to raise tuition considerably in 1996, 1997 and for six consecutive years beginning in 2006 also discriminate against ethnic minorities, who are less financially able to pay the higher tuition compared to the privileged ethnic groups in Hawai'i and thus are excluded from equal access to public higher education.

Institutional discrimination in the UH system and elsewhere in the state also results from the nonenforcement of equal employment opportunity and affirmative action policies and of civil rights laws prohibiting racial discrimination. It is extremely difficult to believe that the highly unequal ethnic stratification system of Hawai'i is the cumulative result of equal opportunity provided to ethnic minorities over the decades. If that is assumed to be the case, then the only explanation for the continued subordinate socioeconomic status of ethnic minorities is that they are to blame for their predicament, particularly their supposed lack of ability or desire to advance themselves. Unfortunately, this is precisely the kind of explanation that has become increasingly accepted in Hawai'i to account for ethnic inequality; in other words, "attributing the outcome [of racial disparities in U.S. society] to the inadequacies of the persons who suffer the condition, not to any as yet undiscovered problems with our own social organization" (Loury 2002: 81). The various forms of institutional discrimination I have discussed, such as raising tuition in the UH system, would not be considered racially discriminatory according to civil rights laws since they are not necessarily intended to deny equal opportunity to particular racial or ethnic groups. However, these decisions or policies do result in unfair or unequal treatment of ethnic minorities as evident in the socioeconomic disadvantages they experience, such as their gross underrepresentation at

UH Manoa and persisting subjugated status in the stratification order of Hawai'i.

## Conclusion

This discussion of the ethnic stratification system brings up the important question of the relation between ethnicity and class as organizing principles of socioeconomic status distribution in Hawai'i. Since I have argued that ethnicity is the primary regulating principle of status allocation, ethnicity therefore trumps class, but not in absolute terms. Young Japanese Americans, Chinese Americans, and Whites from working-class families do not necessarily have greater life chances for socioeconomic advancement than do young middle-class Filipino Americans, Samoans, and Native Hawaiians. However, because they belong to socioeconomically dominant ethnic groups, working-class members of the former groups are more likely to advance socioeconomically than working-class constituents of the latter groups. In contrast, the predominantly working-class status of ethnic minority group members tends to reinforce their subordinate ethnic status, and together they limit their socioeconomic mobility. In sum, the intersection of ethnicity and class as structural principles of Hawaii's stratification system is much more likely to result in socioeconomic advantage for Chinese Americans, Whites, and Japanese Americans than for Samoans, Native Hawaiians, Filipino Americans, and other ethnic minorities because of the greater significance of ethnicity than class in structuring socioeconomic status.

As noted above, ethnicity as the dominant regulating principle does not determine absolutely the distribution of socioeconomic status among individuals and ethnic groups in Hawai'i, although it clearly influences this distribution. Ethnicity is not socioeconomic destiny; it does not constitute a rigid barrier to the educational goals and occupational aspirations of individual members of ethnic minorities, nor is it a guarantee of a privileged lifestyle for members of the dominant ethnic groups. The structural influence of ethnicity (rather than its determinism) in the social stratification system is most apparent among ethnic groups, as opposed to individuals, insofar as the relative positions of ethnic groups in this system (except for Japanese Americans) have not changed very much since 1970, if not earlier. At the same time, a limited number of individuals from the socioeconomically disadvantaged ethnic groups have been able to advance themselves and their families.

Thus, an alternative organizing principle of the socioeconomic status system is individual achievement and merit. If it was the dominant principle—that is, if individuals of whatever ethnicity (or gender) gain access to socioeconomic status based primarily on their personal educational and occupational qualifications and skills in an open, competitive system—then there would be a much more equitable distribution of socioeconomic benefits and opportunities among ethnic groups and obvious indications of upward mobility among the subordinate minorities. However, this has hardly been the case since at least 1970, if not earlier. In this regard, Lipsitz (1998: 15) has contended that in the U.S. economy, "where personal connections prove the most important factor in securing employment, attacks on affirmative action guarantee that whites will be rewarded for their historical advantage in the labor market rather than for their individual abilities or efforts." In the Hawai'i context, Lipsitz's argument applies also to Chinese Americans and Japanese Americans, besides Whites, who are all similarly rewarded for their personal connections and historical advantage in the employment arena, despite the individual abilities or qualifications of ethnic minority group members.

Nonetheless, there is no question that the social stratification order in Hawai'i is relatively open, and that social mobility is very possible, even for members of socioeconomically disadvantaged ethnic groups. However, such advancement is limited to a restricted number of individuals from those ethnic minorities rather than being a collective social process in which the groups themselves or a substantial proportion of their members are engaged. In short, compared to ethnicity, individual achievement and merit as a structural principle is of secondary significance in the social stratification system of Hawai'i.

# 4

# Educational Inequality and Ethnicity

Education has been used by racial and ethnic minorities in Hawai'i and elsewhere in the United States as a means of both individual and collective social mobility. In Hawai'i, ethnic groups that started on the plantation, such as Chinese Americans, Japanese Americans, and Korean Americans, were able to use the public education system to advance themselves socioeconomically, and in the case of the first two groups, to the very highest levels of the social status order. However, public education—including both the Hawai'i state Department of Education (DOE) system from kindergarten through high school (K–12) and the University of Hawai'i (UH) system—no longer serves as a means of group mobility for ethnic minorities. This chapter discusses how public education contributes to the institutionalization of inequality among island ethnic groups and the role of the state government in maintaining educational inequality. My contention is that differences in educational access and attainment among ethnic groups in Hawai'i are primarily the result of policies and practices in the DOE and UH systems and the state government that discriminate against ethnic minorities and thus foster their educational subordination. As the dominant organizing principle of social relations, ethnicity contributes to such unequal treatment of minorities by regulating differential access to educational benefits and rewards, particularly a college degree, and thereby maintains educational inequality in Hawai'i.

## Department of Education System

Perhaps the most significant factor in any comparative discussion of Hawaii's public school system is that it is the only statewide system in the United States. Rather than consisting of hundreds of school districts funded primarily by local property taxes, which is the norm in the continental United States, the DOE receives the bulk of its funding from appropriations by the state legislature. In most states, school districts have the authority to levy taxes, generally property taxes, that provide between 28 percent (Alaska) to 68 percent (Nebraska) of state and local funding for K–12 public education (Office of the Superintendent/Planning and Evaluation Office 2004: 15). The substantial amount of funds for school districts derived from local property taxes in the other forty-nine states almost guarantees differential educational quality provided to students.

In contrast, because Hawaii's statewide funding system eliminates the funding imbalances that result from school districts having widely differing property tax bases and thus revenues, it seemingly should provide equal educational opportunity for individual students, ethnic groups, and schools. Nonetheless as I discuss below, funding disparities from the state legislature still occur among schools that contribute to educational inequality among ethnic groups. Furthermore, since the 1970s the DOE schools have been receiving a declining proportion of the state budget and, consequently, the quality of education provided to students and the condition of the schools have deteriorated markedly. I begin with a brief description of the public school system and its students and teachers.

There are 285 public schools in Hawai'i distributed among the seven inhabited islands, including the smallest island of Ni'ihau. In the 2005–2006 school year, enrollment was about 181,000 students; it peaked in 1997–1998 at about 189,000 and has been declining since then (Office of the Superintendent/Planning and Evaluation Office 2004: 27). In terms of ethnicity, these students include: Native Hawaiian (26 percent), Filipino American (20 percent), White (14 percent), Japanese American (11 percent), Latino (4.6 percent), Samoan (3.6 percent), Chinese American (3.2 percent), African American (2.4 percent), and Korean American (1.4 percent).[1] Thus, the socioeconomically subordinate groups, including Native Hawaiians, Filipino Americans, Latinos, Samoans, and other Pacific Islanders, comprise a majority of public school students. In contrast, the socioeconomically privileged ethnic groups, such as Whites, Japanese Americans, and Chinese Americans, are much less represented in the public schools than they are in the state population and constitute a majority or certainly a plurality of private school students. As I demonstrate below, ethnic minorities are being disadvantaged educationally by the lack of adequate funding provided to the DOE schools and by other government practices and policies much more than the socioeconomically dominant (and underrepresented) ethnic groups.

As for the nearly 13,000 teachers in Hawaii's public schools, the largest ethnic group continues to be Japanese Americans (38 percent), which has probably been the case since the 1960s (Office of the Superintendent/Planning and Evaluation Office 2004: 29). They are followed by: Whites (26 percent), Native Hawaiians (10 percent), Filipino Americans (6.0 percent), Chinese Americans (5.1 percent), African Americans (0.6 percent), Samoans (0.4 percent), and Latinos (0.2 percent). Thus, the two largest groups among students—that is, Native Hawaiians and Filipino Americans—are among the least employed as public schoolteachers, while the two largest ethnic groups among teachers are far less represented as students. Those significant differences in ethnic distribution between students and teachers are more than demographic and concern culture-based learning styles (particularly among ethnic minority students, including immigrants) with which teachers from the dominant ethnic groups may not be familiar. Compounding this problem, the DOE recruits and hires several hundred teachers each year from the continental United States, who comprise a majority of the new teachers hired, because public and private universities in Hawai'i produce less than half the approximately 1,500 new teachers the state needs annually (Office of the Superintendent/Planning and Evaluation Office 2004: 10). These predominantly White teachers are even less culturally prepared to teach in the local public schools since they have had no prior experience in instructing students from Hawai'i as part of their education.

## *Public School Problems*

Since at least the 1990s if not earlier, Hawai'i residents have been regularly bombarded by the local print and television news media with articles and features on the sorry state of the public school system. These troubling media stories are confirmed by various educational and government organizations that rank Hawaii's public schools among the worst in the nation. The American Legislative Exchange Council, the nation's largest bipartisan group of state legislators, rated Hawaii's public schools forty-seventh among the fifty states in a study that evaluated one hundred measures of educational resources and student achievement since 1977 (Kakesako 2000b: A1). The study reported that while the annual amount spent per student increased nationally by 24 percent from 1977 to 1997, such spending in Hawai'i declined 4 percent. Another report, *Measuring Up*, by the nonprofit National Center for Public Policy and Higher Education (2004), gave the state's public schools a grade of C for college preparation, particularly because "small proportions of 11th and 12th graders take and score well on Advanced Placement tests and on college entrance exams."

In its own 1996 report on the status of the public schools issued in the midst of the then ongoing economic slump in Hawai'i, the DOE contended that the state's fiscal crisis was eliminating "hard-won gains" in the public school system and that the system was deteriorating compared to the rest of the nation in all areas from funding to class size (Donnelly 1996: A1). The DOE report noted that, while the state ranked sixth in the nation in per capita income and second in per capita state government revenues, it was last among the fifty states in the percentage of state funding allocated to K–12 public education. Although the DOE report is somewhat dated, I would like to highlight some of its findings to emphasize that the status of Hawaii's public schools has not improved since then and that, at times of fiscal crisis, public education is not a high policy priority of the state government. For the 1994–1995 school year, the state's student/teacher ratio ranked forty-first in the United States with the average class size at twenty-six pupils. The report stated that Hawaii's high schools were by far the largest in the nation at 90 percent bigger than the national average, and its elementary schools were the third largest in size (Donnelly 1996: A1, A6). In 2005 the five largest public high schools in Hawai'i had an average enrollment of more than 2,400 students; at four of those schools, Filipino Americans, Native Hawaiians, and Samoans were a majority of students (Creamer 2005: A7). The DOE report observed that educational studies have demonstrated that small schools, and not just small classes, produce better-achieving students. In 1994–1995, the DOE had a school year of 176 days, the shortest school year in the nation (nine days less than the national average), although it was extended to 183 days in 1997.

More recent information on the status of the Hawai'i public school system is provided in "The Superintendent's Fourteenth Annual Report on School Performance and Improvement in Hawai'i, 2003" (Office of the Superintendent/Planning and Evaluation Office 2004). The report indicated that the percentage of state and local funds allocated to K–12 public education in Hawai'i had declined from 1987–1988 (17 percent) to 1998–1999 (15 percent) with a low of 13 percent in 1992–1993 (2004: 30). In 1998–1999, Hawai'i ranked dead last of the fifty states in such state and local expenditures. Furthermore, between 1987–1988 and 1998–1999, Hawai'i was consistently well below the national average of about 24 percent of state and local expenditures for K–12 public education. Despite its substantially below-average spending on public education, Hawai'i continues to be a relatively wealthy state; in 2000 it ranked third in the nation in per capita state and local government revenues and fourth in per capita state and local government expenditures (Office of the Superintendent/Planning and Evaluation Office 2004: 13). Clearly, public money is not being spent on public education to the extent possible.

As a result of a study commissioned by the state Board of Education in 2005, the extent of the underfunding of K–12 public education has been established.

The study found that the public schools require an additional $278 million per year to provide an "adequate" education to Hawai'i students (Martin 2005a: A1). Conducted by University of Oregon education professor David Conley and the Chicago accounting firm Grant Thornton LLP, the study first identified areas in the school system that needed improvement and then determined 150 expenditure categories and how much additional funds were needed to attain adequacy. Based on the DOE budget for 2003–2004 of $1.7 billion, the 17 percent increase in required funds would boost per-student funding by more than $1,500, from about $8,600 to $10,100. Board of Education member Karen Knudsen remarked on the report's findings in the context of their ongoing struggle for greater state appropriations: "This is definitely something that validates what we've been saying, that schools need more money and that the system is not some huge bloated thing" (cited in Martin 2005a: A9). Obviously, the DOE is never going to receive anywhere near $278 million per year in increased appropriations from the state legislature, but that figure indicates the extent to which the public schools are fiscally unable to furnish even an adequate education to Hawaii's young people.[2] By implication, students, especially from ethnic minorities, are receiving an inadequate education in the DOE schools.

If Hawaii's public schools are providing an inadequate education, they cannot possibly comply with the federal No Child Left Behind Act, which mandates that every school must demonstrate "adequate yearly progress" until 2014 when all students are supposed to meet proficiency standards in core subjects. In 2005, two-thirds of the public schools in the state did not meet their expected reading and mathematics standards under the No Child Left Behind Act (Shapiro and Creamer 2005: A1).[3] However, these goals were met by every school in suburban east Honolulu, which has primarily White, Chinese American, and Japanese American students. In contrast, most schools in west O'ahu, which have a majority enrollment of Filipino American, Native Hawaiian, and Samoan students, failed to achieve the proficiency standards. These and other schools contributed to Hawai'i having the highest percentage of schools (8.5 percent) in the nation in the 2005–2006 school year designated for state-directed managerial and curricular "restructuring," the severest penalty under the No Child Left Behind Act (Martin 2005b: A1).

A significant factor that contributes to the DOE schools not meeting the No Child Left Behind Act proficiency standards is their relatively high proportion of English for Second Language Learners (ESLL), who are predominantly Asian and Pacific Islander immigrants. More than 18,000 students, who represent 10 percent of the public school enrollment, are in ESLL programs (Martin 2005e: A1). At some schools in primarily Filipino immigrant communities, ESLL students are a majority of the student body. Despite being recent immigrants to Hawai'i, these students are expected to meet annual performance standards under the No Child Left Behind Act. The number of ESLL students has grown by more than 40 percent since 2001 and is projected to increase annually by more than one thousand students during the next few years (Martin 2005e: A1). The largest group of ESLL students continues to be from the Philippines, and the second-largest group when combined is from Micronesia—including the Marshall Islands, Chuuk and Pohnpei—who have been immigrating to Hawai'i in increasing numbers since the late 1990s. Other ESLL students (more than one thousand each) are from Samoa, Mexico, Japan, and China.

Another significant problem faced by Hawaii's public school system is its relatively high dropout rate of about 15 percent of entering high school cohorts beginning with the freshman class in fall 2001 (Creamer 2006: A1, A10). Not surprisingly, dropout rates vary widely among high schools and, by extension, ethnic groups, therefore providing another indicator of differential educational attainment among island ethnic groups. High schools that have a majority enrollment of Native Hawaiian, Filipino American, and Samoan students have among the highest dropout rates in the state, such as Wai'anae (29 percent) with the highest, Farrington (23 percent), and Waipahu (21 percent) in 2004–2005. In marked contrast, high schools in which Chinese Americans, Japanese Americans, and Whites together comprise either a plurality or majority of students have among the lowest dropout rates, for example, Wai'akea (2 percent), Kalani (4 percent), and Mililani (5 percent). There is little question that ethnic minorities constitute the great majority of the more than 1,700 students who annually leave Hawaii's public high schools before their entering class has graduated. Unless they earn a high school diploma or its equivalent at some point while they are still young, minority dropouts are likely to end up working at low-paying menial jobs, joining the military, or going to prison where they would join the more than one-third of Hawai'i inmates (the largest number of whom are Native Hawaiian) who also lack a high school degree (Creamer 2006: A10).

An indication of the low policy priority of the public school system are the widely known low salaries of Hawai'i teachers. According to a report by the National Education Association, the average annual salary of the state's public schoolteachers ($44,464) ranked twentieth in the nation, more than $1,400 below the U.S. average ($45,891) in the 2002–2003 school year ("Teacher Pay Ranks 20th in the Nation," *Honolulu Star-Bulletin* 2004: A3).[4] Roger Takabayashi, president of the Hawaii State Teachers Association (HSTA), the union that represents public schoolteachers, observed that if inflation is taken into consideration, the salaries of Hawai'i teachers have actually declined in constant dollars from 1993 to 2003 (cited in "Teacher Pay Ranks 20th in the Nation," *Honolulu Star-Bulletin* 2004: A3).

The below-average salaries of public schoolteachers is a major factor in their high rate of turnover that contributes to the perennial teacher shortage in

Hawai'i, much to the detriment of their majority clientele of ethnic minority students. Between 1999 and 2004, according to HSTA president Takabayashi, the DOE lost about 7,100 teachers, approximately 1,400 to 1,500 a year, including about 400 to retirement and roughly 1,100 for other reasons, primarily salary considerations (cited in Bernardo 2005a: A1, A6). Another indication of the high turnover among public schoolteachers comes from a survey conducted with 2001 graduates of the UH Manoa College of Education. While 80 percent of its graduates generally are employed by the DOE upon graduating, the survey found that only 53 percent of the class of 2001 were teaching in the public schools three years later (DePledge 2005: B5). To be sure, the shortage of teachers is not limited to Hawai'i and is a national problem that only will increase in severity with the imminent retirement of baby boomer educators. But the national shortage of teachers directly affects the state's public schools because most of the new teachers hired each year are from the continental United States.

The DOE also has sought to address the teacher deficit by annually employing about 300 "emergency hires," who have bachelor's degrees but either have not completed all of their teacher licensing examinations or a teacher education program. In other words, they are not fully qualified to be teachers and could be assigned to teach a subject that was not their major in college. This issue of nonqualified teachers in DOE classrooms was raised by the former dean of the UH Manoa College of Education, Randy Hitz, in his commentary on "Five Steps to Improve Schools" that appeared in the *Honolulu Advertiser* (2006: B1). One of his recommended steps is to "Put a quality teacher in every classroom" since, as he noted, numerous studies demonstrate that the single most significant factor affecting student achievement is the quality of the teacher. However, he pointed out that every year the DOE has to hire those three hundred emergency teachers who lack formal training to be instructors because universities in Hawai'i are unable to produce enough of them due to their insufficient funding.

The teacher shortage, the inadequate education provided, the huge size of schools, and other critical problems with Hawaii's public school system are not new, and most of them can be attributed to the lack of sufficient funding of the DOE. The state's economic decline in the 1990s magnified the severity of these problems because funds were not being allocated by the state legislature to address these long-standing issues. One major consequence was that the backlog in school repair and maintenance work ballooned to about $800 million (Shapiro and TenBruggencate 2005: A2). The Honolulu daily newspapers and television news programs regularly highlight the dilapidated condition of Hawaii's public schools, including restroom doors with no locks, leaking roofs, and collapsed ceilings.

As its policy priority in the 1990s, the state legislature continued to support the ailing tourist industry by creating the Hawai'i Tourism Authority in 1998 as the state government's "lead agency and advocate for Hawaii's visitor industry" and by doubling its annual state funding to $60 million. The legislature also approved planning and construction of the Hawai'i Convention Center that also opened in 1998. At a total cost of $350 million, the center is the largest "design-build" project ever initiated by the state government and became its primary lure to attract tourists during the recession-plagued 1990s in Hawai'i. The result has been to increase the state's dependence on tourism rather than to diversify the local economy and create jobs besides primarily in service and sales work. Despite clear evidence of the need for greater funding of public education, state legislators commonly respond to DOE administrators' appeals for increased appropriations by accusing them of overstating their funding problems and of requesting more funds without establishing that it would improve student educational performance (Donnelly 1996: A1).

It might be argued that all public school students suffer as a result of the inadequate funding of the DOE, including Japanese Americans, Chinese Americans, and Whites. However, since ethnic minorities comprise most of the students in the public schools, I consider the underfunding of the DOE system as constituting institutional discrimination against ethnic minorities because they are not being provided with equal educational opportunity by the state government. Instead, they unfairly and unequally bear the burden of the policy decision by state legislators and the governor to provide insufficient funds to the DOE. As a result, K–12 public education is a major factor in the institutionalization of ethnic inequality in Hawai'i, not only in the quality of education provided to ethnic minority students but especially in limiting their access to college.

## *Private School Privilege*

Due to the well-known inadequate funding of the public schools and the consequent myriad educational and other problems that result, Hawai'i has the highest percentage of K–12 private school enrollment in the nation at 16 percent or nearly 35,000 students (Office of the Superintendent/Planning and Evaluation Office 2004: 7). While there certainly are White, Japanese American, and Chinese American students in the DOE schools, these ethnic groups constitute a majority of private school students in Hawai'i. As socioeconomically privileged groups, they have the financial means to avoid the educational deficiencies and other problems of the public school system, such as safety concerns, by sending their children to private schools. More than sixty years ago in *A Century of Public Education in Hawaii*, then UH education professor Benjamin Wist (1940) offered observations that are even more valid in the 2000s: "Independent or private school ventures in Hawaii have been numerous; and it is doubtful whether any other community of similar size, now under the

American flag, has fostered so many of such schools or has enrolled in them so large a proportion of pupil population." Despite being the forty-second most populous state, Hawai'i has 125 private schools, including two of the largest K–12 schools in the United States—Punahou School and Kamehameha School—both with enrollments of about 3,700 students.

Some Hawai'i parents with the necessary financial resources, who tend to be from the socioeconomically advantaged ethnic groups, opt to send their children to private schools beginning with kindergarten in the belief that they will receive a better-quality education than at the local public school. They also believe that such early enrollment will facilitate their children being admitted later to one of the more prestigious private high schools and will contribute in general to their greater educational development for college. If parents live in a community with a very good public elementary school, they may defer private schooling for their children until the sixth grade. At that time when they are about eleven years old, students enter considerably larger and more ethnically and socioeconomically diverse intermediate schools. Parents who had planned to enroll their children eventually in a private school are less willing at this point for them to continue in the public school system, again primarily because of concerns about educational quality. Certainly by the time their children are about to enter high school, parents with private school aspirations will apply at a number of schools to maximize the chances that they will be admitted to at least one. Other parents, including most Japanese Americans, Chinese Americans, and Whites, are sufficiently satisfied with the public schools in their communities such that they have no strong desire for their children to have a private school education. However, these groups generally live in the more expensive urban or suburban communities where the public schools are known for the better quality of education they provide.

The relation of private schools to ethnic inequality in Hawai'i is made evident by considering their annual tuition. In the 2006–2007 school year, tuition for grades K–12 at Punahou School, one of the more costly and highly selective private schools, was $14,725 (Martin 2006: A1), and the average tuition at Hawai'i private schools can be estimated at roughly $10,000 per year. Parents from ethnic minority groups are more likely to lack the financial resources to afford such high tuition and thus have little choice but to send their children to their local public school, whatever the quality of education it provides. Another constraint on obtaining a private school education for one's child is that the total enrollment of these schools has not changed very much since the late 1980s (Office of the Superintendent/Planning and Evaluation Office 2004: 7). Private school enrollment in Hawai'i does not fluctuate with population change because especially the selective schools have stable target enrollment figures and are limited by their facilities.

Private schools, particularly those that are more selective in admissions, contribute to ethnic inequality in Hawai'i through the obvious educational benefits and advantages they provide their primarily Japanese American, White, and Chinese American students. These include smaller classes, better equipped and maintained classroom facilities, current textbooks and other instructional materials, highly educated teachers, and an overall educational environment that fosters student learning. While available in some but not all public schools, private high schools generally offer a wider range of advanced placement and honors classes that enable students to earn college credits before graduating. At the better private high schools, the entire graduating class continues on to college, the great majority of them in the continental United States, including the most academically renown higher education institutions in the nation.

This tendency among private high school graduates to attend a university in the continental United States is evident from the very low "going rate" to the University of Hawai'i at Manoa of graduates from the top private institutions—such as 'Iolani School (10 percent) and Punahou School (7 percent)—in fall 2005 (Institutional Research Office 2006c). The going rate to a university is the percentage of graduates of a given high school who enter that institution in the fall semester immediately following graduation. While the overall going rate of Hawai'i public high school graduates to UH Manoa (9 percent) in fall 2005 is also low, this is because most of these students do not attend college at all. The going rate to UH Manoa of public high schools in ethnic minority communities is extremely low, such as Farrington High School (5 percent) in the Kalihi inner-city area of Honolulu where only twenty-two graduates of the class of 2005 entered Manoa in the fall (Institutional Research Office 2006c). With an enrollment of almost 2,600 students, 60 percent of whom are Filipino American, Farrington is the largest public high school in Hawai'i and is located only about five miles from the Manoa campus. Two other high schools with Native Hawaiian, Filipino American, and Samoan student majorities—Waianae (2 percent, six students) and Waipahu (6 percent, twenty-seven students)—also had very low going rates to UH Manoa in fall 2005 (Institutional Research Office 2006c). It is especially troubling that these poor going rates to the university have not improved much since the 1980s; thus, the educational and broader socioeconomic gap between ethnic minority students at these high schools and the graduates of private high schools continues to increase.

In general terms, private high schools play a significant role in the social and cultural process of preparing Chinese American, Japanese American, and White students to assume their privileged individual and collective positions in Hawai'i society. As discussed in Chapter 3, these students are enabled to enter their positions, not necessarily because they are more intelligent or talented than ethnic minority students, but because of the intergenerational transfer of wealth from their parents that provides them with early educational and other experiential advantages. After graduating from college and, for many of them, continuing on to graduate or professional school, they embark on financially rewarding and upwardly mobile professional careers, although not all of them do so in Hawai'i given the brain drain. However, more than enough of them return to the islands to occupy the relatively high socioeconomic status of their parents and thus to perpetuate the ethnic stratification order in Hawai'i for another generation.

## *State Government Neglect*

Rather than address the teacher shortage, the ever-expanding list of repair and maintenance work, and other critical needs of the public schools identified by the DOE, the state legislature instead has funded its own desired projects and thereby sustained educational inequality among ethnic groups in Hawai'i.[5] For the 2005 legislative session, as in previous years, the DOE and the state Board of Education submitted a prioritized "wish list" of sixty projects for the next two-year budget cycle to the legislature. While the total amount requested for these projects was an unrealistic $543 million, it does indicate the extent of the needs of the public school system. Given limited state funds and a multitude of funding requests from other state and private agencies, there is no way that all of these DOE projects could be supported. In fact, the legislature partly or fully funded only nine of these projects at a total cost of $36.1 million for the first year of the budget cycle; however, it also added sixty-nine projects totaling $63.8 million that were not "high DOE priorities, but were important or popular at schools within the districts that elect those lawmakers" (Brannon 2005b: A1).

Not surprisingly, critics of this long-term practice by legislators, and certainly not only those in Hawai'i, refer to it as simply "pork barrel politics" that serves the interests of politicians seeking reelection rather than the educational needs of public school students. These lawmakers seek to have projects for schools in their legislative districts funded, although they may not be on the DOE priority list, so that they can prominently tout them in their campaign materials for the next election. As longtime Republican state senator Fred Hemmings observed of the funding of DOE projects: "It's not based on need, it's based on political chicanery as far as I'm concerned. Even within the Democratic Party, the . . . power brokers end up with all the gravy. . . . It speaks of petty politics at its worst" (cited in Brannon 2005a: A7). Such political intervention by the more powerful or at least more connected legislators results in funding inequities among the DOE schools, despite Hawai'i having one statewide school district that is not dependent on local property taxes. Such funding imbalances among the public schools are another factor that contributes to educational inequality between students from the socioeconomically dominant and subordinate ethnic groups.[6]

Recent surveys clearly indicate that Hawai'i residents consider the neglected and declining condition of the DOE schools a critical problem and would like to have state government leaders address their concerns. In 2003 a statewide survey of adult Hawai'i residents (n=603) asked them if they would be willing to pay more in state taxes in order to improve the quality of education in the public schools ("77% Would Pay to Aid Schools," *Honolulu Advertiser* 2003: A6). Forty percent of the respondents said they were willing to contribute "significantly" more in taxes, and another 37 percent indicated they would be willing to pay a "little" more. This survey result is remarkable since taxpayers do not very often express their willingness to pay more in taxes for whatever purpose.[7] It very likely reflects the widespread understanding that the DOE faces a very severe problem in trying to educate Hawaii's children with a considerable shortage of funds.

Another survey on public education commissioned by Republican governor Linda Lingle's office in 2004 provides insights into the public's perception of educational problems in Hawai'i. Six hundred registered voters were contacted for the statewide survey by a Republican polling firm based in Virginia (Perez 2004: A11). The survey was paid for by Citizens Achieving Reform in Education (CARE), a private nonprofit, tax-exempt corporation established by the Lingle administration to raise funds and lobby for her K–12 education proposals, chief among which was to replace the elected statewide Board of Education with seven locally elected boards.[8] According to a *Honolulu Star-Bulletin* reporter, the governor "publicly touted" results from the survey that supported her education reform proposals but tried to keep "secret" those that tended to undermine them (Perez 2004: A1).[9]

The reason why the governor tried to prevent the poll results from being released to the public is apparent insofar as the most significant finding was in response to an open-ended question that participants were asked: "What would you say is the biggest problem facing Hawaii's public schools today?" They reported "lack of funding" most frequently (19 percent), followed by "poor quality of teachers" (7 percent), "drugs in schools" (6 percent), and "too much bureaucracy" (5 percent) among a wide range of problems they identified (Perez 2004: A11).[10] When read a list of issues concerning public education in Hawai'i and asked to specify which one they considered most important, the largest number of respondents stated "increasing state funding for public education" (17 percent).[11]

In contrast to the major finding of her own survey, the governor continued to maintain that lack of funding is not the primary problem with the public educational system, but that insufficient funds are being spent at the school level because of what she referred to as a "top-heavy bureaucracy" (Perez 2004:

A11). That the governor would ignore the results of her own survey and resist making them available to the public speaks volumes about the concern, or lack thereof, of state government leaders for public education in Hawai'i. In the mid-2000s, the state government was flush with a huge surplus of funds from increasing tax revenues as a result of Hawaii's booming economy. For the 2005–2006 fiscal year, the surplus was estimated at $600 million, and it was projected at an even larger $700 million for the following fiscal year, according to the state budget and finance director (Martin 2005d: A1). In a major turnaround from the previous year and perhaps contemplating their reelection campaigns, led by the majority Democrats, the state legislature appropriated $303 million in 2006 to the public schools for operating costs, classroom renovation, and repair and maintenance and only $50 million for tax relief (DePledge and Shapiro 2006).[12] However, that still left a $500 million backlog in unfunded repair and maintenance work.

The unwillingness on the part of state government officials to acknowledge, let alone address, a major public problem that the people of Hawai'i are greatly concerned about ultimately explains why educational inequality continues among ethnic groups. Instead of a tolerance of cultural diversity, a tolerance of educational inadequacy has developed in Hawai'i that fosters and maintains ethnic inequality. Educational inequality is even more evident at the postsecondary level when most students from the socioeconomically dominant ethnic groups continue on to college, while most students from the subordinate groups end their formal education with high school.

## University of Hawai'i System

The UH system consists of ten campuses on the four major islands with a total enrollment of more than 50,000 students in fall 2005 (Institutional Research Office 2006a).[13] The flagship campus is the University of Hawai'i at Manoa, a research-extensive institution offering a full range of baccalaureate, master's, professional (for example, law and medicine), and doctoral degrees, located in Honolulu with about 20,000 students. Two other campuses, UH Hilo (3,400 students) on Hawai'i Island and UH West O'ahu (900 students) grant bachelor's degrees, and the latter offers primarily upper-division courses. The seven UH community colleges have a combined enrollment of more than 25,000 students and include four on O'ahu: Honolulu (4,200), Kapi'olani (7,300), Leeward (5,700), and Windward (1,700); and three on the neighbor islands: Hawai'i (2,400), Maui (2,900), and Kaua'i (1,100). After experiencing significant declines in the late 1990s, UH enrollment increased in the early 2000s, particularly at Manoa and Hilo due to concerted efforts to attract students from the continental United States because of the higher tuition they pay.

In terms of ethnicity, the severe disparity between student representation in the public school system and the UH system is quite obvious. Among UH Manoa undergraduates in fall 2005, Chinese Americans (7.1 percent), Japanese Americans (20 percent), and Whites (22 percent)[14] are represented to a much greater extent than they are in the DOE schools, almost twice as much in the case of the first two groups (Institutional Research Office 2006b). Unlike Chinese Americans and Japanese Americans, most White students are not Hawai'i residents, and their enrollment has grown dramatically in the 2000s as a result of UH recruitment initiatives in the continental United States. In contrast, Native Hawaiians (9.1 percent), Filipino Americans (9.3 percent), Samoans (1.2 percent), and African Americans (1.2 percent) are considerably underrepresented as undergraduate students at UH Manoa at less than half their respective percentages in the public schools. Like Whites, most African American students are not Hawai'i residents, and males especially attend the university on athletic scholarship. If not for athletes, African American and Samoan representation at UH Manoa would be substantially lower.

Since UH Manoa is a publicly supported institution, the underrepresentation of ethnic minorities means that they subsidize the college education of the socioeconomically dominant groups, such as Japanese Americans and Chinese Americans, through their lesser enrollment. As taxpayers, Filipino Americans, Native Hawaiians, and Samoans pay state taxes that provide funds for the UH budget appropriation from the state legislature. However, if their children do not attend the university, then those ethnic minority parents and their children do not benefit from their tax payments, which are used instead to support the ethnic groups that are overly represented among the students, faculty, and staff. It might be argued that Japanese Americans and Chinese Americans also subsidize ethnic minorities since many of them send their children to colleges in the continental United States. However, these ethnic groups are not underrepresented at UH Manoa, and their financial status provides them with the option of a continental education for their children that most ethnic minority parents do not have.

The enrollment situation is somewhat better for ethnic minorities in the UH community colleges where in fall 2005 Filipino Americans (18 percent) and Native Hawaiians (18 percent) were the largest groups (Institutional Research Office 2006a). On the other hand, Japanese Americans (14 percent), Chinese Americans (4.2 percent), and Whites (15 percent) have considerably lower representation as community college students than as Manoa undergraduates. This reversal can be explained to some extent by the greater tendency of students from those ethnic groups to enter UH Manoa as first-time freshmen directly from high school rather than start their undergraduate education at a community college. Conversely, the greater presence of Native Hawaiian and Filipino American students in the community colleges than at UH Manoa is because most of them begin their college education in the UH system at the former campuses. Due to stereotyped perceptions of ethnic minority students' academic abilities, they are often advised by high school counselors to start at a community college even though they intend ultimately to earn a bachelor's degree. However, the transfer rate from the UH community colleges to UH Manoa is quite low and even lower for ethnic minority students. Thus, the significant percentages of ethnic minorities in the community colleges are deceiving if it is assumed that most of them will continue on to earn a bachelor's degree.

## *Unequal Opportunity and Affirmative Inaction*

The University of Hawai'i at Manoa (2004) has an established policy on equal opportunity and affirmative action that states:[15]

> The University of Hawai'i is an equal opportunity/affirmative action institution and is committed to a policy of nondiscrimination on the bases of race, sex, age, religion, color, national origin, ancestry, disability, marital status, arrest and court record, sexual orientation, and veteran status. This policy covers academic considerations such as admission and access to, participation and treatment in the University's programs, activities, and services. With regard to employment, the University is committed to equal opportunity in all personnel actions such as recruitment, hiring, promotion, and compensation. Sexual harassment is expressly prohibited under University policy. The University strives to promote full realization of equal employment opportunity through a positive, continuing program in compliance with the affirmative action in employment mandates of federal Executive Order 11246.

I have quoted this policy statement at length to emphasize the comprehensiveness of its scope in encompassing several diversity dimensions that are not always included for protection against discrimination, such as sexual orientation. Besides students, faculty, and staff, the policy also applies to anyone who seeks access to and participates in UH programs and activities, such as campus events. The statement expresses the university's commitment to "full realization of equal employment opportunity" through compliance with federal mandates on affirmative action in employment. While there is much to admire in this clearly and strongly worded statement of UH policy, unfortunately it remains policy rather than being implemented. Having worked at UH Manoa as a faculty member since 1989, I am still unaware of the existence of any racial or ethnic minority faculty affirmative action hiring program that has resulted from the above policy.

The university's ongoing failure to implement its own policy on equal employment opportunity and affirmative action in recruitment and hiring is plainly evident in racial/ethnic minority faculty underrepresentation at UH Manoa. At about one-third of tenured and tenure-track faculty, the university does have one of the highest proportions of minority faculty among research-extensive institutions. However, a major reason for that high percentage is because the academic and research focus of UH Manoa is the Asia and Pacific region, including Hawai'i. Thus, many faculty who were hired as specialists in their respective fields, such as history, literature, or a foreign language, are originally from Asia or the Pacific. More than twenty years ago in the 1983–1984 academic year, racial/ethnic minorities already were 32 percent of UH Manoa tenured and tenurable faculty (Equal Employment Opportunity and Affirmative Action Office n.d.). In short, despite the university claiming to be "An Equal Opportunity/Affirmative Action Institution" and having a formal equal employment opportunity and affirmative action policy, very little progress has been made subsequently in increasing minority faculty representation. The latter is quite obviously not a policy priority, very likely because university administrators and most faculty do not consider the minimal numbers of Native Hawaiian, Filipino American, Pacific Islander, African American, and Latino faculty to be a significant issue that requires their attention.

As a result, like most large universities, Whites comprised a substantial majority (66 percent) of the approximately 1,200 UH Manoa full-time instructional faculty in 2003 as they always have, and White males are the largest group among the faculty (Institutional Research Office 2004a). In many ways, the University of Hawai'i is the last remaining bastion of White colonial rule in the islands, long after the "Big Five" corporations that had dominated Hawaii's economy since the late nineteenth century became fully integrated, even at the highest levels of corporate management. According to federal equal employment opportunity and affirmative action guidelines, racial/ethnic minority faculty at UH Manoa include Japanese (9.7 percent), Chinese (8.3 percent), Native Hawaiian (4.0 percent), Indian (2.6 percent), Korean (2.3 percent), Hispanic (1.8 percent), Filipino (1.7 percent), African American (0.6 percent), Native American (0.4 percent), and "Other Asian/Pacific Islander" (2.5 percent). The Asian and Hispanic faculty include many who very likely were initially hired as international faculty rather than as Asian American or Hispanic American in national origin.

In contrast to the lack of progress in increasing racial/ethnic minority faculty representation at UH Manoa during the past twenty years, women faculty grew by 70 percent between 1983 (21 percent) and 2003 (37 percent) (Institutional Research Office 2004a). This gain resulted from a definite initiative by the university to hire more female faculty that began in the early 1980s and produced the positive outcome that is evident. However, no similar effort has been made to recruit and hire more minority faculty because their limited representation at the university is not seen as a major problem. I consider the university's long-term practice of not implementing its own equal opportunity and affirmative action in employment policy on faculty recruitment and hiring as discriminatory against racial and ethnic minorities, such as Native Hawaiians, Filipino Americans, Pacific Islanders, African Americans, and Latinos, because they are subject to unfair and unequal treatment in the recruitment and hiring process that is clearly evident in their minimal numbers among Manoa faculty. It is inconceivable to me that having only twenty Filipino American and eight African American faculty members at the university is the result of equal employment opportunity, let alone affirmative action.

The continuing failure of UH policy to address racial minority problems and concerns is also evident in the *University of Hawai'i at Manoa Strategic Plan: Defining Our Destiny, 2002–2010* (University of Hawai'i at Manoa 2002). This planning document establishes seven "core commitments" for the university: research; educational effectiveness; social justice; place; economic development; culture, society, and the arts; and technology (University of Hawai'i at Manoa 2002: 3). Each commitment includes a number of related "strategic imperatives" or goals. While several imperatives refer to Native Hawaiians or Hawaiian concepts (for example, *ahupua'a* or land division extending from the mountains to the sea), none of them makes explicit reference to racial or ethnic minorities. Instead, they invoke vague notions of "human diversity" that can refer to just about anything involving differences among human beings. Instead of establishing as an explicit goal to increase the number of racial/ethnic minority faculty and students, under the core commitment of social justice, a strategic imperative states that UH Manoa will "Actively recruit and retain administrators, faculty, staff and students from diverse backgrounds." The latter term of course is much broader than racial or ethnic diversity and can include geographic origin, such as Europe or the continental United States. For the core commitment of economic development, one of the imperatives is to "Increase student enrollment and recruit a greater percentage of non-residents." As I argue below, that is exactly what the university has been doing in the 2000s as a means to increase its revenues since nonresidents pay substantially higher tuition. However, with less emphasis on attracting ethnic minority students from Hawai'i, they continue to be marginalized at UH Manoa. Furthermore, viewing increasing student enrollment as primarily an "economic development" issue clearly indicates that the university is more concerned with the tuition students pay than with the education it provides them.

Given the majority population of Asian Americans and Pacific Islanders among UH Manoa undergraduates, public school students, and Hawai'i residents, it should be an important consideration to have these groups represented sufficiently in the university faculty. While Chinese could be said to be adequately represented among the faculty, such is not the case for Native Hawaiians and Filipino Americans, two groups that are among the largest in the state and the public schools. Their severely minimal numbers as instructional faculty have other detrimental consequences for them beyond their mere underrepresentation; it means that Native Hawaiian and Filipino literatures, histories, cultures, and languages are also underrepresented in the curriculum offered to students and that less research is conducted in those same areas. For Native Hawaiian and Filipino American students, their lesser presence among the faculty means that they have fewer professional role models, informal academic advisors, and advocates available to them who can contribute to their academic success at the university and encourage and assist them in proceeding further in graduate or professional study. Increasing minority representation among the faculty may very well result in greater numbers of ethnic minority students, some of whom eventually may also become faculty.

### *Tuition Increases/Minority Student Decreases*

In the 1990s, UH Manoa attained national distinction as the only public university to undergo seven consecutive years of budget cuts. According to a report by the UH Office on Planning and Policy, state funding for the university declined by 19 percent during that decade (Altonn 1999: A1). In the larger context of Hawaii's overdependence on tourism, those budget reductions are directly attributable to the recession in the state during the 1990s that resulted in less tax revenues for the university's budget allocation from the state government. As one means to deal with the budget cuts, the UH Board of Regents raised resident and nonresident tuition at all campuses in 1996 and 1997. Those increases were the largest at UH Manoa: 50 percent in 1996 and 23 percent the following year for resident undergraduate students. Not surprisingly, enrollment declined throughout the UH system from nearly 50,000 students in 1995 to 45,000 just three years later (Institutional Research Office 1998). At Manoa, enrollment dropped from 19,800 in 1995 to 17,000 students in three years, and all other UH institutions experienced enrollment decreases during the same period. In spring 1996, UH Manoa had one of the largest undergraduate graduating classes in its then nearly ninety-year history because students sought to avoid having to pay the higher tuition by graduating earlier than they had previously planned.

While all ethnic groups in the UH system were impacted negatively by the tuition hikes, they especially hurt ethnic minorities, particularly Filipino Americans, much more than other student groups. Minorities lacked the financial resources to meet the substantially increased tuition compared to the more socioeconomically advantaged ethnic groups, and therefore their enrollment dropped considerably. Beginning in the 1980s, Filipino Americans had been making progressive enrollment gains throughout the UH system, although they continued to be represented below their proportion of public school students. This steady progress continued to the early 1990s when they emerged as the largest ethnic group in the UH community college system at about 20 percent of students and as the largest group at a few of those campuses near Filipino American communities. At UH Manoa, Filipino Americans attained their highest-ever total of students in 1995 (1,900), including both undergraduate and graduate students (Institutional Research Office 1995b: 15). At 14 percent, they became the second-largest ethnic group (after Japanese Americans) among first-time freshmen, that is, students who enter college in the fall immediately after graduating from high school. Boosted by these enrollment gains, Filipino Americans achieved their all-time greatest number in the UH system in 1994 at 7,600 students who represented 15 percent of the total enrollment (Institutional Research Office 1994: 13). While those percentages indicated they still were represented below their proportion of public school students at that time (19 percent), there was a strong belief among UH Filipino American faculty and staff that the future looked extremely promising for continued enrollment growth and that parity representation at the system level would occur by the early 2000s.

However, the tuition increases in 1996 and 1997 brought an abrupt end to hard-won Filipino American advancement in higher education. Their total enrollment in the UH system plummeted by about 1,500 students from 7,500 in 1995 to a low of about 6,000 students in 2001 before finally starting to rebound the following year (Institutional Research Office 2001a; see Table 4.1). The last time the number of Filipino American UH students was that low was in 1990; in short, the tuition hikes had eliminated a decade of progressive gains from which they have yet to recover. As of fall 2005, there were still 1,100 fewer Filipino American students in the UH system than in 1995 (Institutional Research Office 2006a). At UH Manoa, Filipino American undergraduate enrollment decreased six consecutive years from about 1,600 students in 1995 to less than 1,200 in 2001 when the downward spiral finally came to an end.

At UH Hilo, which had an average enrollment of about 2,700 students in the 1990s, the 1996 and 1997 tuition hikes had an even greater negative impact on Filipino American students. As can be seen in Table 4.1, in 1995 there were 200 Filipino Americans, and that figure dropped to 169 students in 2001 before stabilizing in the next several years to about 180 students in fall 2005 (Institutional Research Office 2006a). Filipino Americans are only 5 percent of UH Hilo students, a considerable decline from their highest-ever percentage of almost 11 percent in 1985 (Office of Institutional Research and Analysis 1985a: 13). But perhaps more significantly, during the same six-year period from 1995 to 2001, UH Hilo enrollment expanded from about 2,700 to 3,300

TABLE 4.1 FILIPINO AMERICAN, NATIVE HAWAIIAN, AND WHITE UNDERGRADUATE ENROLLMENT AT UH MANOA, UH HILO, AND UH SYSTEM, 1995, 2001, AND 2005

| | UH Manoa | | |
|---|---|---|---|
| | 1995 | 2001 | 2005 |
| Filipino American | 1,613 (11.0%) | 1,164 (10.1%) | 1,288 (9.3%) |
| Native Hawaiian | 1,165 (10.2%) | 1,122 (9.8%) | 1,252 (9.1%) |
| White | 1,775 (13.6%) | 1,936 (16.9%) | 3,080 (22.3%) |
| | UH Hilo | | |
| | 1995 | 2001 | 2005 |
| Filipino American | 200 (7.0%) | 169 (5.8%) | 177 (5.2%) |
| Native Hawaiian | 522 (18.2%) | 494 (17.0%) | 547 (16.0%) |
| White | 793 (27.6%) | 980 (33.6%) | 1,264 (36.9%) |
| | UH System | | |
| | 1995 | 2001 | 2005 |
| Filipino American | 7,507 (14.9%) | 6,012 (13.%) | 6,371 (12.7%) |
| Native Hawaiian | 6,386 (12.7%) | 6,248 (13.6%) | 6,901 (13.8%) |
| White | 9,715 (19.3%) | 9,106 (19.8%) | 10,688 (21.3%) |

Source: Institutional Research Office, Fall Enrollment Reports, University of Hawai'i, 1995, 2001, 2005; Institutional Research Office, Fall Enrollment Reports, University of Hawai'i at Manoa, 1995, 2001, 2005.

students. In other words, while the university was growing by 22 percent, Filipino Americans were going in the opposite direction toward the same number of students they had in 1991 (Institutional Research Office 1991). The substantial enrollment growth at UH Hilo has been the result of a concerted effort to recruit students from the continental United States rather than from Hawai'i Island, where the university is located, or from other islands in the state. A primary reason for that recruitment target is because nonresident tuition is almost three times greater than that for state residents, and UH Hilo, like other UH institutions in the 1990s, was facing ongoing budget cuts. However, in pursuing out-of-state students, UH Hilo has been grossly violating UH Board of Regents policy established in 2002 that limits their proportion of the enrollment to 30 percent. Since that year, UH Hilo has never complied with that policy, and nonresidents have been nearly 40 percent of Hilo students in most years, while UH Manoa has exceeded the limit once in 2003 (Gima 2007: A1). As is evident, Filipino Americans and other ethnic minority students from Hawai'i have been the sacrificial victims of the University of Hawaii's initiative to address its budget deficits by increasing the recruitment and admission of out-of-state students.

Native Hawaiians are another underrepresented group that suffered enrollment declines because of the 1996 and 1997 tuition increases, although to a lesser extent than Filipino Americans. The reason for their different experience is because Native Hawaiian students have financial assistance available to them through the Ke Alii Pauahi Scholarship Foundation of the Kamehameha

Schools, the federal Native Hawaiian Higher Education Act, and UH tuition waivers designated for Native Hawaiians. These resources served as a means to meet at least some of the higher costs of college for them. As shown in Table 4.1, in 1995 there were about 6,400 Native Hawaiian students in the UH system and, after an initial decrease over the next three years, their number expanded to more than 6,900 in fall 2005 (Institutional Research Office 2006a). At UH Manoa in 1995, Native Hawaiian undergraduates totaled about 1,200, and that figure remained relatively stable until 2000 when it declined to 1,000 students. Since then, their enrollment has gained to nearly 1,300 in fall 2005 (Institutional Research Office 2006b).

In 1995, UH Hilo had 522 Native Hawaiian students who grew in absolute numbers (557) and in their percentage of the total enrollment (20 percent) through 1999 (Institutional Research Office 1999). This latter figure is quite significant because it was the highest representation of Native Hawaiian students in the UH system, even greater than in the UH community colleges and more than twice as high as at UH Manoa that year. However, as evident in Table 4.1, in fall 2005, Native Hawaiians had almost the same number of students (547) but a much lower percentage (16 percent) as they had six years previously because of the considerable expansion in the total number of Hilo students (Institutional Research Office 2006a). Like Filipino Americans, Native Hawaiians also appear to have been victimized by the recruitment campaign to admit more nonresident students from the continental United States.

Since tuition was raised in 1996 and 1997, the ethnic group that has gained the most in enrollment in the UH system is Whites, although like the other groups, they experienced an initial loss. In 1995 there were about 9,700 White students in the UH system (see Table 4.1), and that figure dropped to less than 8,100 three years later, but it began to grow in 1999 and had more than recovered by fall 2005 (10,700) when Whites were 21 percent of the total UH enrollment (Institutional Research Office 1995a, 2006a). In the process, White students became the largest ethnic group in the UH system in 1999 and at UH Manoa in 2002, a distinction they probably last held sometime during World War II before Japanese American veterans began entering in significant numbers (Institutional Research Office 1999; 2002).

Whites actually have been underrepresented at UH Manoa and other UH campuses since the 1970s, if not earlier, because many White students chose to attend college in the continental United States. However, beginning in the 2000s, UH Manoa and UH Hilo sought to recruit and accept a greater number of undergraduate students from the continental United States because of the much higher tuition they pay. As can be seen in Table 4.1, at UH Manoa the percentage of White undergraduates increased from about 14 percent in 1995 to more than 22 percent in fall 2005, and during this period their numbers expanded by 70 percent from nearly 1,800 to almost 3,100 (Institutional Research Office 2006b). This growing number of Whites has been especially evident among first-time freshmen enrolling at UH Manoa where their proportion has nearly tripled from 8.8 percent in 1998, to 17 percent two years later, and to 25 percent in 2003 when they emerged as the largest group, surpassing Japanese Americans for the first time in decades (Institutional Research Office 2003). During this same period, the total number of freshmen grew considerably from 1,500 in 1998 to more than 2,000 in 2003, so this gain clearly has been due to the increased entry of Whites. However, in the process of admitting more White students from the continental United States to UH Manoa, the percentage of first-time freshmen who are Hawai'i residents has dropped severely from 88 percent in 1998 to 69 percent in 2003, thus further limiting the opportunity for local ethnic minority students to receive a college education. My concern with the university policy of increasing the recruitment and enrollment of nonresident students because they pay higher tuition is that it marginalizes ethnic minority students from Hawai'i who have become less of a policy priority to admit. As a result, they continue to be underrepresented in the UH system, as they have been for decades, and I am aware of no UH policy or program that directly addresses this problem.

White students also have played a large role in the enrollment growth at UH Hilo. Table 4.1 indicates that in 1995 there were about 800 White students, and their numbers had been declining during the previous five years (Institutional Research Office 1995a: 15). After an initial decrease following the tuition hikes, they had rebounded by 1998 and began expanding to nearly 1,300 students in fall 2005 (Institutional Research Office 1998; 2006a). In the process, Whites increased their percentage of the UH Hilo student body from 29 percent in 1998 to 37 percent in 2005 and were by far the largest group, a position they have held since 1986.

In terms of their proportion of the state population (39 percent), an argument could be made that Whites are still underrepresented at UH Manoa and in the UH system, although in relation to their percentage of public school students (14 percent), they would be overly represented. However, Whites differ from other ethnic groups, such as Japanese Americans and Native Hawaiians, in having a substantially large in-migrating population from the continental United States, revolving military personnel and their dependents, and transient UH and other college students. These groups continue to provide an external source for the expansion of the White population in Hawai'i, including in the UH system.

As discussed in Chapter 1, in 2005 the UH Board of Regents unanimously approved substantial tuition hikes at every UH campus from fall 2006 through fall 2011. One of the major reasons given by university administrators for the tuition increase was that it would double annual tuition revenues to $198 million during a period of stagnating appropriations from the state legislature

(Vorsino 2005a: A1). At UH Manoa, tuition for resident undergraduates will rise by 140 percent or $816 each academic year for six consecutive years. Tuition thus will more than double from $3,504 in 2005 to $8,400 in 2011. Resident undergraduate tuition for the other campuses will increase by 120 percent at UH Hilo and UH West O'ahu and by 98 percent at the community colleges.

Like the tuition hikes that occurred in 1996 and 1997, those that began in 2006 constitute institutional discrimination against ethnic minorities, including Native Hawaiians, Filipino Americans, Samoans, and other Pacific Islanders. Although the tuition increase applies to everyone, these groups are being denied equal educational opportunity because, being socioeconomically disadvantaged, they are less financially able to pay the higher cost of tuition. Besides being discriminatory, raising tuition contradicts the "mission" of the university as stated in its *University of Hawai'i System Strategic Plan* to "Provide all qualified people in Hawai'i with equal opportunity for high quality college and university education and training" (University of Hawai'i 2002: 4). It also contradicts one of the "Commitments and Core Values" of the university in the strategic plan concerning "Diversity, fairness, and equity" that contends: "Society is best served by ensuring that all populations are represented equitably throughout the University of Hawai'i system." Furthermore, as noted in Chapter 1, the tuition hike contradicts the UH Board of Regents Policy on Nondiscrimination and Affirmative Action since it hardly demonstrates that the "University of Hawai'i is an equal opportunity/affirmative action institution and is committed to a policy of nondiscrimination on the bases of race, . . . color, national origin, [and] ancestry." Based on past history when tuition was raised considerably, already underrepresented ethnic minorities will become even more underrepresented in the UH system, thus perpetuating educational inequality in Hawai'i.

If history is any guide, the tuition increases that started in 2006 will also very likely decrease enrollment throughout the UH system, especially of ethnic minority students. I am not certain that university administrators have a viable plan to ensure that minority students do not experience a substantial decline once again since they assume that students will continue to enroll at their previous levels. The larger question is why tuition is being raised so much when the state had a surplus of more than $700 million in 2006 and 2007. What is the UH administration's proposal for tuition if the economy goes into recession again?

It is evident from the above discussion of the UH system that at times of fiscal crisis, the UH administration responds in the same way as the state government, that is, by seeking to attract transient outsiders to Hawai'i as one of the primary means to alleviate their common problem of declining revenues. The university recruits and admits students from the continental United States, while the state seeks to attract and bring in greater numbers of tourists;

in both cases, the people of Hawai'i ultimately are disadvantaged. More non-resident students mean fewer places for chronically underrepresented ethnic minorities from Hawai'i who will continue to be marginalized in the UH system and therefore cannot avail of public higher education as a means for their socioeconomic mobility. In addition to environmental and cultural damage, more tourists mean greater and continued dependency on tourism as the mainstay of the state economy instead of its diversification toward the creation of more knowledge-intensive jobs, especially for young people completing college. Attracting mobile outsiders to the islands as a means to resolve fiscal crises is a shortsighted and short-term solution to what are fundamental and deeply entrenched flaws in the political economy of Hawai'i, the most obvious of which is the highly unequal distribution of wealth, property, and income among its ethnic groups.

Besides differential access to the UH system, disparities in educational attainment among ethnic groups are evident in their widely differing graduation rates from UH Manoa. A longitudinal study of fall 1990 to fall 2001 first-time freshman cohorts as of 2002 reported the following average graduation rates after six years: Chinese American (72 percent), Japanese American (64 percent), Korean American (51 percent), Filipino American (51 percent), Native Hawaiian (42 percent), White (41 percent), and Pacific Islander (33 percent) (Institutional Research Office 2004b: 10). The UH Manoa average was 54 percent; thus only the former two groups had above-average graduation rates.[16] The comparatively lower rate of White students is probably due to students from the continental United States leaving UH Manoa since their retention rate after two years was only 53 percent; that is, almost one-half of them depart within two years. Differential graduation rates of ethnic groups from UH Manoa and other universities are evident in wide disparities in college completion among them. According to the 2000 U.S. census, the percentages of persons twenty-five years and older with bachelor's degrees or higher among ethnic groups in Hawai'i were: White (31 percent), Japanese American (30 percent), Chinese American (27 percent), Korean American (25 percent), Filipino American (15 percent), and Native Hawaiian (13 percent). For Hawai'i as a whole, the figure was 26 percent, so the three socioeconomically dominant groups are above the Hawai'i average, while Filipino Americans and Native Hawaiians are well below it.[17]

Besides graduation, similar differences exist among Hawai'i ethnic groups in terms of college or graduate school enrollment among persons eighteen to twenty-four years old based on 2000 census data. Ethnic group representation in college or graduate education includes (females first): Japanese American (51 percent, 45 percent), Korean American (50 percent, 44 percent), Chinese American (44 percent, 37 percent), Filipino American (35 percent, 27 percent), White (34 percent, 22 percent), African American (31 percent, 17 percent),

Native Hawaiian (30 percent, 22 percent), and Samoan (24 percent, 16 percent). The percentages for all Hawai'i women (38 percent) and men (28 percent) indicate that both sexes of Japanese Americans, Chinese Americans, and Korean Americans are above their respective Hawai'i figures for college or graduate school enrollment, while males and females of the socioeconomically disadvantaged groups are below their respective percentages. The seemingly anomalous relatively low enrollment status of Whites can be attributed to the inclusion of eighteen- to twenty-four-year-olds associated with the military as enlisted personnel or their dependents, since a high proportion of them are not in college.

The data on enrollment at and graduation from UH Manoa and on college or graduate school enrollment in general clearly demonstrate that the socioeconomically privileged ethnic groups will continue to hold their dominant status in Hawai'i for at least another generation, since their younger population is well represented in higher education. This college education provides them with the necessary educational qualifications and training to enter the same or higher occupational status held by their parents and thus to maintain their overall socioeconomic dominance. In contrast, the below-average college or graduate school representation of eighteen- to twenty-four-year-olds among the aggrieved ethnic groups means that they will remain in their subordinate position for another generation because a substantial majority of their young people is not able to use postsecondary education as a means for their collective social mobility.

## Conclusion

Through a discussion of public education in Hawai'i from "K to 20," that is, from kindergarten in the DOE schools to graduate school at the University of Hawai'i, I have sought to demonstrate that ethnic groups participate and benefit unequally in both of those systems. In addition, I have argued that the consequent disparities in educational attainment among these groups are primarily the result of discriminatory policies and practices against ethnic minorities. Thus, I am less supportive of arguments that seek to explain the differential educational status among ethnic groups in Hawai'i as the result of the different cultural values and beliefs they hold, particularly toward education. Discriminatory policies and practices include the underfunding by the state government of both the public schools and the University of Hawai'i system and the nonimplementation of their equal educational opportunity, nondiscrimination, and affirmative action policies that have much greater detrimental consequences for ethnic minorities than for the socioeconomically dominant ethnic groups. In the DOE schools, where ethnic minorities—including Filipino Americans, Native Hawaiians, Samoans, and other Pacific

Islanders—are a majority of students, inadequate funding continues to result in the deteriorating quality of the educational system that is ranked among the lowest in the nation by various criteria. In the UH system, budget cutbacks by the state legislature through most of the 1990s resulted in substantial tuition hikes in 1996 and 1997 that reduced ethnic minority admissions and enrollment, especially of Filipino Americans. Budget shortfalls also gave rise in the 2000s to a recruitment initiative directed to nonresident students from the continental United States that has further increased the underrepresentation of ethnic minorities from Hawai'i in the UH system. The tuition hikes of 140 percent at UH Manoa and 120 percent at UH Hilo from 2006 through 2011 will again result in a considerable decline in ethnic minority undergraduates from Hawai'i. Clearly, public education does not constitute a site of equal opportunity and upward mobility for aggrieved ethnic minority groups and, in fact, contributes to educational inequality in Hawai'i by restricting minority access to postsecondary education.

As previous U.S. censuses from 1970 to 1990 in Hawai'i have shown (Okamura 1982, 1990, 1998c), Native Hawaiians, Filipino Americans, and Samoans had much lower levels of college completion and enrollment than Whites, Japanese Americans, and Chinese Americans. Since the late 1990s, given the setbacks in admissions and enrollment in the UH system suffered by Native Hawaiians, Filipino Americans, and Samoans, the wide gap in higher educational status between them and the socioeconomically dominant ethnic groups is not being closed at all. Thus, educational inequality among ethnic groups in Hawai'i continues to prevail and is maintained by ethnicity as a structural principle that organizes the highly unequal distribution of educational benefits and rewards. Ethnicity restricts the pursuit of higher education for ethnic minorities by serving as a structural and cultural barrier that limits (although not absolutely) their opportunities to continue along the educational pathway to college completion. Conversely, for the socioeconomically privileged groups, ethnicity facilitates their much greater access to postsecondary education by providing them with greater financial resources for its acquisition.

Over the generations, the restricted entry of ethnic minorities to public higher education has severely constrained their ability to obtain the technical qualifications and skills—particularly a college degree—required for professional, managerial, and white-collar occupations in general. Lacking sufficient access to those more financially rewarding jobs, the socioeconomic advancement of ethnic minorities has been thwarted (see Chapter 3). However, similar to the socioeconomic stratification order, upward mobility in public higher education is possible for ethnic minorities, but it is limited to individuals from those minority groups rather than being a collective process. Each semester, hundreds of Filipino Americans, Native Hawaiians, Samoans, and other Pacific

Islanders graduate from University of Hawai'i campuses with bachelor's or higher degrees, and many of them are the first members of their families to do so. However, the numbers of them who earn a college degree and thus are able to obtain a professional or other position commensurate with their educational qualifications are not large enough for collective socioeconomic advancement to occur. Thus, public higher education in Hawai'i fails to provide an effective means for social mobility for ethnic minorities; consequently, the ethnic status quo of institutionalized and deeply embedded inequality persists, and unequal Hawai'i is maintained.

# 5

# Constructing Ethnic Identities, Constructing Differences

This chapter is concerned with the construction and continuing persistence of ethnic identity among groups in Hawai'i, despite the assimilation that has obviously occurred since immigrants began arriving in the early nineteenth century. The shared identity of an ethnic group is perhaps its most enduring feature, long after it has lost its "traditional" culture of language, religion, beliefs, and values and has acquired the dominant culture of the society. Nonetheless, ethnic identities are always subject to change in their meaning and significance since they are not permanent or natural, but instead variable and contingent. What it means to be Japanese American or Portuguese American in the early twenty-first century can hardly be the same as it was in the late nineteenth century when Japanese and Portuguese began immigrating to Hawai'i. The importance of their ethnic identity to Japanese Americans and Portuguese Americans has also changed, if not declined, over the generations since it does not organize their daily life and collective actions as it did prior to World War II. The same holds true for other ethnic groups in Hawai'i that have all experienced substantial transformations in the significance, meaning, and expression of their respective ethnic identities. Furthermore, these groups have changed their ethnic identities themselves, often in response to varying political and economic conditions they have encountered in different historical periods.

In discussing and analyzing ethnic identity in Hawai'i, I apply the constructionist approach that contends ethnic and racial groups construct or create particular identities by and for themselves under given historical circumstances (Cerulo 1997: 389–390; Cornell and Hartmann 1998: 72–73; Nagel 1994). While different explanations have been offered as to why ethnic and racial groups engage in identity formation, including "happenstance" and "inertia" (Cornell and Hartmann 1998: 99–100) and boundary construction (Nagel 1994: 154), I contend that they do so in order to advance their political or economic interests in competition over valued resources. From this perspective, ethnic or racial identity construction is viewed as a possible strategy a group can use to foster its collective concerns in society when competing with other ethnic and racial groups with comparable goals. Their constructed identity can serve as a means for ethnic and racial groups to mobilize and organize their members in pursuit of common claims and objectives. In this regard, sociologist Karen A. Cerulo (1997: 393) has introduced the concept of "collective agency," which "includes a conscious sense of group as agent" insofar as "[i]dentities emerge and movements ensue because collectives consciously coordinate action; group members consciously develop offenses and defenses, consciously insulate, differentiate, and . . . cooperate and compete" with other groups.

While it might be argued that the group's interests—whether political, economic, or other—should be sufficient themselves for its members to be willing to join in a collective effort to advance them, a shared ethnic or racial identity can underscore how these concerns are specific to the group or are being challenged by other ethnic and racial groups or the state. Cornell and Hartmann (1998: 96) emphasize the "power" of racial or ethnic identity as an organizational basis for collective agency, solidarity, and action: "When it is advantageous to draw a boundary between one set of claimants to opportunities or resources and another, ethnicity and race lend themselves admirably to the task. When there is a need to mobilize persons on behalf of their interests, the invocation of ethnic or racial bonds can be a powerful call to unity."

Even the name that is created or chosen by an ethnic or racial group is a significant aspect of its constructed identity since its meaning or symbolism can serve to mobilize and unite its members. Such a newly created or reconstructed ethnic or racial identity can raise the individual and collective consciousness of group members regarding their shared historical experiences and contemporary status in society and the social and cultural ties that bind them to one another and separate them from others. This increased awareness may result in greater numbers of ethnic or racial group members claiming and asserting their new identity and thereby being more willing to support collective efforts to pursue their political or economic claims or interests, including challenging their unequal status in society.

This activating process is evident in the construction of "Asian American" identity by students and community activists beginning in the late 1960s (Espiritu 1992), which resulted in Chinese Americans, Japanese Americans, Filipino Americans, and other Asians in the continental United States expressing this new racial identity for themselves and the ethnic groups they represented.[1] This new identity then became the organizational basis for advancing the collective concerns of Asian Americans during that tumultuous period, such as opposing the Vietnam War as a racist war, gaining political and economic control over their ethnic communities, and challenging racist stereotypes and other degrading representations of Asians in the United States, for example, as "Orientals." The specific term "Asian" was selected to denote not merely the countries in Asia from where they or their ancestors had immigrated but, more importantly, the common political, economic, and social ties and experiences that Chinese Americans, Filipino Americans, Japanese Americans, and other Asian groups had with each other in the United States. The term "American" was included to emphasize that Asian Americans are indeed American by citizenship or permanent residence, rather than aliens or "perpetual foreigners" as was the widespread misperception, and therefore entitled to the same legal rights and benefits as other Americans.

Identity construction is certainly not the only means engaged in by ethnic and racial groups to further their interests and claims. Other possible collective strategies include political organizing and participating in electoral politics, forming community-based organizations to seek political access or power outside of the electoral arena, or filing lawsuits to have group problems and concerns addressed by the state. Nonetheless, ethnic identity formation can still support these other strategies; for example, a community organization based on ethnic ties can mobilize its members in support of a candidate for political office or in support or opposition to a legal or political issue that directly affects the members of an ethnic group.

Not all ethnic groups engage in identity construction since some groups are politically and economically established such that they have other means or resources to maintain their dominant status in society. These resources include political and economic power or, at the family level, sufficient wealth that can be transferred from parents to children. In contrast, other less-advantaged ethnic groups are prevented from using identity construction to advance their interests because of the political and economic circumstances that confront them. Such conditions include the lesser political power or subordinate economic status of an ethnic group that may result in structural constraints on construction of its ethnic identity. Cultural representations of an ethnic group in the form of stigmatized stereotypes also constitute societal circumstances that can restrict identity formation.

In *Ethnicity without Groups* (2004), sociologist Rogers Brubaker provides a critique of "constructivist" approaches to ethnic identity by questioning if ethnic groups necessarily have identities and if, indeed, they all constitute groups. He contends that (2004: 55):

> even constructivist thinking on identity takes the existence of identity as axiomatic. Identity is always already "there," as something that individuals and groups "have," even if the content of particular identities, and the boundaries that mark groups off from one another, are conceptualized as always in flux. Even constructivist language tends therefore to objectify "identity," to treat it as a "thing," albeit a malleable one, that people "have," "forge," and "construct."

In contrast to such "constructivist thinking," my position is that, while ethnic and racial groups have identities, if only because they have been assigned to them, not all groups can or seek to "forge" and "construct" identities for themselves. By analyzing Japanese Americans and Filipino Americans as examples of ethnic groups in Hawai'i that do not actively engage in identity construction to the same extent as Native Hawaiians and Korean Americans, I believe my approach to identity formation does not contradict Brubaker's.

Lest I be accused of advocating a rational choice approach to ethnic identity construction, my position is that ethnic and racial groups, and certainly not individuals, are not free to create any identity of their own choosing for themselves and, in fact, can be severely limited by the ethnic or racial identities ascribed to them by other groups through denigrating stereotypes. In his critique of rational choice theory as applied to race and ethnic relations by Michael Banton (1980), M. G. Smith (1985: 486) argued that: "It is therefore quite illusory to formulate a general theory of R&ER [race and ethnic relations] as if they are always and everywhere freely created by the rational choice of all parties involved." He emphasized that such choice is often constrained: "Yet if it is assumed that by nature everyone seeks to optimise his or her net advantages, it is essential to recognise the prevalence, bases, variety, aims and conditions of coercion which together ensure that . . . individuals will enjoy . . . radically different freedoms of choice and action" (496). In concluding his critique, Smith (497) asked: "[C]an advocates of RCT [rational choice theory] applied to R&ER explain within the terms and limits of their theory how and why is it that whites have generally enjoyed such superior freedom of choice and opportunities to maximize their individual net advantage, collectively or otherwise, in interracial situations than people of other stocks?"[2]

Nonetheless, it is possible for ethnic and racial groups to seek collectively to change the societal circumstances in which they are situated. They thus can create more favorable social conditions for themselves in which their asserted identity and claims are more likely to be accepted by other ethnic and racial groups in society. Identity construction is therefore an ongoing social and cultural process because both ethnic and racial groups and the political and economic circumstances that surround them are subject to change by the actions of the groups themselves. In this regard, Cornell and Hartmann (1998: 95) attribute much greater transformative and independent power than is warranted to ethnic and racial identities, rather than ethnic and racial groups. They maintain that "identities are capable—via the actions they set in motion—of reconstructing circumstances. Ethnic identity, in other words, is not only a product of circumstantial factors (among other things). At times, it produces circumstances of its own." Ultimately, the groups that create racial or ethnic identities, rather than those identities themselves, set collective actions in motion that can transform political and economic conditions to the advantage of the racial or ethnic groups concerned.

Ethnic identity construction can be seen as having cultural and structural dimensions. The cultural dimension of identity formation pertains to the selective use by an ethnic group of certain aspects of its culture—values, customs, myths, traditions, language, or religion—to create and articulate a distinct identity for itself. This cultural dimension also includes the specific meanings attributed to the group's ethnic identity, such as how it views itself as a constituent group in society, for example, as "hardworking," "family-oriented," or "traditional." By providing a cultural repertoire of resources, culture furnishes a creative element that facilitates the process of constructing an ethnic or racial group's identity and the shared meanings and symbols attached to it. As observed by Nagel (1994: 162): "Culture provides the content and meaning of ethnicity; it animates and authenticates ethnic boundaries by providing a history, ideology, symbolic universe, and system of meaning. Culture answers the question: What are we?" Like ethnic identity, culture also can be reconstructed and transformed by its adherents, and this attribute enhances its utility in identity formation. Under given historical circumstances, an ethnic group may reconstruct certain aspects of its culture—such as traditions, myths, or values—in order to assert a particular identity for itself or to ascribe a particular meaning to its ethnic identity. Alba (1990: 77) has emphasized the interdependent relation between ethnic identity and culture: "Thus, the relationship between identity and cultural activities can be seen as synergistic—each necessary for the other to contribute positively to ethnicity as a social form; that is, ethnic identity without any cultural content represents a pure form of symbolic ethnicity, and an adherence to ethnic culture in the absence of ethnic identity represents a private form of ethnicity that does not feed into the ongoing life of an ethnic community." Ethnic identity and culture thus require each other in order to be constituted as cultural representations articulated for the collective benefit of an ethnic group.

Besides ethnic identity construction, cultural construction also can serve as a mechanism for ethnic mobilization, particularly in ethnic social movements.

Nagel (1994: 165) observes how "Cultural claims, icons, and imagery are used by activists in the mobilization process; cultural symbols and meanings are also produced and transformed as ethnic movements emerge and grow." She notes how such cultural symbols and themes are "borrowed and sometimes repackaged" to advance movement objectives (166). The Hawaiian sovereignty movement (discussed below) provides an example of how cultural values, rituals, and symbols are used strategically to mobilize the community in pursuit of the movement's goals of self-determination and recognition of the rights of Native Hawaiians as the indigenous people of Hawai'i.

On the other hand, the structural dimension of ethnic identity construction concerns a group's relations with other groups in a common society. In this case, identity construction centers on boundary making and maintenance insofar as the group seeks to create a social division or at least a distinction between itself and other ethnic groups. In establishing this boundary, an ethnic group may focus on certain cultural criteria—particularly those significant for constructing its identity—that distinguish its members from nonmembers. Due to acculturation processes and the consequent loss of cultural distinctiveness, an ethnic group can also emphasize common descent or ancestry (real or fictive) among its members as the primary factor in constructing its ethnic boundary vis-à -vis other groups. As Nagel (1994: 162) contends: "Ethnic boundaries function to determine identity options, membership composition and size, and form of ethnic organization. Boundaries answer the question: Who are we?" Conversely, since they establish membership criteria, ethnic boundaries also answer the question: Who are not us? The boundary then can be used by an ethnic group to protect its political and economic resources—such as political rights or land—from nonmembers who seek access to these resources by claiming to belong to the group. The ethnic boundary also can serve as the basis for organizing group members to pursue or protect their shared interests.

Another related aspect of the structural dimension of ethnic identity formation concerns a group's perceived status in relation to other ethnic groups in society. This view of themselves in terms of their relative political or economic power or status is a significant aspect of a group's ethnic identity that also provides certain meanings for their identity that are quite distinct from those that are culture-based. These structure-based meanings might include the perception of an ethnic group that it is "oppressed," "successful," or "poor" in comparison to other groups. Whether the cultural or structural dimension (or both) is emphasized by an ethnic group, identity construction can be understood as primarily about creating and articulating social and cultural differences with other ethnic groups as the primary basis for the expression and maintenance of group distinctiveness toward advancing group-specific rights and claims. As Asian American literature professor Kandice Chuh (2003: 47) maintains: "Thinking deconstructively, we can understand that identity is contingent upon difference, that difference precedes and constitutes identity." In contrast, sameness, or the absence of difference, is not very likely to contribute to the attainment of the particular interests or claims of an ethnic group if it cannot distinguish itself from other comparable groups with concerns of their own. As argued in Chapter 1, ethnic identity signifies social and cultural difference among ethnic groups holding unequal status in society and thus can serve as the organizational basis for a group to foster its specific interests, such as advancing its political and economic status. Ethnic identity formation thus provides a means for aggrieved ethnic groups to disentangle the intersection of ethnic identity and social structure that maintains their subordination in society.

The emphasis on ethnic identity construction may lead to the false understanding that an ethnic group has only one identity and one culture. As noted in Chapter 2, for most ethnic groups, the reality is social and cultural diversity and variability within groups whose members may express different ethnic identities and follow somewhat disparate cultures. These differences in ethnic identity and culture may be based on citizenship, class, generation, or gender within a group. Among Asian Americans and Latinos, a primary contributing factor in such internal diversity is ongoing post-1965 immigration that has resulted in a major division between the American-born and immigrant sectors within both racial groups and within specific ethnic groups such as Filipino Americans and Mexican Americans. As discussed in Chapter 2, while Hawai'i-born and Philippine-born Filipino Americans belong to the same ethnic group in Hawai'i, they affirm distinct identities, practice different cultures, and speak different languages at home. Thus, ethnic or racial identity construction tends to obscure or neglect such cultural and social differentiation in the effort to create and advance particular meanings for the common identity of an ethnic or racial group and therefore can be considered a form of "strategic essentialism" (see Lowe 1991).

By applying the constructionist approach, I discuss why and how some ethnic groups in Hawai'i are actively engaged in structural and cultural processes of identity construction. These groups include Native Hawaiians, Korean Americans, particularly the "1.5" generation, and locals. These groups occupy differing political and economic positions in Hawai'i society and thus have different resources and strategies available to them in using identity formation as a means to advance their collective concerns and interests. They also encounter and have experienced different economic, political, and historical conditions in Hawai'i and hence have responded in different ways at different times. In Chapter 6, I review Japanese Americans as an example of an ethnic group that does not have to employ identity construction because of their already dominant political and socioeconomic status in Hawai'i. I also discuss how and why Okinawan Americans or *Uchinanchu* differentiate themselves from Japanese Americans through identity formation processes. Chapter 7 reviews Filipino Americans as an example of an ethnic group that has been precluded from constructing its own ethnic identity by the constraining societal conditions with which they must contend, especially their historical and contemporary racist stereotyping by other groups. Through description and analysis of ethnic identity construction, this and the following two chapters demonstrate the significance of ethnicity as a cultural representation that signifies social and cultural difference among ethnic groups. I also show that ethnic identity formation serves as a means for some groups to contest political and economic inequality in Hawai'i.

## Native Hawaiians: *Kanaka Maoli* Identity

Of the three groups discussed in this chapter, Native Hawaiians provide the most significant example of strategically employing identity construction to advance political and economic interests and objectives.[3] It is not coincidental that since the emergence in the 1970s of the sovereignty movement that seeks self-determination for Native Hawaiians, they have constructed and asserted a collective identity for themselves as the indigenous people of Hawai'i. This political identity and status foster the attainment of their major goals of greater political and economic power and formal recognition of their rights and entitlements as the native people of Hawai'i, including sovereignty. In pursuing these collective political and economic objectives, Native Hawaiians differentiate themselves socially and culturally from all the other groups in the islands that, as they point out, arrived as immigrants and thus do not have the ancestral ties to Hawai'i that Native Hawaiians can claim. As Native Hawaiian scholar and sovereignty leader Haunani-Kay Trask (2000: 1) asserts: "As the indigenous people of Hawai'i, Hawaiians are Native to the Hawaiian Islands. We do not descend from the Americas or from Asia but from the great Pacific Ocean where our ancestors navigated to, and from, every archipelago. . . . The lesson of our origins is that we are genealogically related to Hawai'i, our islands, as family." Being the indigenous people of the islands, Native Hawaiians emphasize that they are not just another ethnic group or minority, like Chinese Americans or Korean Americans, but have a very different legal and political status in Hawai'i since they are not immigrants to the state. Instead, they are a native people whose homeland was colonized by the United States with the overthrow of the Hawaiian monarchy in 1893, and thus they have a legal and political relationship to the United States recognized by Congress in numerous acts that ethnic groups in Hawai'i lack.

The Native Hawaiian case brings out the significance of both the cultural and structural dimensions of identity construction. In terms of the cultural dimension, Native Hawaiians employ particular aspects of their traditional (pre-contact) culture—such as language, religion, and values—to articulate their social and cultural distinctiveness from other island groups.[4] This is evident in the Hawaiian term *kanaka maoli*, literally "real or true people," that they use to express their collective identity as the indigenous people of Hawaiʻi.[5] Using a term from their own language instead of English is a powerful symbol that underscores the cultural uniqueness of Native Hawaiians compared to ethnic groups in Hawaiʻi that simply refer to themselves as Caucasian, Chinese, or Japanese that is indicative of their desired assimilation into American culture and society. But as Trask (2000: 6, emphasis in original) reiterates: "Hawaiians are not engaged in identity politics. . . . *The struggle is not for a personal or group identity but for land, government, and international status as a recognized nation.*" As I have maintained, identity construction is a means toward an end, including economic and political objectives, rather than an end in itself.

Besides the cultural and political significance of the term kanaka maoli, Native Hawaiians have chosen it to represent their identity because an increasing number of non-Hawaiians claim they are "Hawaiian" due to their birth or long-term residence in Hawaiʻi. They thus equate being Hawaiian with being a Texan or a New Yorker, instead of understanding or acknowledging that Hawaiians are not merely residents of a state but a native people with a distinct culture, history, religion, language, and ancestral ties to Hawaiʻi. While some non-Hawaiians may not hesitate in referring to themselves as "Hawaiian," they are far less likely to claim being kanaka maoli. Already in the 1980s, sovereignty leader and then professor of medicine Kekuni Blaisdell (1989: 11, emphasis in original) remarked on this disturbing trend among non-Hawaiians:

> Accentuating the pain of every Native Hawaiian is the increasing use, and therefore misuse and abuse, of the term "Hawaiian" to refer to what is clearly *not* Hawaiian and sometimes even anti-Hawaiian. To kanaka maoli, the Royal Hawaiian Hotel, Hawaiian Airlines, . . . and non-Hawaiian residents of Hawaiʻi are not Hawaiian. . . . [I]f non-Hawaiians are Hawaiian, then who or what are Hawaiians? . . . This failure of non-Hawaiians to respect the distinctive identity of Hawaiians as *the* aboriginal people of Hawaiʻi in Hawaiʻi with special rights is humiliating.

The emphasis on traditional culture, such as language, in the construction and expression of Native Hawaiian identity can be attributed to several factors. One basic reason is that they were prohibited from practicing various highly significant aspects of their culture, such as language, religion, and dance, following Western contact; thus, the great interest in these cultural traditions is an effort to retrieve what was forcibly taken away from them. The much greater concern to maintain and practice their traditional culture clearly differentiates Native Hawaiians from most ethnic groups in Hawaiʻi that have become largely acculturated over the generations to American culture. Certainly for Native Hawaiians, practicing certain aspects of their traditional culture contributes to the articulation of their unique identity as the indigenous people of Hawaiʻi. This is the primary reason that symbols of Hawaiian traditional culture, including language, religion, dance, and dress, are prominently featured in their political demonstrations (see below) because they represent the self-determination that Native Hawaiians had before the arrival of Europeans and Americans. However, it must be understood that their political movements are not concerned with a nostalgic return to a romanticized past but instead are very much focused on gaining greater power and control over their collective lives and lands in the present and immediate future.

As for culture-based meanings of being Native Hawaiian, there can be no doubt that construction of their identity as the indigenous people of Hawaiʻi and the sovereignty movement have resulted in much greater pride and consciousness in being Hawaiian. Until the 1970s, feelings of inferiority and inadequacy were common among Native Hawaiians, including youth, because of the widespread denigrating stereotypes of them as dumb, lazy, violent, and criminally inclined (Kanahele 1982: 22–23). However, during that decade, the emergence of the Hawaiian "cultural renaissance" resulted in a revitalization of their values, customs, and beliefs in traditional dance, music, language, religion, sports, medicine, and arts and crafts (25–27). Writing on "The New Hawaiians" in the early 1980s, historian George Kanahele (25) astutely observed: "Among Hawaiians there is a new kind of awareness about themselves and their problems. . . . [W]hat is happening is part of the quest for a higher sense of communal pride and renewed sense of identity as Hawaiians." The Hawaiian cultural renaissance and the sovereignty movement have led Native Hawaiians to contest their racist stereotyping and advance their political goals by reclaiming and redefining their identity with new positive meanings. A primary source of cultural meanings of Hawaiian identity are traditional values—such as *aloha ʻaina* (love for the land)—that underscore their ancestral relationship to the land and other natural resources of Hawaiʻi (Trask 1984: 125). Similarly, in advancing a "definition of [American Indian] tribal identity," Native American studies scholar Eva Marie Garroutte (2003: 118, 135) contends that it is "founded on traditional notions of kinship," particularly the "traditional value of reciprocity" in relating to others and on "relationship to ancestry" or common ties of descent.[6]

With regard to the structural dimension of identity construction, Native Hawaiians seek to affirm and maintain the boundary between themselves as the native people and other groups by emphasizing their ancestral origins in Hawaiʻi that those other groups lack. In fact, the Hawaiʻi Constitution formally defines a Native Hawaiian as a person who can trace descent to the people who were living in Hawai'i prior to 1778 when European contact occurred. Compared to sociological definitions of an ethnic group that focus on a shared culture as one of its most distinctive features, the state definition of a Native Hawaiian is very realistic in not requiring knowledge or practice of Hawaiian culture since much of it was lost with their forced acculturation following contact. This does not mean that Native Hawaiians do not have a culture, only that the state does not require an individual to demonstrate any aspects of that culture to be legally considered a Native Hawaiian.[7] Questioning the relevance of cultural definitions of American Indian identity, Garroutte (2003: 80) argues: "Can we . . . enforce identity definitions that inevitably exclude precisely those who have already suffered the greatest degree of cultural loss and its profound consequences?" However as I discuss below, the state definition of a Native Hawaiian has in effect been legally challenged by non-Hawaiians desiring rights and resources designated only for Native Hawaiians.

While there certainly are different meanings of being Native Hawaiian, structure-based meanings pertain to their perceived political and economic power and status in relation to other groups in Hawai'i. One such meaning for some Native Hawaiians is that they are a colonized people in their own homeland and thus "politically subordinated" (Trask 2000: 2–3). For some of those who consider Native Hawaiians to be colonial subjects of the United States, being Native Hawaiian means not being American. Other Native Hawaiians might view themselves more generally as a politically and socioeconomically oppressed group in Hawai'i compared to other groups evident in their poor health status, low educational and occupational attainment, and high proportion of welfare recipients, homeless, and incarcerated (see Okamura 1998c; "Special Report," *Honolulu Star-Bulletin* 1993: A6). The different meanings of being Native Hawaiian are important in underlining that, like ethnic groups in Hawai'i and elsewhere, Native Hawaiians articulate diverse collective identities with different meanings and have varying political and economic concerns depending on their class, age, and other social characteristics.

Even before the emergence of the sovereignty movement in the 1970s, Native Hawaiians were successful through their community organizing and political protests in changing to some extent the political and economic circumstances they faced in Hawai'i. These changes were evident in a constitutional amendment approved by a majority of Hawai'i voters in 1978 for the establishment of the Office of Hawaiian Affairs as a state government agency led by elected Native Hawaiian trustees that would provide programs and services only to Native Hawaiians. Another constitutional amendment that was adopted in 1978 made Hawaiian one of the official languages of the state of Hawai'i. In addition, the sovereignty movement has made the people of Hawai'i more aware of the historical injustices and abuses and contemporary subjugation and marginalization of Native Hawaiians and more accepting of the notion that, as the indigenous people of the islands, they have unique rights and claims and are not just another ethnic group among the many others.

However, the *Rice v. Cayetano* (then governor of Hawai'i) decision of the U.S. Supreme Court issued on February 23, 2000 constitutes a major change, if not setback, in the legal and political circumstances that Native Hawaiians must contend with in seeking their political and economic objectives. The Court's decision gave non-Hawaiians the same right as Native Hawaiians to vote in elections for trustees of the Office of Hawaiian Affairs (OHA). Prior to the *Rice* decision, only Native Hawaiians could be elected as trustees of the agency, but it also led to the loss of that right. The Supreme Court ruling resulted from a suit filed by Harold "Freddy" Rice, a White missionary descendant and wealthy Hawai'i Island rancher, who challenged the state's restriction on voting in OHA elections only to Native Hawaiians as racially discriminatory. The *Rice* decision has ushered in what I have referred to as the "Post-Rice" era of ethnic relations in Hawai'i that has been distinguished by increasing legal challenges to Native Hawaiian rights and entitlements by non-Hawaiians who seek to have the same rights and benefits previously granted by federal and state law only to Native Hawaiians (Okamura 2002: 135). As a result, construction and articulation of kanaka maoli identity has come to serve more as a means to protect and maintain, rather than advance and obtain, their rights and claims from lawsuits. Based particularly on common ancestry, Native Hawaiian boundary making has been employed to prevent non-Hawaiians from accessing their entitlements and resources by excluding them from being considered group members.

However, since the *Rice* decision, non-Hawaiians seeking admission to the Kamehameha Schools, a private prekindergarten through twelfth grade educational institution, have been successful by advancing other group membership criteria by which they claim the same rights as Native Hawaiians.[8] Established in 1884 by the will of Princess Bernice Pauahi Bishop, the schools are a $6 billion nonprofit, charitable trust that annually educates about five thousand Native Hawaiian students on campuses on the three major islands. These students are admitted according to Kamehameha's policy that gives "preference" to Native Hawaiians. However, in a case settled in 2003, a non-Hawaiian, twelve-year-old boy, Brayden Mohica-Cummings, was accepted to the Kamehameha Schools even though his non-Hawaiian mother had falsely claimed in his application that he was Hawaiian. After the schools rescinded his acceptance, he filed suit through his Sacramento, California-based attorney, Eric Grant, contending Kamehameha's admissions policy violated federal antidiscrimination laws, although the schools do not receive any federal funds (Daysog 2003c). The reason that many non-Hawaiians want their children to attend the Kamehameha Schools is because of the excellent college preparatory education provided that is comparable to that offered at the more academically prestigious private schools in Hawai'i but at a much lower cost of about $3,200 per year (2006–2007).

As for claiming to be Hawaiian, the boy's mother, Kalena Santos, said she had been adopted by a Native Hawaiian father and therefore was raised as a Hawaiian; she asserted that her son was similarly Hawaiian because she had raised him. Thus, contrary to the state definition of a Native Hawaiian based on descent rather than culture, Santos advanced a cultural definition of being Hawaiian. After a U.S. District Court judge ordered the Kamehameha Schools to admit Mohica-Cummings pending a decision in his lawsuit, the schools' Board of Trustees, in a controversial decision, voted to admit him and allow him to attend Kamehameha through the twelfth grade on the condition that he drop his suit (Daysog 2003c). Their concern was probably that if he prevailed in court, the schools would have to revise their admissions policy drastically not to give preference to Native Hawaiian applicants.[9] Strong Native Hawaiian opposition to the Mohica-Cummings lawsuit and the boy's acceptance by the trustees was evident in the more than 84,000 signatures collected by the Na Pua Ke Alii Pauahi (The Children of Princess Pauahi) organization (Daysog 2003b).

In 2007 the Kamehameha Schools reached an out-of-court settlement in the *John Doe* lawsuit against them that an anonymous non-Hawaiian student had filed four years earlier. He challenged the schools' admissions policy as racially discriminatory after he had twice been denied acceptance because he has no Hawaiian ancestry. John Doe's suit was filed on his behalf by John Goemans, the lawyer for Freddy Rice in his suit against OHA, and by constitutional law attorney Eric Grant, the lawyer for Brayden Mohica-Cummings in his lawsuit against the schools. In a 2003 ruling in the suit, a U.S. District Court judge in Hawai'i found that Kamehameha's admissions policy "serves a legitimate remedial purpose by addressing the socioeconomic and educational disadvantages facing native Hawaiians, . . . and revitalizing native Hawaiian culture" (cited in Apgar 2006). However, in 2005 the decision of two of the three judges on a 9th U.S. Circuit Court of Appeals panel in San Francisco overturned the previous ruling and found that the schools' admissions policy "constitutes unlawful race discrimination" and "operates as an absolute bar to admission for non-Hawaiians" (cited in Barayuga 2005a: A1). Commenting on the court's decision, Goemans (cited in Apgar 2005b: A7) contended that it "is a reaffirmation of everything found in Rice, that all these programs are all race-based. This case sets precedents for other cases [challenging programs only for Native Hawaiians] and dramatically raises the national visibility of what exists in Hawaii and has grown since the 1970s, this pernicious racism." Goemans's remarks indicate the significance of the *Rice* decision as itself a major precedent in providing the legal basis for contesting other programs, both public and private, designated for Native Hawaiians.[10]

Goemans's reference above to "racism" in Hawai'i is ironic insofar as he views non-Hawaiians as somehow the victims of racism and racial discrimination by Native Hawaiians because the former are denied the privilege of benefiting from private programs such as the Kamehameha Schools that are fully funded by Native Hawaiian financial resources. For Goemans and other advocates of neoconservative racial politics, racial discrimination is fundamentally a denial of individual rights, whether those of Whites or non-Whites; thus, from their perspective, even a subjugated group like Native Hawaiians can commit discrimination against Whites. Goemans's mention of "national visibility" indicates why the California-based Grant was an attorney in the two cases against the Kamehameha Schools. Like the *Rice* case, the suits are of national significance because they are part of the nationwide neoconservative movement to abolish all race-based educational, employment, and government programs designated for the benefit of racial minorities. For those who support this movement, the Kamehameha Schools' admissions policy is no different from race-based affirmative action policies in higher education that they strongly oppose and are committed to challenge in courts across the nation.

Shortly after the court's decision in the *John Doe* suit was announced, the Kamehameha Schools sought and were later granted an "en banc" hearing of the case by a larger panel of judges. After rehearing the case in 2006, fifteen judges of the 9th U.S. Circuit Court of Appeals ruled by an 8 to 7 vote that the schools' admissions policy does not violate federal civil rights laws and has a legitimate remedial purpose of rectifying educational and economic disadvantages suffered by Native Hawaiians (Barayuga 2006). However, in spring 2007 the attorneys for John Doe filed a petition to have the U.S. Supreme Court hear the case. Had the Court ultimately decided against the Kamehameha Schools, the disastrous consequences for Native Hawaiians cannot be overstated. They would have lost their right of access to their most highly valued educational institution that, besides providing a means of socioeconomic advancement for many Native Hawaiians, develops future community leaders and contributes to the development of Hawaiian culture.

The same 9th U.S. Circuit Court of Appeals ruled in 2007 that the plaintiffs in the *Arakaki v. Lingle* (governor of Hawai'i) suit have no legal standing to challenge state of Hawai'i funding of OHA with state taxes, but the court did not dismiss the suit that was filed initially in 2002. The case was returned to the U.S. District Court in Hawai'i to determine if any of the plaintiffs are eligible "in any other capacity" (Da Silva 2007: A6). As a legal remedy, the suit seeks to have the state of Hawai'i abolish OHA and the Department of Hawaiian Home Lands (DHHL) and have their assets returned to state control for the benefit of all Hawai'i residents. The fourteen plaintiffs in the *Arakaki v. Lingle* suit, representing different ethnic groups in Hawai'i, maintain that OHA and DHHL are race-based programs and therefore violate the equal protection clause of the Fourteenth Amendment of the U.S. Constitution because they discriminate against non-Hawaiians (Apgar 2005c: A6).[11] As is evident since the *Rice* decision, lawsuits against Native Hawaiian rights and entitlements represent Native Hawaiians as a "race," instead of recognizing them as the native people of Hawai'i, and so argue that programs or institutions established for their benefit are "racially discriminatory" because they are based on "racial preference."

The initial U.S. Circuit Court of Appeals ruling on August 2, 2005 in the *John Doe v. Kamehameha Schools* suit in John Doe's favor generated immediate and widespread protests by the Native Hawaiian community, not only in Hawai'i but also in the continental United States. That very day, Native Hawaiian attorney Trisha Kehaulani Watson addressed a crowd that had gathered at the Kamehameha Schools administrative office, stating that the court's ruling should be a "wake-up call" to Native Hawaiians to take a collective stance that "we are a nation of people who stand together. So today, don't see this as a day we lost the 9th Circuit Court's decision. I hope five years from now we look back and say this is the day Hawaiians said, 'We have had enough,' and from this day forward, we move as one nation" (cited in Barayuga 2005a: A7).

The following Sunday, the Native Hawaiian community held a large rally at 'Iolani Palace, the former residence of Hawaiian monarchy, that brought together more than ten thousand people in solidarity (Vorsino 2005b: A1). The two-hour demonstration featured chants and prayers in the Hawaiian language and speeches by Kamehameha Schools' trustees and officials who declared their determination to oppose any legal challenges to their admissions policy. The schools' chief executive officer, Dee Jay Miller, told the crowd, "All over the world, Hawaiians are standing as one. When we leave here today, we are one." As in Watson's remarks, the emphasis on sharing a common Native Hawaiian identity served as a strategic means toward collective agency to unite the community to protect their rights of access to their highly valued institution.

As is common in political demonstrations by Native Hawaiians, traditional cultural symbols were evident among many of them in the rally at 'Iolani Palace. Some of the men wore *malo* or loincloths, while some women and men were dressed in *kihei*, a loose-fitting garment tied over the left shoulder. Many other participants wore red T-shirts with the expression "*Ku I Ka Pono*" or "Justice for Hawaiians," which were produced for a 2003 rally after the Kamehameha Schools court cases had emerged, and since have been worn by Native Hawaiians at other political gatherings. Protest signs also were written in the Hawaiian language. After the rally, the participants marched to the Royal Mausoleum where Princess Bernice Pauahi Bishop is buried, many carrying

Hawaiian flags inverted as a sign that the Hawaiian nation is in distress. Other demonstrations and marches were held the same day on the islands of Hawai'i, Maui, Kaua'i, and Moloka'i, and in the continental United States in California, Oregon, and the East Coast that manifested the rapid mobilization of the Native Hawaiian community in opposition to the court decision. As noted by Trask (2000: 5), such protest gatherings have the "power" to raise the collective consciousness of Native Hawaiians of their indigenous identity through the "political education" they provide:

> The substance of the "nation" is made obvious when thousands of Hawaiians gather to protest the theft of their sovereignty. The power of such public rituals to de-colonize the mind can be seen in the rise of a new national identification among Hawaiians. After the 1993 sovereignty protests at the ['Iolani] Palace of our chiefs, Hawaiians, especially the youth, began to discard national identity as Americans and reclaim indigenous identification as Natives.[12]

Yet another legal challenge to Native Hawaiian entitlements in the Post-Rice era is directed against tuition waivers and lower tuition rates provided to some Native Hawaiian students by the University of Hawai'i. This university policy came under investigation by the Office of Civil Rights of the U.S. Department of Education, including a site visit to the University of Hawai'i (UH) at Manoa in 2004, after a civil rights complaint was filed in 2002 by John Goemans (Gima 2005a: A6).[13] He contended that providing tuition waivers for Native Hawaiians and permitting out-of-state Native Hawaiians to pay the significantly lower resident tuition rate are racially discriminatory (Dunford 2004: A8). Similar federal discrimination investigations were conducted in 2004 at several other universities, which is indicative of how in the aftermath of the *Rice* decision, Native Hawaiians have become racialized and viewed not as a native people but as a racial minority comparable to African Americans or Latinos.

Five months after the U.S. Supreme Court issued its *Rice* decision in February 2000, U.S. senator Daniel Akaka introduced what has become commonly known as the "Akaka Bill" or the Native Hawaiian Government Reorganization Act. This bill establishes that Congress finds Native Hawaiians to be an indigenous people and authorizes a process by which they can form a "native Hawaiian governing entity" for self-governance (Reyes 2005a: A12). It provides federal recognition of Native Hawaiians comparable to that accorded to more than five hundred Native American and Alaska Native groups. Among other reasons, the bill was introduced to protect Native Hawaiian rights and programs, such as OHA, from further lawsuits such as the *Rice* case. It provides for the Office for Native Hawaiian Relations, established and funded by

Congress in 2004, in the U.S. Department of Interior to serve as a liaison between the Native Hawaiian governing entity and the federal and state governments. The bill authorizes the federal and state governments to negotiate with the Native Hawaiian entity on issues such as the transfer of lands, natural resources, and other assets; the protection of existing native rights to those lands and resources; and the delegation of governmental powers to the Native Hawaiian government (Reyes 2005a: A12).

Opinions differ widely among Native Hawaiians, as they do among other Hawai'i residents, on whether they support or oppose the Akaka Bill. Those in favor of the bill include Native Hawaiian institutions, such as OHA, the Kamehameha Schools, and the Native Hawaiian Bar Association. Other supporters include Governor Linda Lingle, the state legislature, the entire Hawai'i congressional delegation, and 68 percent of Hawai'i residents, according to a 2005 public opinion survey paid for by OHA (Borreca 2005). Supporters of the bill maintain that federal recognition is a starting point for further advancement and protection of their rights and claims by a Native Hawaiian government in future negotiations with the U.S. and Hawai'i state governments.

Opponents of the Akaka Bill include a coalition of Native Hawaiians called *Hui Pu* (group to unite) and other sovereignty leaders and supporters who generally advocate the formation of an independent Hawaiian nation. They view the bill as perpetuating colonial control over Native Hawaiians by making them "wards" of the U.S. government like Native Americans under the Bureau of Indian Affairs. Sovereignty leader Kekuni Blaisdell contends that the Native Hawaiian governing body established through the Akaka Bill would be a "puppet government" of the United States because it requires the approval of the U.S. secretary of the interior (cited in Apgar 2005a: A6). Blaisdell further argues: "The Akaka Bill is an attempt to turn us into native Americans so that we can continue under the heel of the U.S. invader and colonizer of our homeland. . . . But when we see the plight of the American Indians and the Alaska natives, we certainly don't want to be similarly treated and have our lands taken and our trusts violated." Akaka Bill opponents also include those in Hawai'i who are most strongly against any government recognition of Native Hawaiian rights and claims, such as attorney William Burgess, leader of the Aloha for All group, and former *Honolulu Advertiser* publisher Thurston Twigg-Smith whose grandfather, Lorrin Thurston, was one of the leaders of the 1893 overthrow of the Hawaiian monarchy. Their position is that the Akaka Bill is "race-based" and therefore unconstitutional since it discriminates against non-Hawaiians on the basis of race by allowing only Native Hawaiians to participate in the process of establishing a governing entity. Beyond Hawai'i, opponents of the Akaka Bill include the U.S. Department of Justice, almost all Republicans in the U.S. Senate, and the U.S. Commission on Civil Rights. In a 2006 report, the commission concluded that the bill would "discriminate on the basis of race or national origin, and further subdivide the American people into discrete subgroups accorded varying degrees of privilege" (cited in "Akaka Bill Faces Crucial Vote," *Honolulu Star-Bulletin* 2006).

Even after substantial revisions had been made since its introduction, the Akaka Bill was blocked from being voted on for several years by procedural measures initiated by several Republican senators opposed to it. In 2006, the U.S. Senate took a procedural vote that prevented the bill from moving to a final vote on the Senate floor. While the bill received a majority fifty-six votes, it needed sixty votes to advance. Nonetheless, even if the bill had been approved by the Senate, its passage by the U.S. House of Representatives and signing into law by President George W. Bush were doubtful given strong Republican opposition to it.

The constant legal and political challenges to Native Hawaiian rights and entitlements following the *Rice* ruling in 2000 demonstrate the superficiality and invalidity of the Hawai'i multicultural model in representing ethnic relations in the state. If the people who generously extended their aloha to newcomers to their islands are themselves denied just and fair treatment in their own homeland, where are the tolerance, harmony, and aloha spirit that are supposed to distinguish Hawai'i as a multicultural society? The model is analytically bankrupt in providing any explanation of what has been occurring to Native Hawaiians since the *Rice* decision.

## Korean Americans: 1.5-Generation Identity

Korean Americans of the 1.5 generation construct and affirm a distinct ethnic identity that distinguishes them from their first- and second-generation counterparts (Danico 2002, 2004).[14] These generational distinctions pertain to the post-1965 Korean American community rather than to the descendants of the first Korean immigrants who arrived in Hawai'i between 1903 and 1924 and include fourth- and fifth-generation members. As a result of post-1965 immigration, these more recent immigrants and their descendants constitute a majority of Korean Americans in the state. The Korean American case indicates the significance for ethnic identity construction of internal segments within an ethnic group and how they each can have a distinct identity that differentiates them from the others.

Based on her research on 1.5-generation Korean Americans in Hawai'i, sociologist Mary Yu Danico has argued that the 1.5 generation refers to Koreans who immigrated during their formative years such that they were old enough to have developed memories of living in Korea and young enough to have attended intermediate or high school in the United States. As a result, "1.5ers" become bicultural in Korean and American cultures and bilingual in the Korean and English languages. While they may not speak Korean fluently, Danico states that they are able to converse in Korean, and they speak English with little or no Korean accent; however, the specific social, cultural, and class experiences of individual 1.5ers following immigration affect their degree of bilingualism and biculturalism. The life experiences of the 1.5 generation differ significantly from those of immigrants (like their parents) who arrive in the United States at an older age, and from those of the second generation who have no background of living in Korea. In general terms, the first generation speaks English with a discernible accent, feels more comfortable speaking Korean than English, identifies as Korean, and continues to follow Korean cultural values and norms. In contrast, the second generation speaks English as their primary language—including Hawai'i Creole English, although some of them can also speak Korean—considers themselves more local or American than Korean, and does not identify strongly with Korean culture. As Danico (2002: 148) observes: "What makes these 1.5ers distinct . . . is their lack of identification [with] and their consciousness of not being first or second generation but 'somewhere in-between.' The feeling of being 'neither'—and, to some extent, invisible—has demarcated 1.5ers from other Korean Americans in Hawai'i." Given their bilingual and bicultural abilities, members of the 1.5 generation are able to switch their generational and ethnic identities "in varying situations as first, 1.5, or second generation or as Korean American, local, or Korean" (Danico 2004: 7).

Danico (2004: 151) emphasizes that becoming 1.5-generation Korean American is "a process of discovery" rather than simply a demographic fact of birthplace and immigration. She maintains that young Korean immigrants are not 1.5ers when they arrive in the United States and that not all of them will become 1.5-generation members since it involves a socialization process of meeting and interacting with other 1.5ers as they become adults. Through this process, they develop an understanding of what it means to be 1.5-generation Korean American and discover their shared ethnic identity with others who have similar experiences of having been child immigrants while growing up in Hawai'i and who contradict prevalent stereotypes of Korean immigrants (182). Danico (2002: 148) argues that it is the demeaning stereotypes of Korean immigrants in Hawai'i as bar hostesses, taxi drivers, and small vendors catering to tourists that lead the 1.5 generation to construct their own ethnic identity because of the resulting embarrassment and shame they feel being Korean American. These stereotypes depict Korean immigrants as sexually loose (young women), pushy, hot-tempered, money-hungry, and rude. Danico adds that, insofar as the 1.5ers hold the same negative perceptions of Koreans, they have themselves internalized the stereotypes held by non-Koreans. Thus, part of the process of becoming a 1.5er is no longer feeling ashamed and embarrassed about being a Korean immigrant. The degrading representations of Korean immigrants and their relegation to service occupations comprise major aspects of the societal conditions that confront Korean Americans in Hawai'i.

Consequently, 1.5ers seek to dissociate themselves from first-generation Koreans and their stigmatized identity, as is clear in a comment by a 1.5-generation Korean American college student about Korean immigrants at her high school (cited in Danico 2002: 155): "They were too 'cliquey'; they only spoke Korean, hung out with Koreans, and isolated themselves from others. We did not want to hang out with just Koreans, particularly those at our school. We wanted to blend in with the rest of the school and wanted to associate with local students." The "we-they" categorical opposition in this 1.5er's statement makes clear the division she perceived between 1.5ers like herself and Korean immigrant students, some of whom could have been of the 1.5 generation. On their part, adult members of the first generation, including their parents, consider 1.5ers as being more like the second generation and do not accept them as fully Korean because they tend to lack language fluency and cultural competency in not being entirely cognizant of expected behavioral norms.

As expressed in the student's comment, affirming a local identity is a very important means by which at least some 1.5-generation Korean Americans differentiate themselves from Korean immigrants since the latter, as well as other immigrants and newcomers in general, are not viewed as local. Expressing a local identity is much more common among working-class 1.5ers than among their upwardly mobile middle-class counterparts. Members of the 1.5 generation can claim a local identity by gaining knowledge of local culture, including the ability to speak pidgin English, and by developing close friendships with Korean American and non-Korean locals. However, 1.5ers often are not accepted as local by second-generation Korean Americans who, having been born and raised in Hawai'i, consider themselves local and view 1.5ers as immigrants. Much like 1.5-generation Korean Americans, their second-generation counterparts also wish to dissociate themselves from the degrading representations of Korean immigrants in Hawai'i. The lack of acceptance by second-generation Korean Americans combined with the desire of 1.5ers to distance themselves from the first generation leads 1.5-generation Korean Americans to construct and affirm a separate ethnic identity for themselves. Danico (2004: 157) maintains that another interest individual 1.5ers have in asserting their own ethnic identity is greater access to employment. She states that when seeking work they emphasize their bilingual skills and their ability to serve a multiethnic clientele, including Korean immigrants and locals.

At a more collective level, a Korean American organization in Hawai'i that consists predominantly of the 1.5 generation (90 percent) is the Honolulu Korean Junior Chamber of Commerce (hereafter, Jaycees), established in 1994 (Danico 2004: 160). Due to international Junior Chamber of Commerce rules, members of the Jaycees must be between twenty-one and thirty-nine years of age. Thus, they are relatively young compared to the members of the more established Korean American community organizations that have a primarily first-generation and older membership such as the Korean Chamber of Commerce. The Jaycees can be considered a professional, college-educated, middle-class group that has the communication and intercultural skills to interact with members of the larger society, including the news media, that first-generation community leaders may lack. Certainly, there are many second-generation Korean Americans of the appropriate age group who are middle-class professionals and could join the Korean Jaycees if they wished. However, efforts by the Jaycees to recruit second-generation members have not been very successful because "Korean culture and Korean American community affairs" are not their primary social concern and, having assimilated into local culture, they want to join less ethnically based organizations (178).

According to Danico (2004: 165), the Jaycees are highly concerned to assert a positive ethnic identity for Korean Americans by challenging prevalent stereotypes of them as temperamental, aggressive, clannish, and materialistic immigrants who speak English with an obvious accent: "They hope to create a new image of Korean Americans as articulate, community-oriented, and open to all of Hawaii's ethnic groups." The Jaycees seek to accomplish this objective by various service activities for both the Korean American and local communities, such as sponsoring golf tournaments and an annual U.S. citizenship drive that is open to all immigrants. They thus advance an ethnic identity for the Korean American community as being more local than immigrant. The Jaycees also can be seen as employing ethnic identity construction to contest the socioeconomic subordination of Korean immigrants as tourist-industry service workers. The Jaycees demonstrated their advocacy role on behalf of the Korean American community when some of them responded to an article that they found offensive in one of the Honolulu daily newspapers about a golf tournament won by a Korean woman professional, Se Ri Park (Danico 2002: 150). Ironically, the article was written by a local Korean American sportswriter, Bill Kwon, who made reference to Ke'eaumoku Street in Honolulu that is well known for its hostess bars or, as they are commonly called, "Korean bars" because some Korean immigrant women work in them along with other women. Kwon wrote: "They're dancing in the streets of Seoul. And, I imagine, on Keeaumoku too; especially during happy hour . . . Maybe there even might be a Club Se Ri on Keeaumoku some day" (Kwon 1998: D1). In response, a member of the Jaycees wrote to the newspaper's editor:

> We are not exactly sure what Mr. Kwon was trying to express, . . . but one can't help but think that all Koreans live on Keeaumoku, or that all Koreans attend "happy hours," or that all Koreans engage in liquor businesses (i.e., "Club Se Ri"). What is most certain however is that Mr. Kwon's comments stereotype Korean Americans as being at least

> associated with these activities. In effect and in a subtle way, Korean Americans are attributed with socially undesirable characteristics. . . . It is possible that Mr. Kwon was trying to add humor to his article, however, this type of humor is not only offensive to Korean Americans but can lead to racist treatment toward Korean Americans.

In submitting his letter, the writer and other Jaycees members who sent similar letters of protest to the newspaper were seeking to change the societal circumstances to which they are subject, particularly the stigmatized stereotyping of Korean Americans by the news media. This example of blatant stereotyping by the print media demonstrates how those with the power to represent others, even members of the same ethnic group, can be absolutely ignorant of how their writings denigrate others. It is significant that the sportswriter himself is Korean American, although very likely descended from earlier immigrants than the post-1965 Koreans in Hawai'i. In making no reference to his shared ethnicity with them in their letter to the editor, it seemed that the Jaycees almost considered him to belong to another ethnic group, or at least to view local Korean Americans as significantly different from immigrant Koreans like themselves.

Danico (2004: 166) contends that because of the bilingual and bicultural skills of their members, the Jaycees can serve as a "bridge," not only between first- and second-generation Korean Americans, but also between the Korean American and local communities. As stated by a Jaycees leader (cited in Danico 2004: 179): "We as 1.5[er]s can understand the needs of the Korean American community, but at the same time understand how to deal with the American culture. Our method of communicating with non-Koreans is more likely to bridge the relationship with the [Korean American] community and the others." Constructing a distinct "in-between" identity for themselves facilitates the assumption by the 1.5 generation of this mediator role for the Korean American community that enables them to address its political and economic concerns. Danico (2005) notes the possibility for 1.5ers to mobilize Korean Americans to have a greater "political voice" in Hawai'i. Such political activism is not necessarily limited to electoral politics; the Jaycees' protest of the news media's demeaning representation of Korean Americans is an example of such political advocacy. Representatives of the 1.5 generation are particularly suited to play a mediating role on behalf of the Korean American community since the first generation generally lacks the English language and intercultural abilities to work with the larger Hawai'i society, and the second generation lacks the desire to associate themselves closely with the Korean American community and its problems and concerns. Furthermore, the third- and fourth-generation descendants of the pre–World War II Korean immigrants do not have social and cultural ties with the post-1965 community, especially language, and thus cannot or do not wish to play this intermediary role for the Korean American community.

The 1.5-generation Korean American case highlights that ethnic groups, especially immigrant minorities, are internally culturally and socially diverse, and thus ethnic identity construction is a form of self-representation that may obscure significant differences, if not cleavages, within a group. It should not be surprising that members of the 1.5 generation would assume a leadership role in such ethnic identity formation for the Korean American community given their more proficient English language skills, higher educational attainment, and greater political awareness compared to the first generation. While those attributes are also held by the second generation, 1.5ers have a stronger sense of Korean American identity and closer ties to the Korean American community.

## Globalization of Local Identity and Culture

During the infamous Massie case of 1931, the term "local" was first used to categorize collectively people from Hawai'i, in particular, the five young men accused of kidnapping and raping Thalia Massie, the twenty-year-old White wife of a navy lieutenant. As "local" was used in accounts of the trial that appeared in the *Honolulu Advertiser*, it referred to the birth and upbringing in Hawai'i of the five working-class youths, that is, two Native Hawaiians, two Japanese Americans, and a Chinese-Hawaiian. Their racial and class status and origins in the islands contrasted sharply with those of their White, military accusers from the continental United States, and those social and cultural differences signified the primary cleavage in Hawai'i during the pre–World War II period between non-Whites and Whites. No doubt, some Whites had been born and raised in the islands, but they were of a far more privileged class than that of Native Hawaiians and the descendants of the immigrant plantation groups.

Historian John Rosa (2000: 100) has discussed the various ways that books, television dramas, and historical tours about the Massie case have contributed to the "cultural production of local identity" and preserved the collective memory of the case into the twenty-first century "as an event with strong meaning for locals." He maintains that the case itself and subsequent narratives of it "have consistently served as a means to express local identity as a cultural identity continually in the making." Other sources that contribute to this continual making of local identity include the everyday cultural practices, norms, and values followed by local people that are or become part of local culture in Hawai'i.

Yet another significant source of the cultural production of local identity are articles that appear quite regularly in newspapers and magazines published in Hawai'i. My interest in these journalistic discussions of local people and their cultural practices is because of their frequency of publication and wide circulation by the print media. Like newspaper articles on Hawai'i as a multicultural model, they have the potential at least to influence hundreds of thousands of readers. Insofar as they express popular understandings of local culture, these articles convey certain meanings and symbols of that culture and representations of local people and their practices and beliefs. However, through this dissemination process, the media can reinforce certain commonly accepted views about local identity and culture that are stereotypic in nature and that do not reflect significant changes in their definition. In this section on local identity, I discuss the problems in representation that can result from journalistic descriptions of local people and from their limited focus on interpersonal relationships. I also review a few scholarly works and my own survey on the concept of local.

Despite the importance of being local to the people of Hawai'i, journalistic discussions of local culture and identity often take a humorous approach. In a 2002 essay titled "You Know You're a Malihini [Newcomer] Starting to Turn Local When . . . ," *Honolulu Advertiser* columnist and playwright Lee Cataluna raised the issue of newcomers becoming local over time: "What about the people who didn't grow up here, but who have put in some serious time and effort to understand and adopt the culture? When do they know they've turned the corner to local-ness?" (Cataluna 2002: A25). She suggested that a list should be compiled for them of various cultural indicators such as: "You know you're local when you get irked by people who act too 'Mainland' "; and "You know you're turning local when you go to the beach and aim for the shade. People from cold places sit in the sun." While intended to be funny, Cataluna's discussion of local identity at least correctly emphasized that its definition is based on cultural criteria rather than mere birth or upbringing in Hawai'i, since those "who didn't grow up here" can still "adopt the culture" and "turn local" over time.

Cataluna's column was a response to what she referred to as "You know you're local if . . ." lists regularly sent by e-mail among Hawai'i residents that include well-known references to local culture. These lists very likely originated after 1996 when the *Honolulu Advertiser* asked its readers to complete the above phrase and published the results, most of which also had a humorous tone ("You Know You're Local if . . ." *Honolulu Advertiser* 1996: D1, D3). According to the newspaper's editors, the submissions "fell neatly" into six major categories that they gave titles in Hawai'i Creole English, with food the most frequently mentioned category: "Grinds: The foods we love," "Clo's [clothes]: Slippers and anykine," "Talk Story: The way we talk," "No Big Thing: Our philosophy," "Local Style: Stuff we do," and "Da Fax: You outta [ought to] know." Besides food, the other categories refer to the casual attire commonly worn in Hawai'i, including "rubber slippers" or flip-flops; the use of pidgin English; cultural norms and values that emphasize an easygoing, casual, and considerate attitude; common lifestyle practices; and cultural knowledge about Hawai'i and its peoples.

Consistent with the generally humorous approach to local culture and identity evident in readers' responses, the article was accompanied by cartoon drawings of local people engaged in activities mentioned in some of the submissions, such as wearing rubber slippers with formal attire. The numerous responses sent in by the general public represent popular conceptions of local culture, and the six major categories into which the submissions were classified could be interpreted as indicating the cultural practices, symbols, and values that local people consider most distinctive about their culture. However, the racialized, gendered, and classed image that is conveyed about local people from the readers' responses and the cartoon drawings is to some extent of a stereotypical overweight, non-White male who eats plate lunches, wears a T-shirt, speaks pidgin English, has a carefree attitude toward life, and knows much local trivia about Hawai'i but perhaps not much about the rest of the world.[15] Such a distorted representation of local people obscures not only the many locals who do not conform to that overgeneralized image but, more importantly, the many significant political and economic issues that confront local people and their culture and about which they are concerned.

Another newspaper article that reinforced stereotyped notions of local culture and people is an "analysis" of the firing of then University of Hawai'i president Evan Dobelle by the UH Board of Regents in 2004, supposedly because he had "flunked 'Locals 101'" (DePledge and Creamer 2004: A1). According to the authors of the front-page article in one of the Honolulu dailies, "While Honolulu has long been as cosmopolitan as any large city on the Mainland, an intense localism still defines many social and business relationships, and Dobelle's East Coast confidence sometimes came across as arrogance." In contrast to Dobelle, one of the local persons interviewed for the article maintained that being local involves "that whole sense of humility and self-deprecation, the need to listen." As a recent newcomer to Hawai'i, Dobelle apparently lacked the humble, reserved, and laid-back temperament that locals tend to idealize as characteristic of themselves. According to the authors, these social and cultural deficiencies on Dobelle's part contributed to his inability to get along with members of the UH Board of Regents and to his ultimate downfall. The article thus perpetuates the stereotyped view of how a local person relates interpersonally with others and incorrectly elevates that belief to a major factor in the firing of a president of a research-extensive university.

An article in *Hawaii Business* magazine (Choo 2004), "Local Style for Lolos" ("stupid" in Hawaiian), also related the termination of Dobelle's presidency to his lack of facility with local culture and local people.[16] The cover story is subtitled "Should Lessons on Hawaii's Cultural Landscape Be an Elective or a Requirement?" implying the importance of local cultural knowledge for newcomers. A sidebar article on "How to Do Business Local Style" purported to provide seven "tips for the wayward newcomer on doing business local style" given that "Hawaii has a truly unique business climate" (Youn 2004: 27–28). Intended for the "Mainlander" who would like to conduct business in Hawai'i, the various words of advice are very comparable to the major categories in the "You Know You're Local if . . ." newspaper article and thus also contribute to the essentializing of local persons and their behaviors. For example, the "No Big Thing: Our philosophy" category is apparent in the tip "Don't confuse slow with incompetent" because, while the pace of business in Hawai'i may be slower than in the continental United States, "it doesn't mean the people here can't close deals."[17]

Similar to the articles on the termination of Dobelle as UH president, the various suggestions offered to the newly arrived businessperson have a narrow focus on interpersonal interactions in doing business in Hawai'i that are assumed to be governed by local cultural norms and values. However, one of the local businessmen interviewed for the article pointed out that "people [including locals] tend to confuse how locals choose to socialize with how they do business" (cited in Choo 2004: 29). In other words, local cultural practices and norms relevant to informal social interactions do not necessarily apply to formal business transactions. Furthermore, the narrow concern with interpersonal relationships obscures that, at least in some of the more economically significant business transactions, representatives of Hawai'i-based companies are dealing with much more financially powerful transnational corporations and not merely socially inept newcomers from the continental United States or Asia who are unfamiliar with local cultural practices. From this political economy perspective, the cultural differential that privileges locals over nonlocals in conducting business in Hawai'i is reversed, much to the disadvantage of locals. I maintain that a truly local way of doing business in Hawai'i gives priority to the economic and political interests and concerns of local people rather than to simply closing a deal successfully. The poststatehood expansion of Hawaii's tourism-dependent economy has resulted in the concerns of local people being regularly overridden by corporations based in the continental United States, foreign investment firms, tourist industry and land developers, and transnational corporations.

Besides reinforcing stereotyped views of local people and their supposed behaviors, the print media also contribute to the reification of social boundaries through their discursive practices that contrapose local with nonlocal categories, such as between local and Haole that ignore changes in the definition of local that have resulted in the notion of "local Haoles." The categorical opposition between local and Haole is evident in a newspaper article on the still unsolved beating death in 2002 of a forty-three-year-old White male carpenter who had lived in Wahiawa, a military town on O'ahu, for more than twenty years (Antone 2002: A1, A9). His widow is quoted describing her husband: "That's what kills me because even though he was haole and had blue eyes, he was just so local. He was such a good person, he loved everybody." She believes that someone started a fight with her husband because they thought he was "just another GI" instead of a long-term resident of the community. Similarly, a friend of the deceased described him in the article: "He could speak the pidgin, he loved Hawaii. He was a friendly guy that would stop and talk to anybody." This article highlights the discursive contrast between local and Haole and is based on a violent incident between a White male and what are assumed to be locals. It thus reifies the historical social boundary between the two groups, but in so doing neglects the fluid nature of that boundary and its transgression by local Haoles, perhaps including by the deceased victim in this case.

The frequency of articles published on local identity and culture by the print media raises the question of why there is such a concern with these issues among Hawaii's people. I contend that the reason for this interest is because of the ongoing cultural and economic globalization of Hawai'i that threatens the persistence of local culture and identity. These external threats to Hawaii's people and their distinctive ways of life obviously are not new and, in the late 1960s and early 1970s, gave rise to the first significant change in the construction of local identity. This new meaning of local emphasized a shared appreciation of the land, peoples, and cultures of the islands and a commitment to maintaining control of Hawaii's political and economic future from outside forces of change such as foreign investment, tourism development, immigration from the continental United States, and immigration from Asia and the Pacific (Okamura 1980). However, the myopic view of local culture noted above, focused on interpersonal relationships, results in an inability to perceive the larger national and transnational political, economic, and cultural context in which local people and their culture are situated, especially in opposition to those external forces.

The globalization of Hawai'i, particularly in terms of global consumer culture, has increased markedly since the late 1980s with the arrival of the "big box" retail outlets such as Costco, Wal-Mart, Kmart, and Best Buy. The spread of global consumer culture is visually evident in the dramatic transformation of Ala Moana Center beginning in the early 1990s from a popular local institution opened in 1959, with many of its stores and shops found only in Hawai'i, to somewhat of a trendy shopping mall that could be found anywhere in suburban America since it has many of the same shops and restaurants.[18] The buyout and replacement of Liberty House, a 150-year-old retail establishment in Hawai'i, by Macy's in 2001, and the opening of upscale designer boutiques that cater to free-spending Japanese tourists rather than sales-conscious local shoppers are symptomatic of the ongoing economic and cultural globalization of Hawai'i.

Driven by transnational capital, globalization threatens to eliminate or at least substantially reduce the cultural uniqueness of Hawai'i and is one of the principal reasons why there is an ongoing concern among islanders with local culture and its various manifestations. Far from referring merely to being born and raised in Hawai'i or to having the intercultural skills to interact appropriately with others, local identity has come to represent an assertion of resistance against the increasing cultural and economic globalization of Hawai'i. Unfortunately, this opposition lacks the collective and organized nature of local community struggles in the 1970s, such as at Kalama Valley, Ota Camp, and Waiahole and Waikane Valleys (Nakata 1999; Okamura 1980). In those struggles, local people resisted eviction from their communities by land developers that was part of a larger opposition movement to the uncontrolled economic development of Hawai'i, including tourism expansion. Since the 1990s, a more apparent manifestation of opposition to the globalization of Hawai'i, including loss of local control, is the ongoing movement of islanders to the continental United States noted in Chapter 2; however, they thereby express their sense of powerlessness to control the political and economic future of Hawai'i. Given the never-ending threats to local culture, it would be a terrible tragedy for Hawaii's people if all that eventually remains of local culture is eating Spam, wearing rubber slippers, remembering a few expressions in pidgin English, and going to Las Vegas for a vacation.

To gain an understanding of the changing meaning of local identity, especially among young people, I conducted a brief survey in my Japanese Americans in Hawai'i course in Ethnic Studies at UH Manoa in 2005. Students were asked to respond to an open-ended question: "What does being local mean to you?" They also provided general background information about themselves such as their sex, age, ethnicity, place of birth, length of residence in Hawai'i, and if they can speak pidgin English. The reason for the latter question is because speaking pidgin is generally assumed to be a clear cultural indicator of being local. However, over the years I have met an increasing number of college students whom I would consider to be local but who cannot speak pidgin.

The sample consisted of 126 students who completed the survey and provided 174 responses to the question since many students wrote replies that referred to different ways of being local. I did not include the statements from students who had lived in Hawai'i for less than three years because they tended to reply in very general terms that could apply to anyplace; for example, "I guess being local is when one lives somewhere for quite a long time and is familiar with that environment." As for the demographic background of the respondents, the great majority of them had lived all or most of their lives in

Hawai'i (94 percent) and was born in the islands (82 percent). Their median age was twenty-one years old, and a majority was male (56 percent). In terms of ethnicity, the largest group of respondents was Japanese American (25 percent) and was followed by students who were Japanese and some other ethnicity (15 percent), including Chinese, White, or Filipino. Fourteen percent of the respondents said they were Japanese and Okinawan, and next were Hawaiian (14 percent), Filipino American (8 percent), Korean American (7 percent), and Chinese American (6 percent) students.[19] Since a majority of the respondents was full or part Japanese American, the sample is not representative of UH Manoa students or of eighteen- to twenty-four-year-old residents of Hawai'i, but the responses do provide insights into contemporary views of local identity and culture.

The survey results indicated that, for the students, being local has a predominantly cultural meaning, as evident from the more than three-fourths of their responses that referred to cultural factors (77 percent). Nearly one-third of the responses stated that being local means knowing local culture, customs, values, or traditions (31 percent). As one student wrote: "Being local means being able to assimilate oneself into Hawaii's 'salad bowl' culture." For this and other students, there is a local culture that has developed over time from the mixing or blending of the cultures of different ethnic groups in the islands and which nonlocals have not assimilated. Another cultural factor reported by the students was appreciating or understanding the diverse cultures of Hawai'i (17 percent) as apparent in the following statement: "Local to me means not only being born and raised here, but having an appreciation for the many histories, cultures, and [ethnic] groups here. Local also means being . . . open to the rich diversity found in these islands." This response emphasizes not only an appreciation of Hawai'i and its ethnic groups but also of the diverse cultures of those groups rather than a singular local culture. This meaning of local includes valorizing the cultural diversity of Hawai'i and being familiar with the cultural practices of different ethnic groups. The next most frequently stated cultural criterion of being local was speaking pidgin English and/or eating local foods (15 percent) that I combined because they often were mentioned together, probably because they both are somewhat stereotypic behaviors of local people. The survey question on speaking pidgin English indicated that a significant minority of students do not speak it (29 percent) and that a higher proportion of females (38 percent) than males (21 percent) said they do not. The last significant culture-based criterion of being local was having the "aloha spirit," being laid-back, or having respect for others (14 percent).[20] As a student commented: "Being local everyone has a common ground to stand on and we all respect each other and the place that we come from regardless of cultural/ethnic background. There are still many variations between ethnicities and the types of lifestyles and occupations, but if you're 'local' there's still a common set of values and respect for each other and the Islands. It may be a naive perspective, but the "Aloha Spirit" promotes that idea." This response highlights certain cultural values, such as aloha and respect, in how local people relate to one another and is very consistent with the "tradition of tolerance and peaceful coexistence" dimension of the Hawai'i multicultural model discussed in Chapter 1.

A small minority of students maintained that being local means being born and raised or having grown up in Hawai'i (19 percent) that was the initial meaning of the term in the 1930s. It should not be surprising at all that major changes in the meaning of local identity have occurred since Hawai'i itself and the relations among its constituent ethnic groups also have changed dramatically since that decade. Although the students are not representative of Hawaii's population, as young people, their responses may indicate the direction of changes in the definition of being local, for example, toward a greater emphasis on cultural criteria.

As for scholarly discussions of local culture and identity, sociologist Laura Edles conducted an "informal" survey in 2001 of 128 UH Manoa students who were asked to respond to the open-ended question: "What does being 'local' mean to you?" (Edles 2004: 57). She similarly notes that the great majority of her respondents (91 percent) defined local in "cultural" terms rather than in a "racial" or "ethnic" way, clearly defining local as a "way of life" and/or "attitude" and specifically rejecting "racial" and/or "ethnic" notions (61). As one student commented: "Being local to Hawai'i is a feeling, something deep down inside that ties you to this land and its people, truly understanding the way of life here, clothes, language, eating habits" (cited in Edles 2004: 57). Nonetheless, Edles (61) observes that this "inclusive, explicitly 'de-racialized' notion of local is not uncontested," given that for some Hawai'i residents the "notion of 'local haoles' is absurdly oxymoronic," that is, Haoles are not and cannot become local. Thus, while she contends that cultural definitions of local are a "response to the implicit assumption that 'local' *does* mean a specific 'racial' and/or 'ethnic' group" (58, emphasis in original), these definitions are really a response to the common assumption that local does not mean Haole since they are the major racial/ethnic group that historically has not been considered local until the emergence of the notion of local Haoles in the 1990s.[21]

Local Haoles can be contrasted with "mainland" Haoles and "military" Haoles who, as recent newcomers to Hawai'i with a tendency to associate primarily among themselves, are definitely viewed as nonlocal. Haoles are not the only ethnic group in Hawai'i among which distinctions are made between its local and nonlocal segments since similar differences are evident in the contrast drawn between local and immigrant Filipinos or between local and immigrant Koreans. These differences between locals and immigrants of the same ethnic group, which emerged in the early 1970s as a result of the post-

1965 immigration of Filipinos and Koreans, are an early indication of the greater significance of cultural rather than racial or ethnic criteria in the meaning of local identity.

In her article on local Haoles, Keiko Ohnuma (2002) addresses the question of whether the notion of "local Haole" is a contradiction in terms. Focusing on what she refers to as the "dominant discourse of 'local vs. haole,'" she contends that "oppressions currently felt and culturally remembered are linked with the Other, the West—and thus readily equated to the visible sign of whiteness, the resented military, tourists, malihini [newcomers] and kama'aina [longtime residents] alike." While local versus Haole was the dominant discourse and social division in Hawai'i since the 1930s, by the late 1960s and early 1970s, local stood in categorical opposition to other groups besides Haoles, including non-White groups such as Asian and Pacific Islander immigrants, Japanese tourists, and foreign (predominantly Japanese) investors in Hawai'i. Since World War II, the presence of African American servicemen was and continues to be another reason that the military is not considered local. While Ohnuma (277) recognizes that Haoles can be considered local, she does not seem to understand that the primary social and cultural category opposed to local is nonlocal, and that nonlocal includes much more than Haoles and thus cannot be equated only with Whiteness or the West.

In the early 1990s, I argued that as a result of the ongoing globalization of Hawaii's economy and the consequent marginalization of Hawaii's people, "local identity has been maintained as an expression of resistance and opposition, albeit unorganized, to such outside domination and intrusion" (Okamura 1994: 174). However Ohnuma (2002: 282) contends that: "Rather than a stance of resistance, localism becomes a liability, as the ideology of 'Local vs. *haole*' increasingly is experienced as local vs. global." According to her, localism is a liability because "by definition [it] stands opposed to upward mobility. Its badges and codes of belonging, such as speaking pidgin, tend to preclude fluency in the wider world," and thus presumably disadvantage local people in resisting the global. This position is based on her essentialist, if not racist, perception of locals, or at least of what she maintains is "the 'most' local . . . the dark-skinned, pidgin-speaking, working-class people who answer to the archetype" (282). Local people are actually quite diverse in terms of race, ethnicity, culture, and class, even including the fair-skinned and upwardly mobile. Furthermore, speaking Hawai'i Creole English does not mean that one cannot speak standard English since one linguistic ability does not preclude the other. Localism is a liability only if it is misunderstood as consisting merely of "culture and attitudes" that operate in interpersonal relationships. However, viewed as asserting a commitment to Hawai'i and its peoples and cultures, local as a shared identity serves as the basis of collective agency to contest the penetration by nonlocal forces that threaten local communities. As observed by historian Arif Dirlik (1996: 22), by the early 1990s, "local movements, or movements to save and reconstruct local societies, have emerged as the primary (if not the only) expressions of resistance to [global] domination."

Another contrasting category with local is Native Hawaiian, understood as denoting the indigenous people of Hawaiʻi. As noted above, this political identity and status has gained increasing significance since the 1970s as a result of the Hawaiian sovereignty movement. Trask (2000: 4) contends that the term "local" has been advanced particularly by Asian Americans in Hawaiʻi because it obscures their complicity in "maintaining institutional racism against Natives" and in continued Hawaiian dispossession of land and sovereignty. By claiming a common local identity with Native Hawaiians and their ties to Hawaiʻi, locals can blame Haoles for the historical and contemporary subjugation of Native Hawaiians. However as Trask (2) observes: "Calling themselves 'local,' the children of Asian settlers greatly outnumber us. They claim Hawaiʻi as their own, denying indigenous history, their long collaboration in our continued dispossession, and the benefits therefrom." As a result, some Native Hawaiian sovereignty advocates have dissociated themselves from local identity since it implies a common social status and identity shared by Native Hawaiians and the descendants of the immigrant groups recruited to work on the plantations. Such a common status diminishes the uniqueness of Native Hawaiian claims to land, sovereignty, and other indigenous rights.

As apparent from the above discussion, local identity continues to change in its significance and meaning in response to both internal changes in the relations among ethnic groups in Hawaiʻi and external changes in Hawaii's relation to the world. This should not be surprising since, as I have argued previously (Okamura 1994: 165): "local identity can be seen to derive its significance primarily from structural rather than cultural factors. This structural dimension of local identity is based on the categorical opposition between groups considered local and those considered nonlocal, including haole, immigrants, the military, tourists, and foreign investors." This categorical opposition between local and nonlocal underlies the ongoing changes in the meaning and importance of local culture and identity. Along these lines, sociologist Evelyn Nakano Glenn (2002: 15) has argued that race is a "relational concept" insofar as racial categories (such as Black or White) "are positioned and therefore gain meaning in relation to each other." She continues that such "oppositional categories" are "inherently unstable," although stability is attained by representing the categories as "hierarchical." Thus, in the Hawaiʻi case, local tends to be privileged, although not necessarily empowered, over nonlocal categories, including Haoles, African Americans, Asian and Pacific Islander immigrants, tourists, the military, and foreign investors. Nonetheless, all of these nonlocal groups have been perceived as constituting political, cultural, and economic threats to the primacy of local people, culture, and identity in Hawai'i and thus have contributed in different ways to the instability in the fundamental opposition between local and nonlocal categories. These threats and the local opposition generated against them have resulted in substantial changes in the significance and meaning of local identity from the 1960s to the 2000s, evident in its reconstruction and reaffirmation. These changes have emphasized both the structural and cultural dimensions of local identity rather than simply birth and upbringing in Hawai'i and the cultural ability to get along with others of differing ethnicity.

## Conclusion

This chapter has shown how some groups use ethnic identity construction to advance their political or economic concerns in the larger context of their cultural representation by and social relations with other ethnic groups in Hawai'i. The groups discussed have different interests in creating distinct identities for themselves that range from restoring sovereignty among Native Hawaiians to contesting denigrating representations among 1.5-generation Korean Americans to resisting the globalization of Hawai'i among local people. In constructing their respective identities, all of the groups assert cultural and structural differences with other ethnic groups. All three groups thus can be seen to use both the cultural and structural dimensions of ethnic identity formation in representing themselves, although in varying ways. Native Hawaiians especially employ aspects of their traditional culture—such as language, rituals, values, and myths—to express their unique identity as kanaka maoli that distinguishes them from all other ethnic groups in Hawai'i. At the same time, they create a structural boundary with other island groups by emphasizing Hawaiian descent or ancestry as the primary criterion for being considered Native Hawaiian. The Native Hawaiian case underscores how identity signifies cultural and social difference, if not uniqueness, as the principal basis for advancing their claims and entitlements to land and other resources in Hawai'i.

Another common feature of ethnic identity construction among the three groups is that they all seek to change for their advantage the societal circumstances that confront them. The 1.5-generation Korean Americans challenged the demeaning cultural representations of Korean immigrants as sexually loose bar hostesses and rude taxi drivers that, as prevalent stereotypes, are a dominant aspect of the societal conditions that Korean Americans must contend with in unequal Hawai'i. In the 1970s, local people contested expanding economic and political control of the islands by transnational corporations, foreign investors, and other external forces by organizing community-based struggles against tourism and land development projects. The identity formation initiatives of the three groups also demonstrate that political and economic circumstances themselves change, whether or not groups seek those changes. This is especially evident in the increasing constraints that Native Hawaiians have encountered in maintaining their indigenous rights and entitlements since the emergence of the Post-Rice era in Hawai'i and its legal and political challenges against them.

Finally, all of the cases clearly indicate how ethnic identities change in their meaning, significance, and expression over time, especially as a result of actions initiated by a group. Such changes are particularly evident among Native Hawaiians since the 1970s, even in the terms used to express their identity—from Hawaiian to Native Hawaiian to kanaka maoli—and in the greater political and cultural importance attributed to their identity. Similarly, since its emergence in the 1930s, local identity has been reconstructed to have a much more significant meaning than being born and raised in Hawai'i, and in the 2000s is articulated in opposition to the cultural and economic globalization of the islands. However, mobilizing and organizing this resistance based on a shared local identity and culture may not be as politically important to local people as it was in the 1970s; in other words, the significance of being local may have declined in Hawai'i since that time.

# 6

# Japanese Americans: Toward Symbolic Identity

In contrast to the ethnic groups and their cultural and structural processes of identity construction discussed in Chapter 5, Japanese Americans do not have to become actively engaged in the formation of their identity because of the dominant social status they hold in Hawai'i. For the same reason, Chinese Americans and Whites are other examples of such ethnic groups in Hawai'i. These ethnic groups have other means than identity construction by which they are able to maintain themselves in their privileged position in society. This is not to argue that Japanese Americans do not assert an ethnic identity or that they are perceived in generally positive terms by other ethnic groups since that is not the case. Instead, this chapter discusses why Japanese Americans have less of a need for ethnic identity formation as a way to advance their collective interests and concerns compared to other ethnic groups in Hawai'i. It also reviews the articulation of their ethnic identity through certain cultural values and norms, different meanings of being Japanese American between the third and fourth generations, and the symbolic expression of Japanese American identity. This chapter highlights the changing and diverse meanings of ethnic identity among Japanese Americans that reflect their relatively high political and socioeconomic status in Hawai'i. In addition, it includes a

---

Excerpts from "Making Yonsei" are used with the permission of Carrie Takahata.

discussion of how and why Okinawan Americans or *Uchinanchu* (overseas Okinawans) construct a distinct ethnic identity culturally and structurally to distinguish themselves from Japanese Americans given that the boundary between these two groups has become less rigid over time.

## Limited Identity Construction

Japanese Americans do affirm a generalized ethnic identity that emphasizes their "success" in Hawai'i as evident in their established middle- and upper middle-class status and their significant accomplishments in politics, business, government, education, and community life (Kotani 1985: 152). Many Japanese Americans believe that their socioeconomic and political success is the cumulative result of their own determined efforts and family and personal sacrifices, with each generation contributing to the progressive mobility and well-being of the next. According to this model minority version of Japanese American history and ethnic identity, the *issei* or first generation struggled with the oppressive living and working conditions on the plantations so that they could provide a better life for their children, the *nisei* (second generation). Despite being American-born, the second generation had to prove their loyalty to the United States in order to gain their equality and rights as American citizens. Thousands of young men did so by joining the U.S. military during World War II, while women contributed to the war effort on the home front through volunteer activities. The *sansei*, or third generation of baby boomers born for the most part after the war, was the first generation of Japanese Americans with viable aspirations for college and a professional career and embodied their working-class parents' dreams of middle-class life, particularly through higher education. The fourth-generation *yonsei* have been referred to as the "spoiled generation" because supposedly, unlike the previous generations, they need not struggle to advance themselves and are able to garner the benefits and privileges gained from the hard work, perseverance, and sacrifices of the previous generations. For most yonsei, attending college is a given and, for some, whose parents have entered the upper middle class, their expectations include private school education through high school, college in the continental United States, and possibly graduate or professional education in preparation for a financially rewarding professional career, either in Hawai'i or the continental United States.

Thus, while Japanese Americans affirm a general view of themselves as a socioeconomically successful ethnic group in Hawai'i, they do not actively construct an identity with a more specific meaning than that. Given their already dominant socioeconomic status in the islands, they do not need to articulate an ethnic identity that can be used to advance their economic and political interests. As discussed in Chapter 3, Japanese American families have the income and other wealth resources, such as home ownership, to provide for themselves and the future financial security of their children without having to rely on the creation of a collective ethnic identity to foster their socioeconomic status. Japanese Americans also are well represented politically among elected and appointed officials at the state and county levels such that they have greater political power than most ethnic groups. As a result, the societal circumstances faced by Japanese Americans, either individually or collectively, are much less restrictive for them in seeking to maintain their power and privilege in Hawai'i compared to those that are confronted by subjugated groups.

An indication that the Japanese American community does not believe it needs to advance its political and socioeconomic status in Hawai'i, and thus does not have to become involved in ethnic identity construction as a means to do so, occurred during the 2002 election campaign for governor. In that election, one of the reasons given for the defeat of the Democratic candidate, then two-term lieutenant governor Mazie Hirono, a Japanese American, was that she did not receive sufficient campaign contributions and therefore was outspent by more than $2 million by her Republican opponent and the eventual winner, Linda Lingle.[1] Besides being the first woman elected governor of Hawai'i, Lingle became the first Republican to hold that office in forty years.

As the governor's race was being contested in fall 2002, the Japanese Cultural Center of Hawai'i was able to raise $9 million from community donations to pay off its long overdue bank loans and prevent the imminent sale of the building and property where the center is located. Based on a list of donors published in the *Hawai'i Herald*, a Japanese American community newspaper, the great majority of them, at least by last name, was Japanese American. Thus, if those donors and other Japanese Americans thought that it was very important to have a Japanese American elected as governor, they could have contributed substantially more to Mazie Hirono's campaign, especially since most Japanese Americans vote Democratic. The last time a Japanese American was elected governor was in 1982 (George Ariyoshi), and I do not believe that most Japanese Americans consider it a major political priority to have another elected in the near future because it will not make much of a difference in their socioeconomic status.[2]

As another example of limited identity formation, when Japan emerged as an economic superpower during the late 1980s, Japanese corporations spent billions of dollars buying hotels, office buildings, golf courses, and other commercial real estate in Hawai'i. Nonetheless, this massive spending spree did not have a harmful impact on Japanese Americans as a result of their racialization as Japanese nationals. While there was some public resentment expressed against such foreign investment and control of Hawai'i, most island residents realized that such corporate investments were far beyond the financial means of the great majority of local Japanese. Thus, there was no collective effort or even need on the part of Japanese Americans to distinguish themselves from Japanese nationals.

Instead of ethnic identity construction, at least some Japanese Americans have resorted to defensive ethnicity,[3] that is, actions taken by an ethnic group to protect its interests, resources or privileges in response to a perceived threat from external forces, including other ethnic groups (Okamura 2002: 133). Some Japanese Americans have sought to maintain their interests in certain economic and political arenas—such as government contracts and jobs and access to political power—through favoritism for members of their own ethnic group rather than being more egalitarian and inclusive of others. Defensive ethnicity also is quite evident in the illegal campaign contributions that many Japanese Americans were found to have made or admitted they made as a result of investigations by the state Campaign Spending Commission in the early 2000s (Daysog 2003a: A3). Many Japanese American (and other) contracting, engineering, architecture, and other firms seek to enhance their access to lucrative state and county government contracts by contributing to the election campaigns of gubernatorial and mayoral candidates, particularly incumbents, whether they are Japanese American or not. However, between fall 2001 and 2003, 60 percent of the companies fined or prosecuted for making excessive or false-name campaign contributions in Hawai'i were owned or co-owned by Japanese Americans (*Hawai'i Herald* 2003). Instead of constructing a positive ethnic identity, such illegal activities contribute to the widespread perception that Japanese Americans are primarily concerned with maintaining themselves in power and excluding other ethnic groups from equal access.

Like Asian Americans in the continental United States, the relatively high socioeconomic status of Japanese Americans in Hawai'i leads to the question of whether or not they are becoming White.[4] With regard to the issue of Asian Americans becoming White, sociologist Min Zhou (2004) contends that such a prediction is "premature and based on false premises," much like the model minority stereotype of Asian Americans. As she argues, "their [Asian Americans'] experience suggests that whitening has more to do with the beliefs of white America, than with the actual situation of Asian Americans." Zhou concludes that "becoming white or not is beside the point" since "the bottom line" for Asian Americans is that they "still have to constantly prove that they are truly loyal Americans" rather than "forever foreigners." Although Japanese Americans in Hawai'i no longer need to establish their loyalty as Americans, a response similar to the one above could be made to the question of whether or not they are becoming White. In Hawai'i, Whiteness has been decentered by local identity and culture, particularly since the reconstruction of local identity in the 1970s. White is not the "unmarked category against which difference is constructed" (Lipsitz 1998: 1) and that serves as the unquestioned normative standard by which non-Whites are evaluated, as it does in the continental United States. Despite their long-term political and economic power and privilege in the islands and their being the largest group since the 1960s, Haoles continue to be viewed and often treated as the racialized and cultural other in Hawai'i. Thus, the question of whether or not Japanese Americans in Hawai'i are becoming White also is "beside the point." A much more relevant question is whether Haoles are becoming local since local identity and status are far more central to island culture and society than Whiteness is.

## Cultural Dimension of Ethnic Identity

In distinguishing themselves as an ethnic group, Japanese Americans tend to emphasize certain cultural values and norms centered on the family that they believe are especially characteristic of their group. The cultural values considered particularly important by Japanese Americans include: sacrifice for the well-being and future security of one's children, a concern for the education of one's children, and a sense of duty and responsibility to one's parents. One reason for this focus on family-related values and norms to differentiate themselves from other ethnic groups is because by the 1960s, as a result of acculturation into local and American cultures, the Japanese language and Buddhist religion were no longer dominant cultural institutions among Japanese Americans, although they still were being practiced (Kotani 1985: 149–150). However, this emphasis on particular cultural elements does not necessarily constitute ethnic identity formation by Japanese Americans because it does not result in the assertion of a clearly defined ethnic identity or of a specific meaning for their identity.

These family-centered values appear to be related to *kachikan* or the traditional cultural values brought by Japanese immigrants to Hawai'i in the late nineteenth and early twentieth centuries. Their symbolic importance to the Japanese American community is evident in their being the subject of the very first display of the Historical Gallery of the Japanese Cultural Center of Hawai'i, the major permanent exhibit on Japanese Americans in the state. Thirteen kachikan are represented in Japanese with their English equivalents (for example, *koko* or filial piety) and are etched in *kanji* or Chinese characters in granite pillars about four feet high.[5] These pillars are meant to replicate *dohyo*, wooden guideposts that were set along roads to guide travelers in nineteenth-century Japan (Hayashi 2002: A8). In similar fashion, the kachikan are supposed to guide Japanese immigrants and subsequent generations of Japanese Americans in their daily lives in their adopted homeland of Hawai'i. Their representation in stone pillars, rather than wooden posts, signifies their permanent or at least long-lasting importance for the Japanese American community. The Japanese Cultural Center of Hawai'i (2001) published a booklet on the thirteen kachikan that provided a definition and examples of each of them, drawn predominantly from first- and second-generation Japanese American experiences. One of the authors of the booklet maintained that, "This [kachikan] may have started from the issei, but it certainly is valuable for the fourth generation, fifth, and others" (cited in Hayashi 2002: A8). This statement is indicative of the belief among many older Japanese Americans, whose parents raised them with kachikan, of their continuing relevance, despite the obvious cultural and social changes among Japanese Americans over time.

These traditional cultural values do not have the same significance or meaning that they had when Japanese immigrants brought them to Hawai'i more than one hundred years ago. Even in Japan, the thirteen kachikan are not observed to the same extent as they were in the late nineteenth century, so there is no reason they still should have the same importance they once had for Japanese Americans in Hawai'i. Some of the kachikan have changed over time to have very different meanings, such as *gisei* or sacrifice. When Japanese immigrated to Hawai'i, gisei included the sacrifices that children made for the benefit of their parents, such as older siblings dropping out of school to work and contribute their earnings to help support their generally large families. Such sacrifice is evident in Milton Murayama's *All I Asking for Is My Body* (1988), a historically accurate novel of the struggles of a Japanese American family on a sugar plantation on Maui in the late 1930s. Tosh, the Hawai'i-born oldest son in the family, constantly complains to his parents that, because he had to help them pay off the family debts, he could not continue on to high school as he wished and instead was "slaving in the cane fields" (Murayama 1988: 42). According to the novel's narrator, Tosh's mother responds, "'[H]ere you work only one year and you talk big. Look at . . .' and she named all the number one sons in Kahana who'd been working for their parents for ten years and more" and giving them their plantation earnings. However, when second-generation Japanese Americans became parents themselves, sacrifice referred to what they gave up, such as spending their savings on themselves, so that their children could have greater opportunities in life, such as a college education. In terms of parent-child relationships, this completely opposite meaning of sacrifice is also held by sansei parents and very likely continues among yonsei as more of them have children of their own.

The kachikan *haji* or shame continues to serve to some extent as a constraint on inappropriate behavior among Japanese Americans. In the past, parents commonly admonished their children explicitly or implicitly "not to bring shame to the family." However, shame as a social deterrent against deviant behavior is not as significant as it may have once been for Japanese Americans. The worst mass killing in Hawai'i history occurred in 1999 when Byran Uesugi, a forty-year-old sansei employee of a copying company in Honolulu, shot and killed seven of his coworkers in their office building.[6] Still armed, he then fled to a wooded park where the police negotiated with him to surrender and, after several hours, he finally did. During the negotiations, his father was asked by a television news reporter why he did not speak to his son and urge him to give himself up. The father replied that if he did have the opportunity to talk to his son, he would tell him to shoot himself instead of surrendering to the police. My interpretation of the father's response is that, as a nisei, he believed that by the heinous act his son had committed, he had brought such horrendous shame to their family, and not just to himself, that the only way the son could possibly atone for his mass murder was to commit suicide. Instead of doing so, however, Uesugi eventually surrendered and was later tried and convicted of multiple homicides. In this case, shame as a traditional Japanese norm obviously had much greater cultural significance for the father than for the son, and this lesser importance of shame as a restraint on socially unacceptable behavior very likely prevails among the third and fourth generations of Japanese Americans.

Thus, the cultural basis of Japanese American ethnic identity is Japanese American culture, not Japanese culture—and certainly not the Japanese culture brought to Hawaiʻi by the immigrant generation. Japanese American culture has developed over the generations beginning especially with the *nisei* second generation as they were acculturated into American beliefs, values, and norms by their education in Hawaii's public schools and as they socialized with their peers from other ethnic groups. With the continuing development and changes in their culture in Hawaiʻi, Japanese Americans certainly have become less culturally Japanese (for example, language, religion, and traditional practices), but there still remains a clear affirmation of being Japanese American. Although they have been harshly criticized since the 1970s by some of the politically and economically disadvantaged groups in Hawaiʻi, such as Native Hawaiians and Filipino Americans, one does not find a lack of pride or feelings of shame attached to their ethnic identity among Japanese Americans. I attribute this definite affirmation of Japanese American identity to the relatively high political and socioeconomic status of the community such that they can ignore to some extent the antagonism and censure from other ethnic groups, although they certainly are aware of them.

## Sansei: Being Local

Criticisms of and resentment against Japanese have long been expressed in Hawaiʻi since the early 1900s when it became apparent that they, by then already the largest ethnic group in the islands (40 percent), intended to remain on a permanent basis. This anti-Japanese movement continued through World War II but, with the rise in political and economic status of Japanese Americans in the postwar decades, it had a very different quality. By the mid-1970s, a clear "anti-Japanese backlash" had emerged, particularly as a result of the overrepresentation of Japanese Americans in state government jobs and elected political office. These positions included as governor, lieutenant governor, two U.S. senators, two (of four) county mayors, and a plurality of state legislators (about 40 percent). Other ethnic groups hence viewed Japanese Americans as "dominating and controlling" island politics and government to their exclusion (Kotani 1985: 158). These groups, especially Native Hawaiians and Filipino Americans, contended that Japanese American "success" had been attained at their expense insofar as they had been discriminated against and marginalized as Japanese Americans advanced themselves politically and socioeconomically (Trask 2000). According to these subordinate minorities, Japanese Americans had obtained far more than their fair share of political and economic power and resources by unfairly excluding others. Furthermore, they appeared unwilling to share those benefits and opportunities more equitably with other ethnic groups, as evident from their continuing high proportion of elected and appointed officials and state government workers such as teachers.

As a politically powerful and economically privileged group, Japanese Americans could have responded to the antagonism and criticism from other ethnic groups by constructing an ethnic identity that asserted their solidarity with and support of these groups and their concerns in the larger context of multiethnic Hawai'i. This did occur in the 1970s when the third (sansei) generation of Japanese Americans, then young people in their twenties and thirties, articulated an identity for themselves as local, together with other ethnic groups as part of the reconstruction of local identity. As a result, local identity came to have a much more significant meaning than mere birth and long-term residence in the islands and instead represented an appreciation of and commitment to the land, cultures, and peoples of Hawai'i (Okamura 1980). Members of the sansei generation actively participated in and supported local community struggles that established a multiethnic resistance movement against external forces of economic development and change that were viewed as threatening the very quality of life in Hawai'i. In 1971 a sansei female community activist expressed the very different perspectives toward Hawai'i and its peoples held by her generation and by the second generation of their parents (cited in Miyazaki 1994):

> Today there are many Japanese [American] people who are trying to become rich and trying to be haole. . . . [T]hey joined the American Army and fought with the 442nd Combat Team. They went to universities and got good-paying jobs that haoles usually held like doctors, lawyers and teachers. They now have the kind of greediness that the rich haoles showed the local people how to have. These Japanese

> should stop and think about their position. Are we going to remain local or become more and more haole? . . . Are we going to continue to make money by kissing the asses of the rich haoles and at the same time screw our own local people be they Hawaiian, Chinese, Japanese, Filipino, Puerto Rican, Samoan, Portuguese or Black?

In aligning themselves with other local ethnic groups, the sansei affirmed not just a shared local identity but also their solidarity with those other groups that had begun to express resentment of Japanese Americans as they gained political and economic power. This woman's statement also advances a division between sansei and nisei, who nonetheless are local, because some nisei had attained the same class status as Haoles who were definitely considered nonlocal in the 1970s.

While an undergraduate student at the University of Hawai'i (UH) Manoa in the mid-1970s, UH law professor Eric Yamamoto (1974: 99–100) provided one of the earliest analyses of the reconstruction of local identity by third-generation Japanese Americans. For his liberal studies thesis, "From 'Japanee' to Local: Community Change and the Redefinition of Sansei Identity in Hawaii," he interviewed eighteen- to twenty-four-year-old sansei on O'ahu of middle-class status and found: "In its simplest sense, the Sansei are reacting to both changes in community and other group's reactions towards Japanese Americans as a result of changes in community, and creating a new identity for themselves. This identity centers around being local, of Hawaii. . . . This identification [as local] places the Sansei, Hawaiians, and certain other groups in supportive rather than adversary roles." A common local identity thus served as a means to bridge the emerging social and political cleavage that was becoming evident between Japanese Americans and other local groups in the anti-Japanese backlash of the 1970s (see Kotani 1985: 158). The sansei were especially concerned with "removing . . . the stigma of being classified as 'establishment Japanese Americans' that applied to politically and socioeconomically privileged nisei" (Yamamoto 1974: 108).

Yamamoto (1974: 101) contended that the sansei "assumes a social identity of being Local and maintains a value-orientation close to ethnic values" such that they are "Local externally and Japanese American internally." He concluded that being local for the sansei was a "compromise: a coping mechanism for being true to those aspects of Japanese [American]-ness that are valued, true to one's commitment to Hawaii and its people, and accommodating to the western social structure that pervades" (101). Rather than viewing local identity as an integral part of being Japanese American for the sansei, Yamamoto (100) argued that "Sansei identify themselves more closely to local than to Japanese [American]." While there may have been a substantial proportion of sansei in the 1970s who did identify more with being local than with being

Japanese American, I wonder if Yamamoto's generalization applied equally to men and women.

The assertion of a local identity by and for sansei is evident in the concluding chapter titled "The Sansei Generation" in Roland Kotani's *The Japanese in Hawaii: A Century of Struggle* (1985). The book was published in commemoration of the hundredth anniversary of Japanese immigration to Hawai'i in 1985 when sansei were a majority of Japanese Americans. Kotani's chapter features profiles on sansei such as "The Working Couple" and "The Politician." Sansei himself and a former ethnic studies instructor at UH Manoa, Kotani sought to represent the couple as local by downplaying their middle-class status and noting their plantation background. Despite both having college degrees, they are described as "the working couple" because the wife has a clerical position and the husband a blue-collar job as a boilermaker at the Pearl Harbor naval shipyard. As Kotani (1985: 151) observed, they "have discovered that the 'AJA success story' doesn't pay the bills."

The sansei politician featured in Kotani's chapter is then state representative David Hagino who is pictured wearing a *palaka* shirt (1985: 157), symbolic of a position paper titled "Palaka Power" which Hagino wrote that was circulated at the state Constitutional Convention in 1978. Palaka was a durable cloth used to make the work clothes of plantation field laborers, and Palaka Power came to represent the interests and concerns of local people during the convention, as delegates discussed proposed changes to the state constitution.[7] In his paper, Hagino recommended measures to control economic development and population growth, to protect the land, to provide land reparations to Native Hawaiians, and to establish community control of the mass media (163). Other sansei are depicted in the chapter as participants and supporters of local community struggles against proposed land development projects that would have resulted in the eviction of farmers, such as at Wai'ahole and Waikane valleys on O'ahu in the mid-1970s. Kotani concluded, " 'Palaka Power' demonstrated that the AJA youth of the statehood era were no longer merely 'ethnic' Japanese [Americans] but full-fledged members of a local multiethnic Island community."

The affirmation of a local identity for the entire Japanese American community, and not just the sansei generation, is apparent in a statement prominently displayed on a wall in the Historical Gallery of the Japanese Cultural Center of Hawai'i: "We are no longer only Japanese American, we are local. We have learned from others. We have absorbed their values and traditions while we have preserved our own. We are proud of our mixed heritage—our local Hawaiian way of life." This pronouncement makes clear that Japanese American identity and culture are not based only on Japanese culture but have incorporated cultural elements from Native Hawaiians and the other ethnic groups that immigrated to Hawai'i. This appreciation of and familiarity with the different peoples and cultures of Hawai'i is a major dimension of the local identity of Japanese Americans.

## Symbolic Ethnicity

Yamamoto's (1974) contentions that the sansei viewed being Japanese American "close to ideal in terms of interpersonal value-orientation" and that they were "Japanese American internally" indicate that being Japanese American was quite significant for them in their daily lives. In other words, rather than being expressed once a year on important Japanese American holidays such as New Year's Day, being Japanese American was very much part of the everyday experience of sansei insofar as they maintained interpersonal values proximate to Japanese American values. In this regard, Herbert Gans (1979, 1992) introduced the concept of "symbolic ethnicity" to explain the persistence of ethnic identity among acculturated and assimilated third- and fourth-generation "ethnics" by which he referred to White ethnic groups, including Jews, Italians, and Poles. He hypothesized that these generations have less interest in their "ethnic cultures and organizations" and greater concern with maintenance of their ethnic identity, "with the feeling of being Jewish, or Italian, or Polish, and with finding ways of feeling and expressing that identity in suitable ways" (1979: 7). Gans contended that symbolic ethnicity "above all . . . is characterized by a nostalgic allegiance to the culture of the immigrant generation, or that of the old country; a love for and a pride in a tradition that can be felt without having to be incorporated in everyday behavior" (9). The cultural practices that are transformed into ethnic symbols need to be "visible and clear in meaning" and "easily expressed and felt" by third-generation members without interfering in other aspects of social life. Gans gave as examples of such ethnic identity symbols, holidays, rites of passage, foods, state and national politicians (of non-Irish ancestry), and ancestral homelands, since they are either temporally or physically remote from everyday life (9–10).

To the extent that symbolic ethnicity is primarily concerned with the maintenance of ethnic identity through the selective use of certain cultural practices, it can be viewed as a form of ethnic identity construction. However, Gans (1979: 9) emphasized the "expressive" rather than "instrumental" functions of symbolic ethnicity as it becomes "more of a leisure-time activity and los[es] its relevance, say, to earning a living." Thus, symbolic ethnicity is not focused on analyzing how ethnic groups construct their identity to advance their economic or political interests or how and why they assert a specific meaning for their identity. In a subsequent essay, Gans (1992: 45) did note Glazer and Moynihan's view of ethnic groups as "political interest groups" and added that "employers, workers, homeowners and other citizens often have political or economic interests, and they will still play an ethnic card if that is useful for advancing these interests." It is significant that Gans did not state that ethnic groups have economic or political interests and are concerned with advancing them, but class-based groups (for example, employers, workers, and homeowners) have such interests. This relative lack of emphasis on ethnicity might be due to Gans's (1992: 45) understanding of "the American tradition of using ethnicity as a surrogate for class," that is, what appear to be ethnic group interests are really class interests, which is clearly a reductionist argument.

In distinguishing symbolic ethnicity "above all" by a "nostalgic allegiance" to the culture of the immigrant generation or of their home country and by "the feeling of being Jewish or Italian," Gans (197, 9) appeared to diminish the significance of economic or political concerns or problems of ethnic groups. Indeed, in his interpretation of Gans's concept of symbolic ethnicity, Alba (1985: 173, emphasis added) noted that "ethnics attempt to maintain some *psychological* connection with their origins, as a way of retaining some ethnic 'spice' in their identity." Given his focus on assimilated White ethnic groups, Gans's relative lack of concern with the political and economic aspects of ethnic identity formation should not be surprising since those groups do not have to contend with the same kinds of race-related exclusionary barriers faced by racial minorities. In his only reference to race and racial minorities in his first article on symbolic ethnicity, Gans (1979: 15) noted that since World War II, "the ethnics have been able to shoulder blacks and other racial minorities with the deviant and scapegoat functions they performed in an earlier America, so that ethnic prejudice and 'institutional ethnism' are no longer significant, except . . . at the very top of the societal hierarchies." He continued that "the costs of being and feeling ethnic are slight," and this generalization can be attributed to the White racial identity and consequent privileged social status of White ethnics. In marked contrast, racial prejudice and institutional racism continue to be highly significant for racial minorities at most levels and sectors of American society. The increasing significance of symbolic ethnicity does not necessarily mean the decreasing significance of race for both White ethnics and non-White minorities. As observed by sociologist Mary Waters (1990: 156) with regard to non-White minorities: "Who your ancestors are does affect your choice of spouse, where you live, what job you have, who your friends are, and what your chances are for success in American society, if those ancestors happen not to have been from Europe."

In *Ethnic Options: Choosing Identities in America*, Waters (1990) provided a much needed concern with race and race relations for Gans's initial conception of symbolic ethnicity. She accounted for the persistence of symbolic ethnicity, which she sometimes substituted with "symbolic ethnic identity," among middle-class White Americans as partially due to "its ideological 'fit' with racist beliefs" (147).[8] Waters (158, 163) contended that middle-class Americans of European descent experience their ethnicity symbolically as a matter of individual and voluntary choice, as a source of enjoyment, as not having much influence in their everyday lives, and as lacking in social costs. However, this view, together with the belief that their European ancestry and that of racial minorities can be equated and are therefore "interchangeable," prevents them from understanding the qualitatively different experiences of non-White minorities in U.S. society, such as racial discrimination that White Americans believe is the same in degree and in kind as that encountered by their immigrant ancestors decades earlier (160, 163). As Waters argued (156): "For the ways in which ethnicity is flexible and symbolic and voluntary for white middle-class Americans are the very ways in which it is not so for non-white and Hispanic Americans."

According to Henry and Bankston (1999: 1), the concept of symbolic ethnicity has been applied to several White ethnic groups, including Jewish Americans (Zenner 1985), Finnish Americans (Kivisto 1989), Armenian Americans (Bakalian 1993), and Polish Americans (Rokicki 1995). In notable contrast, it has not been used to explain the very different experiences of ethnic minorities, such as Chicanos or Japanese Americans, perhaps because of their lesser degree of assimilation into American society, although Japanese Americans can be considered one of the most assimilated non-White ethnic minorities, at least socioeconomically.

As a frequently cited example, Italian Americans have been discussed as an ethnic group whose ethnicity has become symbolic (Alba 1985). The following description of Italian Americans (Cornell and Hartmann 1998: 76) also would apply to Japanese Americans in Hawai'i:

> Few first-generation Italian immigrants remain. Most Italian Americans are now of the third or fourth generation in the United States. Many have married non-Italian Americans; many are the children of these marriages. Few speak Italian. Decreasing numbers live in neighborhoods that are heavily Italian American. Most have become part of the economic, political, and cultural mainstream of U.S. society. . . . [F]ar fewer Italian Americans experience their ethnic identity as thick. Most may still identify as Italian Americans and may do so proudly, but in fact that identity organizes little of their daily lives.

While just about all of the above description applies to Japanese Americans, the following does not: "For most of them [Italian Americans], it [Italian American ethnicity] has become the stuff of holidays and stories and old photographs. . . . [T]hey have gone from being to feeling Italian" (Cornell and Hartmann 1998: 76). For most Japanese Americans, their ethnic identity constitutes much more than merely a feeling, and they still have a definite consciousness of being Japanese American. One reason for this conscious awareness of their ethnic identity is because it is a source of considerable pride for most Japanese Americans, an identity they readily claim rather than one from which they seek to dissociate themselves. Another reason is the significance of ethnicity, instead of race, in structuring social relations in Hawaiʻi that results in Japanese Americans, Haoles, Samoans, and other ethnic groups relating to each other as ethnic groups rather than in terms of panethnic racial categories, such as Asian American, as is the case in the continental United States. In the latter, Italian Americans have become White, and their social relations in American society are based primarily on their White racial identity, thus lessening the significance of being Italian American to them and to other Americans.

## Yonsei: Feeling Japanese American

As for the latest adult generation of Japanese Americans, local poet Carrie Y. Takahata's poem, "Making Yonsei," is one of the few texts, literary or academic, about the fourth-generation or yonsei Japanese American experience in Hawaiʻi (Takahata 1998). The poem is written from the voice and perspective of a yonsei daughter speaking to her sansei mother and expresses the generational differences and cultural changes among Japanese American women. Yonsei herself, Takahata insightfully captures and portrays the cultural experiences and social status of a certain segment of her generation, that is, those who are female, socioeconomically privileged, and for whom their Japanese American and local identities have become symbolic in contrast to those of the sansei, as represented by her mother.

In the opening verse, the daughter faults her mother for her own inability to speak Hawaiʻi Creole English, which is not uncommon among privileged yonsei women, because her mother did not speak it to her: "Mom, / what are you saying? / What'd you mean, / *How come I don't know?* and *What kind / Japanese are you?* Don't act / like I'm supposed to know these words. You / never told them to me before. You always said, / *three* not *chree* / *I am* not *I stay/ like that* not *li dat.*" The mother's question to her daughter about what kind of Japanese person she is indicates her expectation that her daughter, being local Japanese American, should know how to speak pidgin English like herself. While the mother can speak pidgin, she is depicted as being perhaps an executive with her own secretary (a stereotypical occupation of sansei women), indicative of the relatively higher-class status of herself and her daughter: "*Call me at the office and if my secretary answers, give me a page; if I don't / answer within five / minutes, call my cell; I'll keep it on just for you,* / you told me that." In addition to the daughter's local identity becoming symbolic, so has her Japanese American identity evident in her knowledge of Japanese American cultural practices being limited to traditions observed once a year on holidays, such as New Year's Day when families set off firecrackers at midnight and eat *ozoni* soup in the morning.[9] The daughter demonstrates her knowledge of the symbolic importance of the main ingredients in the soup: "the konbu [seaweed] for happiness, / the mochi [rice cakes] to make the family stick, / the soba [buckwheat noodles] for long life."

The concluding verse highlights the cultural differences between the mother and daughter as perceived by the mother's male "friend" who is probably Haole:[10] "He looks at you / and that's what he sees; / he looks at me / and wonders / what went wrong." What the mother's friend sees is the "little Local Japanese" woman who is willing to do things for him, such as "teach him" Japanese words and "show him" how to eat Japanese food, an implicitly submissive role that the daughter is critical of her mother for assuming in order to attract her friend: "You only use these words [pidgin] now / because you know your friend / likes them." As a result, the friend thinks that something has gone amiss with the daughter because she appears to be so unlike her mother, that is, nonlocal and non–Japanese American. Insofar as the daughter does not speak pidgin, she is representative of yonsei women of her higher-class segment of Japanese Americans. However, most yonsei, especially males and both females and males from the neighbor islands, continue to speak pidgin as an expression of their local identity. Thus, while the daughter does not represent yonsei women in general, "Making Yonsei" brings out the social, cultural, and class diversity of that generation and, by extension, of the Japanese American community.

To gain some understanding of the changing meanings of Japanese American ethnic identity, especially among the yonsei generation, I conducted a short survey in my Japanese Americans in Hawai'i course at UH Manoa in 2005.[11] Given my primary interest in the views of the yonsei students from Hawai'i in the class, I included several questions on generational status, ethnic background, age, and length of residence in Hawai'i that enabled me to separate their responses from those of non-yonsei and non–Japanese American students. I obtained responses from sixty-five yonsei students, including thirty-six females and twenty-nine males, who constituted 43 percent of the students who completed the survey form in class (150).[12] Less than one-third of the respondents are Japanese only (31 percent), while 43 percent are Japanese and some other ethnicity or race, and 23 percent are of Japanese and Okinawan ancestry. The median age of the students is twenty years, and the great majority (92 percent) of them has lived all their lives in Hawai'i. As young college students, they are not representative of the yonsei generation, many of whom are in their thirties and employed, but their responses do offer some insights into yonsei understandings about Japanese American identity. As shown below, some of the students' replies to the survey questions can be interpreted as expressions of symbolic ethnicity among fourth-generation Japanese Americans.

The students answered two open-ended questions: "What does being Japanese American mean to you?" and "In what ways are you Japanese American?" I purposely limited the number of survey questions so that fuller replies might be given by the students, which to some extent was the case. Since most Japanese Americans in Hawai'i refer to themselves as "Japanese," I used the former term to remind the students that they are Japanese American so that they would use that term when appropriate. Nonetheless, as evident below, most of the students used the term "Japanese" rather than Japanese American in their responses. Many of the students provided more than one response to a given survey question; for this reason, the percentages for the different responses to each question are based on the total number of responses to a question rather than the number of students who completed the survey. There were 83 responses for the first question and 102 responses for the second question.

With regard to the first question on the meaning of being Japanese American, the most frequently given response referred to Japanese ancestry, descent, or ethnicity (21 percent). As a male yonsei wrote: "It means being of Japanese ancestry but being an American citizen." Most students who replied in this way did not mention any cultural aspects of being Japanese American such as values or customs. This may be an indication that they do not think of any of their cultural values or activities as specifically Japanese American. Common descent (real or putative) or a common ancestral homeland certainly is a defining characteristic of ethnic groups in the United States (Cornell and Hartmann 1998: 19), especially acculturated ones like Japanese Americans.

The second most numerous response provided by the students on what it means to be Japanese American concerned following or practicing "Japanese culture" (including values), "Japanese customs," or "Japanese traditions" (18 percent). Yonsei women replied in these cultural terms much more than their male counterparts, perhaps because they engage in cultural practices and traditions to a greater extent than yonsei men. In their responses, both female and male students referred to "Japanese" rather than Japanese American culture, implying that they meant the culture or customs brought to Hawai'i by Japanese immigrants. As a yonsei woman stated: "I think being Japanese American is still doing and celebrating Japanese culture;" or as another woman remarked: "Being a Japanese American means setting/following traditions like generations before." It appears that the students do not have an understanding of Japanese American culture that has developed and continues to develop in Hawai'i and that includes not only elements that can be traced historically to the culture brought from Japan by immigrants but also practices, values, and beliefs from the local culture of Hawai'i and from American culture. Since they apparently have difficulty identifying aspects of Japanese American culture, the students focus on what seems to them as unambiguously "Japanese," that is, customs and traditions of the immigrant generation, in order to define being Japanese American.

Not surprisingly then, in their replies some of the students appeared to dichotomize being Japanese American into separate Japanese and American cultural components, as can be seen in the following statement: "A Japanese American continues to follow the culture of Japan and also integrates the culture of America into their (*sic*) lives." This dualistic perspective does not allow for a syncretic Japanese American culture and perhaps ethnic identity. The emphasis on Japanese culture also is evident in the students' responses to the other survey question in which they stated the ways they are Japanese American by references to Japanese culture, customs, or traditions (see below).

Fifteen percent of the students indicated that being Japanese American for them means being "proud" of what their ancestors achieved after immigrating to Hawai'i.[13] In a representative response, a yonsei woman remarked: "Coming from a long ancestral train, I feel proud of the accomplishments that my family and ancestors have achieved. I understand all of the struggles and hardships that Japanese Americans have endured and feel empathetic for those in the past who had to go through rough times to allow myself and my generation the benefits we are fortunate to have today." Her pride in being Japanese American comes from an appreciation and understanding of the "struggles and hardships" that her ancestors and Japanese Americans in general overcame that have enabled her and other yonsei ("my generation") to have the "benefits" that are theirs. While she does not specifically mention them, those material benefits include greater educational and occupational opportunities and a comfortable middle-class lifestyle that most yonsei have available to them compared to previous generations of Japanese Americans. This student's comments are very consistent with the overall "success story" of Japanese American history in Hawai'i subscribed to by many Japanese Americans, not only yonsei. As a yonsei, she situates not only herself but her entire generation in the larger historical context of the Japanese American experience in Hawai'i as the fortunate beneficiaries of the perseverance and sacrifices of the previous generations to provide a better life for their children.

The students' responses that assert their appreciation for the "accomplishments" of their ancestors, especially the issei, can be viewed to some extent as expressions of symbolic ethnicity, particularly the "nostalgic allegiance to the culture of the immigrant generation" that Gans contended is characteristic "above all" of his concept (1979: 9). In the yonsei case, this allegiance or appreciation is not to the culture of Japanese immigrants in Hawai'i but to the immigrants themselves for their historical contributions to the relatively privileged status of yonsei. Furthermore, their nostalgia is understandably not based on a longing for a return to the "rough times" endured by their ancestors in the past, but on a romanticized view of that past in which Japanese Americans were able to overcome "hardships" and obstacles and to advance themselves economically primarily through their own hard work, determination, and sacrifice. This popular romanticization of the historical "struggles" of especially the issei and nisei generations is a major component of the success-story version of Japanese American history in Hawai'i. This is not necessarily false since undoubtedly there were racist barriers that Japanese Americans had to contend with in the past. However, by the 1970s, as they gained political power and rose in socioeconomic status, Japanese Americans began to be accused of engaging in the same kinds of discriminatory actions against other ethnic groups to maintain themselves in power (see Kotani 1985: 159; Trask 2000).

Regarding the second question on the survey, "In what ways are you Japanese American?" the most frequently given answer pertained to following "Japanese culture," "Japanese customs," "Japanese traditions," or "Japanese cultural values" (36 percent), that together ranked second among the responses to the first question. Again, students overwhelmingly referred to "Japanese" rather than Japanese American culture, customs, or traditions, as in the following comment by a yonsei woman: "I am Japanese American in that although I live in America and was brought up with the 'American' culture, my family (ex. grandparents) still taught me about the Japanese culture and practice some of it today." Students also tended to dichotomize Japanese and American cultures as they did in their replies to the first question. A yonsei male remarked: "I have adopted both Japanese traditions as well as American because of being raised in both cultures at the same time (Family 1st, obedience to parents, different martial arts, etc. . . . then American ones like 4th of July, Christmas, etc.)." Instead of practicing Japanese American culture, this student, as well as others, indicated that they observe two distinct cultures. Respondents who reported following "Japanese traditions" generally did not specify them or they mentioned trivial traditions like taking one's shoes off after entering a home, perhaps indicative of their lack of knowledge of how they are Japanese American culturally.

In their replies related to Japanese culture, customs, or traditions, many of the students (predominantly women) noted the role of their family in observing together or teaching them about the culture. As stated by a yonsei female: "I follow some Japanese culture through food, attending festivals, and getting taught aspects of the culture through family." Family, including grandparents, provides the means for the maintenance and transmission of Japanese American culture through everyday interactions, in addition to family celebrations of holidays and cultural events.

The second most numerous response to the question on ways of being Japanese American concerned the observance of "Japanese" holidays and annual cultural events (18 percent). Holidays included New Year's Day, Girls' Day (March 3) and Boys' Day (May 5), while cultural events referred to *mochi* (rice cake) pounding on New Year's Day or *bon* dances held in the summer.[14] More than twice as many responses in this category were from women compared to men, indicative perhaps of their greater participation in Japanese American cultural activities. A yonsei woman commented: "Our family from the nisei are all very close. I participate in local Japanese culture such as new year's mochi pounding, Buddhist ceremonies. I enjoy learning about my culture." While very much a minority perspective, the student's reference to participating in "local Japanese culture" is significant because it indicates an understanding that she and other Japanese Americans in Hawai'i follow Japanese American culture and not the Japanese culture of the immigrant generation. Holidays such as New Year's Day or cultural events such as bon dances are observed according to a local Japanese cultural style that has evolved over the decades and that has incorporated elements from other ethnic groups, for example, the Chinese American custom of setting off firecrackers on Chinese New Year's Day. Several students noted the consumption of Japanese food, such as ozoni soup or mochi on New Year's Day, as part of how they celebrate holidays. Note that these are the same holidays and cultural activities mentioned by the yonsei daughter in Carrie Takahata's poem "Making Yonsei." Several students indicated that they are Japanese American because of their ability to speak Japanese as a result of having learned it in high school or college, again emphasizing a definitely Japanese cultural practice, although a considerable majority of Japanese Americans lack that ability.

The celebration of annual holidays or events can be interpreted as expressions of symbolic ethnicity by Japanese Americans insofar as they concern cultural activities that occur infrequently, are sources of enjoyment generally observed with family and relatives, involve the eating of special "ethnic" foods, and do not interfere with the daily activities in which yonsei and other Japanese Americans are involved. The remoteness of these holidays and cultural events from everyday life makes them ideally suited to be symbols of Japanese American ethnicity. As observed by Alba (1990: 306): "Symbolic ethnicity is concerned with the symbols of ethnic cultures rather than with the cultures themselves[;] . . . the cultural stuff of ethnicity continues to wither, and thus ethnic identity tends to latch onto a few symbolic commitments," such as New Year's Day among Japanese Americans. In her informative master's thesis titled "Yonsei Japanese American Women in Hawai'i," Juri Ishikawa (2006: 28) argued that "compared to the previous generations of Japanese Americans in Hawai'i, the ethnic identity of Yonsei Japanese American women in Hawai'i has become less significant to them, and their ethnic identity is expressed symbolically." From her structured interviews with thirty yonsei women, she also found that they used cultural symbols to assert their ethnic identity, including "Japanese cultural traditions" such as New Year's Day observances, special Japanese foods consumed on holidays, and Japanese middle names (32).

Another frequently stated way of being Japanese American reported by the yonsei students is their Japanese ancestry or descent (16 percent), which was the most numerous response to the first question on what it means to be Japanese American.[15] In nearly half of the replies, students again dichotomized the way they are Japanese American by referring to their ancestry as Japanese and their citizenship as American, as shown in the following example: "Although I follow Japanese culture, I am not Japanese American because of this one fact. I am Japanese American because I have Japanese blood, and was born an American citizen." Respondents generally did not mention that they followed any cultural practices or customs as part of their answer, which was also the case in the responses to the first survey question concerning Japanese descent or ancestry.

The students' responses to the two questions on the meaning of being Japanese American and on the ways they are Japanese American can be combined to provide their composite view of Japanese American ethnic identity. Clearly, the yonsei students consider Japanese culture, customs, and traditions and Japanese ancestry as most significant to them in what it means to be Japanese American and in how they are Japanese American. They also expressed being Japanese American symbolically in their responses concerning observing annual holidays and cultural events and having pride in the achievements of their ancestors. The expression of symbolic ethnicity by fourth-generation yonsei should not be surprising since Japanese Americans have attained a relatively high socioeconomic and political status in Hawai'i comparable to, if not higher than, that of White ethnic groups in the continental United States, despite not being of European ancestry. Like most White ethnic groups, Japanese Americans also are distinguished by limited immigration from their ancestral homeland, thus increasing the likelihood that their ethnic identity will be expressed symbolically since their "ethnic" culture has declined over the generations and has not been revitalized by post-1965 immigrants. Thus, Japanese Americans in Hawai'i, at least their fourth generation, may be one of a limited number of non-White ethnic groups that assert their ethnic identity symbolically.[16]

## Okinawan Americans: Born-Again *Uchinanchu* Identity

In marked contrast to Japanese Americans, Okinawan Americans or *Uchinanchu* provide an example of an ethnic group in Hawai'i that actively constructs a distinct ethnic identity for themselves. In particular, they seek to differentiate themselves from Japanese Americans, an ethnic group in which they can claim membership since Okinawa was a prefecture of Japan when Okinawans began immigrating to Hawai'i in 1900.[17] As noted by Kaneshiro (2002: 84): "The main component of Uchinanchu identity has always been the deeply rooted need to separate and distinguish itself from Japanese [American] identity." The major concern of Okinawan American community leaders and other group members is that their distinct ethnic identity and community will disappear if they do not continue their efforts to maintain them in Hawai'i. The loss of Okinawan American ethnic identity already has occurred in the continental United States where most Okinawan Americans have assimilated into Japanese American identity, and Okinawan identity is claimed primarily by immigrants from Okinawa. A yonsei student from California, who was enrolled in a course on ethnic identity I taught at UH Manoa in 2002, wrote in a paper about his lack of awareness of his Okinawan ancestry while growing up (S. A. 2002):

> I remember the first day of class we talked about Okinawan or Uchinanchu identity. What we talked about that day was the most I had ever learned about my identity. It was funny because during the lecture we talked about the significance of Uchinanchu identity in Hawaii and how it is basically non-existent on the [U.S.] mainland, which is exactly how I felt during that discussion. I was kind of lost when I started hearing certain words like "Uchinanchu." That was the first time in my life that I had ever heard that word. . . . Until recently, I had never even thought about saying that I was Okinawan. I would just say that I was Japanese. When I was growing up in southern California, my parents always told me that I was Japanese. I had heard from my older cousins about being Okinawan, but I never really understood what that meant.

The Okinawan American community in Hawai'i is aware of what has already occurred in the continental United States among Okinawan Americans who do not even inform their children of their Okinawan ancestry. Consequently, their primary interest in constructing their ethnic identity is to maintain the ethnic boundary that differentiates them from Japanese Americans.

The Okinawan American case in Hawai'i highlights the importance of historical and social circumstances for analysis of the construction and persistence of ethnic identity. When Okinawans were immigrating to Hawai'i as plantation labor recruits and picture brides during the first two decades of the twentieth century, their homeland, the formerly independent Ryukyu Kingdom, was a prefecture of Japan, so they were Japanese by nationality. However, in Hawai'i, Okinawans were not fully accepted as Japanese by the *naichi,* or Japanese from mainland Japan, because they spoke their own language and followed their own customary practices and beliefs. Moreover, Japan had gained formal authority over the Ryukyu Islands (Okinawa is the largest island) only in 1872, and they had become incorporated as a prefecture in 1879, just six years before Japanese labor migration to Hawai'i began.

In Hawai'i the naichi were extremely prejudiced against Okinawans and looked down on them as racially and culturally inferior or, as observed by Makoto Arakaki (2002: 138), as the "Japanese other." The naichi held racialized stereotypes of Okinawans as short, dark, and hairy compared to themselves. Okinawan cultural practices, such as married women having tattoos on their fingers, were considered primitive, and their *Hoogen* language was perceived as rough (Ueunten 1989: 37). As a result of Chinese cultural influences in the Ryukyu Kingdom, Okinawans had more pork in their diet than did naichi, so many of them became pig farmers, and by 1940 they operated almost half of such farms in Hawai'i. However, the entire Okinawan American community suffered the common fate of pig farmers in various parts of the world of being considered "dirty" and hence undesirable by naichi. Even the term "Okinawa" was used by them as a racial epithet directed against Okinawans. Due to the hostile attitudes against and avoidance of Okinawans, very little intermarriage occurred between them and naichi immigrants that continued into the second generation.

There were two primary responses on the part of Okinawan Americans to the prejudice and discrimination against them from Japanese Americans. One response was to form their own separate and cohesive community apart from Japanese Americans as evident in their own community organizations and economic institutions. The most important of these community groups was a federated organization, the Hawaii United Association of Okinawan People, established in 1951, which consisted of individual Okinawan organizations such as locality clubs (*sonjin-kai*) based on ancestral ties to a district or town in Okinawa. This association developed from relief efforts by the Okinawan American community following the devastation of Okinawa toward the end of World War II. Between 1945 and 1949, they collected and sent 150 tons of clothing, medical supplies, farming tools, pigs, and milking goats to Okinawa and later assisted in establishing the University of the Ryukyus (First Worldwide Uchinanchu Conference Booklet Committee 2003: 33). In 1995, the association changed its name to the Hawaii United Okinawa Association and continues to provide the corporate representation of the Okinawan American community separate from that of the United Japanese Society for the Japanese American community.[18]

Perhaps the major economic institution among Okinawan Americans was the large number of restaurants, cafés, and drive-ins that were started and continue to be operated by them. The first of these dining establishments was established in 1921, and by 1935 it was estimated that Okinawan Americans operated more than two-thirds of such businesses in Honolulu. Instead of viewing themselves in competition with one another, Okinawan American restaurant and café owners offered their support and advice to other Okinawans who wanted to enter that business by helping them to gain work experience and get started. Due to such assistance, Okinawan Americans became established in the retail and wholesale food service industry in general by the mid-1930s and have continued that economic prominence in the 2000s. One of the primary reasons for this cooperation and support provided to other Okinawan Americans was to foster the overall socioeconomic success of their community and thus to demonstrate to Japanese Americans that they were equal to or even more successful than them (Ueunten 1989: 38).

Another important means by which Okinawan Americans maintained a separate community was by inmarrying, a practice that was closely adhered to by members of the first and, for the most part, second generations. Endogamy is no longer strictly followed, and there is considerable intermarriage, which began in the 1970s with the coming-of-age of the third generation, between Okinawan Americans and Japanese Americans and with other ethnic groups in Hawai'i.

The other completely different response among Okinawan Americans to the hostile attitudes from Japanese Americans was to assimilate or "pass" into Japanese American identity as a means to escape their prejudice and discrimination (Arakaki 2002: 132). Some Okinawan families began to use the Japanese pronunciation of their last name written in *kanji* or Chinese characters instead of how their name was customarily pronounced in their own language. It was thought that this change in pronunciation made their family names sound more Japanese. Thus, the Okinawan family name Yamagusuku became Yamashiro, Tsukazan was changed to Tsukayama, and Gibu became Yoshitake (Higa 1981: 142; cited in Ueunten 1989: 37). In other cases, Okinawan last names, some of which are relatively long, were shortened, as in Shimabukuro becoming Shima. Nonetheless, although family names have been changed in some cases, they still remain one of the most distinctive ethnic markers of Okinawan ancestry in Hawai'i.

Another means of assimilating into Japanese American identity was that in many cases, immigrant parents decided against teaching the *Hoogen* language to their children so that it is generally not spoken by second-generation Okinawan Americans except in a "pidgin" form (Chinen 2006). They are more likely to be able to speak Japanese as a result of having attended Japanese language school in their youth at the insistence of their parents. Other customary practices, such as those related to religious rituals, also were not continued by Okinawan immigrants in Hawai'i.

While it is stated above that the success and proliferation of Okinawan American restaurants and cafés demonstrated how they were able to form their own economic institutions separate from those of Japanese Americans, those businesses also indicated the Okinawan American tendency toward assimilation. Dining establishments owned by Okinawan Americans overwhelmingly did not serve Okinawan food because, according to some of their owners, Okinawan dishes were not marketable to the larger public in Hawai'i. Instead, they offered "American" food and thereby increased their potential clientele to a substantially larger non-Okinawan population (Higa 1981: 42). However, in contrast to Japanese American restaurants, Okinawan American–owned restaurants and cafés also did not have Okinawan family names or words as part of their name; instead, they had names in English such as Columbia Inn or Rainbow Drive-in. By not using Okinawan names, it could be argued that these businesses sought to avoid distinguishing themselves as Okinawan American.

As for the societal circumstances confronting Okinawan Americans, much of the bigotry and discrimination from Japanese Americans declined after World War II as the second generation of both groups matured into adulthood and began to assume leadership roles in their respective communities and the larger society. Relations between the two ethnic groups also improved because they grew up together in the same plantation camps or urban neighborhoods, served together in the war effort either abroad or in Hawai'i, and shared a common status as "second-class citizens" under Haole domination (Ueunten 1989: 41).

As a result of processes of cultural assimilation and loss of traditional culture beginning with the second generation of Okinawan Americans, the cultural distinctiveness of Okinawan American ethnic identity became less apparent. While most third-generation Okinawan Americans were raised as such by their parents and were told they differed from Japanese Americans, they were not necessarily told how they differed from them (Kaneshiro 2002). Another factor contributing to the decline of Okinawan American identity was, as noted above, the substantial decrease in prejudicial attitudes and discriminatory treatment toward Okinawan Americans by second-generation Japanese Americans after World War II (82). This decline in negative treatment continued with the third generation of Japanese Americans, many of whom had close friendships and intermarried with Okinawan Americans and did not carry any of the biases of the previous generations because their parents did not transmit anti-Okinawan sentiments to them.[19] As a result of intermarriage, many fourth-generation Okinawan Americans are of Japanese and Okinawan ancestry or have other ancestries (for example, Hawaiian). They can legitimately assert membership in those other ethnic groups, thus threatening the persistence of Okinawan American identity. Also, the prejudice against Okinawan Americans has decreased so much that their younger generations, even those who are fully Okinawan by descent, have no difficulty claiming to be Japanese American.

In the context of these ongoing threats to the maintenance and continuity of Okinawan American identity, what has been referred to as "a turning point in the history of the Okinawan community in Hawai'i" occurred in 1980 when thirty-five mostly third-generation Okinawan Americans between the ages of eighteen and thirty-five went on a "leadership and study tour" of Okinawa (Arakaki 2002: 136). This twelve-day visit was sponsored by the Okinawan prefectural government as part of the commemoration of the eightieth anniversary of Okinawan immigration to Hawai'i (134). The Okinawan government and people were quite willing to host Okinawan Americans from Hawai'i because of their deep sense of gratitude for the substantial assistance provided them in the aftermath of World War II that they have never forgotten (Chinen 2006). The tour participants were all representatives of Okinawan locality clubs and were selected from more than two hundred applicants, indicative of the great interest among young Okinawan Americans to visit their ancestral homeland. In addition to lectures given by university professors on the history, culture, economy, and politics of Okinawa, the visitors had the opportunity to spend three days in their relatives' home, including a visit to their grandparents' birthplace, which they all considered especially significant (Arakaki 2002: 134). As observed by Arakaki (134–135), the impact of the tour experience on the participants was such that many of them gained a "new understanding and appreciation of their cultural heritage [that] connected the participants to their Okinawan identity and roots."

The 1980 tour was particularly important for Okinawan Americans because of the influence that its participants soon had on their community. Upon returning to Hawai'i, they assumed leadership positions in Okinawan American community associations, including serving as president of the Hawaii United Association of Okinawan People for three consecutive terms after 1981. The tour members also formed an organization for young people like themselves who were interested in maintaining Okinawan identity and culture that they called the Young Okinawans of Hawaii. The emergence of this group encouraged other sansei to become involved in Okinawan American community affairs and "revitalized" the community (Arakaki 2002: 136).

In terms of its structural dimension, Okinawan American identity is constructed by asserting its social distinctiveness from Japanese American identity in order to maintain the ethnic boundary between them. As noted above, the Hawaii United Okinawa Association (HUOA) is a federated organization that represents the Okinawan American community. It has its own Hawaii Okinawa Center that was built in 1990 before a similar community center was established by Japanese Americans five years later. Another Okinawan American community center opened on Maui in 1992. Since 1982, the HUOA has organized an annual Okinawan Festival that was such a success in revitalizing the community in its early years that it had to be relocated twice to larger venues. Since 1990, the two-day festival, which is the largest ethnic celebration in Hawai'i, has been held at Kapi'olani Park in Waikiki during the Labor Day weekend where it is attended by an estimated fifty thousand Hawai'i residents and some Okinawans in tour groups from the homeland. They all have the opportunity to enjoy musical and dance performances by artists and groups from Hawai'i and Okinawa and to partake of various Hawai'i Okinawan dishes. It is a matter of considerable pride to Okinawan Americans that they are able to organize such successful large-scale projects as the festival and the community center, while Japanese Americans have been less successful with such ventures, despite their much larger population (Ueunten 1989: 110). By having their own representative organization, community center, and community festival, Okinawan Americans demarcate an ethnic boundary and affirm their structural distinctiveness from Japanese Americans.

As for the cultural dimension of Okinawan American identity construction, food remains a distinguishing feature of their ethnic group, particularly *andagi*, a deep-fried, doughy confection served at Okinawan American community and family events that many non-Okinawans in Hawai'i recognize and consume as an Okinawan pastry. However, due to the loss of the Okinawan language, folk religion, and other cultural practices and beliefs, Okinawan classical and folk music and dance have come to represent "Okinawan culture" in Hawai'i (Kaneshiro 2002; Ueunten 1989: 111). Cultural performances are especially significant as expressions of ethnic identity since they can be conducted in public to large numbers of both members and nonmembers of an ethnic group. In the Okinawan American case, music and dance troupes regularly perform at community gatherings such as voluntary organization functions and family celebrations such as wedding and retirement parties. These cultural performances are comparable to the cultural significance that *hula* dances and Hawaiian music have among Native Hawaiians for the maintenance of their traditional culture, especially language, and the articulation of their collective identity as the indigenous people of Hawai'i.

Okinawan music and dance groups often include a few young Okinawan Americans who have gone to Okinawa to be formally trained in their specialization at universities and other training schools. They believe that the kind of formal training they received can be obtained only in Okinawa from master performers or teachers; therefore, they were willing to spend a year or longer learning their particular art form and becoming certified as an instructor themselves by passing formal examinations. Subsequently, they returned to Hawai'i to teach others who are interested in learning and performing Okinawan dance and music in organized troupes, some of which have formal affiliations with musical ensembles in Okinawa. As a result of this transnational transfer of cultural knowledge from the homeland, Okinawan culture as represented by folk and classical music and dance has undergone a significant revitalization in Hawai'i since the 1990s.

In addition to cultural performances, Okinawan American identity is also expressed through return trips to Okinawa. It is not uncommon for third- and fourth-generation Okinawan Americans in Hawai'i to visit their ancestral homeland but generally not only as tourists. These trips to Okinawa can be compared to a pilgrimage, albeit secular, since they can result in transition to a new social status, that is, a stronger sense of one's ethnic identity as Okinawan American or Uchinanchu as a consequence of being in the land of one's ancestors. Okinawan Americans are often able to contact and visit their relatives in Okinawa, a transnational kinship connection that most Japanese Americans have lost.[20] The former also often travel together to Okinawa on "study tours" organized by Okinawan American locality or cultural clubs to learn about Okinawan culture and history. No doubt many Japanese Americans travel to Japan, including members of the third and fourth generations, but they tend to go as tourists rather than to visit relatives or to study Japanese language and culture with others. Furthermore, upon their return to Hawai'i, these sansei and yonsei do not initiate or engage in any collective efforts to reconstruct Japanese American ethnic identity either culturally or structurally, although they may pursue their own individual interests.

In making such return visits to Okinawa, third- and fourth-generation Okinawan Americans articulate a diasporic identity that generally is associated with the immigrant and second generations of ethnic minorities, as in the case of Filipino Americans (Espiritu 1994; Okamura 1998b; Strobel 1996). Rather than being merely a dispersed overseas community, a diaspora consists of the transnational relations that connect an overseas community socially, economically, or culturally with its homeland (Okamura 1998b: 17). Starting especially with the 1980 leadership tour to Okinawa, a diasporic identity based on transnational connections with their homeland began to characterize the Okinawan American community. This diasporic identity distinguishes Okinawan Americans from Japanese Americans who do not constitute a diaspora because of their lack of collective transnational ties to Japan. As noted by Arakaki (2002: 133): "During the 1980s and 1990s, as communications and interaction between the Hawai'i Okinawan community and Okinawa became more frequent, Okinawan [American] identity in Hawai'i moved beyond its Hawaiian social space." In other words, being Okinawan American is not limited to their social and cultural experiences in Hawai'i because for an increasing number of Okinawan Americans, the meaning of their ethnic identity includes knowledge and appreciation of their ancestral homeland, including their relatives and Okinawan culture and history.

Beginning in the 1980s, the more frequent use of the term "Uchinanchu" (overseas Okinawan) by Okinawan Americans in Hawai'i to identify themselves individually and collectively has served as a powerful cultural symbol of their diasporic identity and as an expression of their reconstructed ethnic identity. Using a word for their ethnic identity from their own language (which generally is not spoken by them), rather than from Japanese or English, strongly proclaims the cultural and structural distinctiveness of Okinawan Americans from Japanese Americans.

In renewing relationships with their relatives and participating in study tours, Okinawan Americans establish diasporic or transnational relations with them and their Okinawan homeland; thus, they can be seen to affirm a diasporic identity for their community or at least for a significant segment of it. A sansei participant in the 1980 leadership tour described his sense of connection with his ancestral homeland: "From the moment I arrived at the Naha Airport [in Okinawa], I had the feeling of belonging, the feeling of returning home, the feeling that this is where my ancestors came from" (cited in Arakaki 2002: 134). Insofar as it is asserted by members of the third and fourth generations rather than by immigrants, this diasporic identity differentiates Okinawan Americans from Japanese Americans in Hawai'i and from other Asian American and Pacific Islander groups in the United States.[21]

Contributing to the development of this notion of an Okinawan American diasporic identity were initiatives of the Okinawan prefectural government and the Okinawan people that began more actively in the 1980s to maintain closer ties with overseas Okinawan communities in the United States and Latin America (Arakaki 2002: 133).[22] In 1990 the concept of a global Okinawan diaspora was realized when the Okinawan government hosted the first Worldwide Uchinanchu Festival for Okinawans living abroad.[23] With the development of this global Uchinanchu network, Okinawans at home and abroad have advanced the "Uchinanchu spirit" as "the common bond" with previous generations and Okinawan diasporic communities dispersed throughout the world. The Uchinanchu spirit has been defined by sansei and yonsei Okinawan Americans from Hawai'i who participated in a 1993 leadership tour to Okinawa as consisting of five basic elements: "(1) an open, giving, sharing, supportive, helping, and encouraging heart; (2) fellowship and cooperation; (3) hard work; (4) Okinawan cultural awareness; and (5) emphasis on family." Many other Okinawan Americans in Hawai'i would subscribe to this definition of the Uchinanchu spirit, and some refer to it using a term in the Okinawan language as the "spirit of *yuimaaruu*" (mutual help). The Uchinanchu spirit constitutes a major cultural element of the meaning of being Okinawan American for many members of the third and fourth generations. However, one can question the notion of an essentialized and dehistoricized Uchinanchu spirit that serves as the "common bond" among all Okinawans, past and present wherever they may be found.

In his insightful master's thesis on "The Maintenance of the Okinawan Ethnic Community in Hawaii," Wesley Ueunten (1989: 108) contended that: "The Okinawan ethnic community in Hawaii represents an interesting case since its membership consists largely of people who voluntarily assert their Okinawan identity. That is, membership in the Okinawan ethnic community is not determined merely by one's Okinawan ancestry but also by one's actions in affirming his/her Okinawan heritage. A person thus becomes part of the Okinawan ethnic community by 'getting involved' in its activities."

If Okinawan Americans do not assert their ethnic identity, then they are likely to be considered and to consider themselves Japanese American or, if they are of some other ancestry in addition to Okinawan, then they could claim it as their ethnic identity. Ueunten (1989: 108) maintained that Okinawan American identity "ironically" appeared to be the "greatest" among their third and fourth generations who have more in common culturally and socially with other local people in Hawai'i and Americans in general than with second-generation Okinawan Americans. He noted the "resurgence of interest in asserting Okinawan identity" in the 1980s, despite the decline in the "antagonism" between Okinawan Americans and Japanese Americans, and a concurrent "revitalization of the Okinawan ethnic community" (12, 111). This revitalized interest in Okinawan American identity occurred during that decade (and not earlier) principally because the societal circumstances confronting the community—particularly Japanese American prejudice against them—had become considerably less harsh by then and, as stated above, third-generation Okinawan Americans began to be more actively involved in the community, especially in leadership roles. Thus, the reconstruction and reassertion of Okinawan American ethnic identity has been led by their third and fourth generations.

I refer to these third- and fourth-generation Okinawan Americans who are concerned with affirming their ethnic identity as the "born-again Uchinanchu." Under the influence of their parents, they may have grown up thinking they were Japanese American but later learned they are Okinawan by descent, and then began to assert they are Okinawan American or specifically "Uchinanchu." In other cases, they may have known they were of Okinawan ancestry but were unaware of how they differed from Japanese Americans. The born-again Uchinanchu can vary considerably in how they articulate their ethnic identity. Some may simply claim to be Uchinanchu or Okinawan American in their daily life and not be concerned to express their identity either structurally or culturally. Others may affirm their ethnic identity structurally by being an active member or officer in an Okinawan American community organization and by participating in its activities such as sports leagues.[24] Those who are much more committed to Okinawan American identity can assert it culturally by learning to perform Okinawan music or dance with a group of similarly minded individuals. Although admittedly they are only a small minority of the Okinawan American population, they nonetheless play a highly significant role in constructing and expressing the cultural and thereby social distinctiveness of their community.

The Okinawan American case is important because it demonstrates that an ethnic group may engage in ethnic identity formation primarily to differentiate itself from other comparable groups. In other words, for Okinawan Americans, establishing the cultural and structural boundaries between themselves and

Japanese Americans is the principal end in itself of identity formation rather than a means to obtain, for example, greater political or economic power. Nevertheless, ethnic boundary construction is highly important for Okinawan Americans since the absence of difference with Japanese Americans could potentially result in the loss of their ethnic identity and community. The incorporation of a diasporic identity as part of their reconstructed ethnic identity by third- and fourth-generation members also makes the Okinawan American case significant, if not unique, among Asian American and Pacific Islander ethnic groups.

## Conclusion

Interviewed in a documentary on ethnic relations in Hawai'i, "The Politics of Plate Lunch" (1997), Eric Yamamoto argued that a reconstruction of Japanese American ethnic identity should emphasize social values of justice and equality: "My own hope, my own aspiration is that this new AJA [Americans of Japanese Ancestry]/local identity for Japanese Americans in Hawai'i will be one that reclaims the notion of justice in how we relate to each other, that reclaims the notion of fairness and equality in how we deal with economic institutions, and how we act politically."

Yamamoto's emphasis on "reclaiming" the ideals of justice, fairness, and equality refers to the social values advocated and practiced by the nisei generation in the 1950s and 1960s as legislators, union leaders and members, and Democratic Party officials and supporters. However, like kachikan, these values have lost much of their importance to Japanese Americans as they subsequently gained in political power and economic status. Japanese American elected politicians, Democratic Party leaders, union officials, educators, and community representatives who consistently advocate social justice and equality for Hawaii's people are clearly in the minority compared to most Japanese American public officials and leaders who espouse a more conservative mainstream position. Perhaps fully aware of this situation, Yamamoto expressed an appeal to the Japanese American community based on its dominant political and economic status to assume once again a leadership role in fostering a socially just and equal Hawai'i. Certainly, Japanese Americans continue to be a politically and socioeconomically advantaged group, as evident from their being the largest group of state legislators and one of the largest groups of workers in Hawai'i, particularly in higher-status occupations. These positions of power and influence enable them to work to eliminate ethnic inequality and discrimination in Hawai'i.

# 7

# Filipino Americans: Model Minority or Dog Eaters?

Since they were recruited to work on the plantations in 1906, Filipino Americans have encountered great difficulty in asserting their own conception of their ethnic identity and having it accepted by other groups. Instead, in many ways, Filipino American ethnic identity has been and continues to be defined by non-Filipinos through racist stereotypes and other denigrating representations that are pervasive throughout Hawai'i society. Filipino Americans thus are an example of an ethnic group that has been precluded from using identity construction as a means for their collective political and economic advancement. Identity formation is certainly not the only or the principal means for socioeconomic and political mobility for Filipino Americans (and other subordinate ethnic minorities); however, it can have a collective significance for an ethnic minority that other means, such as higher education or electoral politics, do not necessarily provide. Having a Filipino American governor of Hawai'i for eight years (1994–2002) hardly resulted in their socioeconomic advancement.

This chapter discusses both historical and contemporary processes of the racist representation of Filipino Americans and their pernicious effects on Filipino American identity and social status in Hawai'i. It begins with a discussion of the political, economic, and social causes and consequences of the gross overrepresentation of Filipino men among those executed during the territorial period in Hawai'i from 1900 until 1957 when capital punishment was abolished. The chapter analyzes how the Honolulu daily newspapers, in their coverage of the murder trials and hangings of Filipino men enhanced the dominant stereotypes of them as being prone to violence, emotionally volatile, and criminally inclined during the 1920s through the 1950s. I argue that, in turn, these stereotypes very likely contributed to the high rate of conviction and sentencing to death of Filipinos. As for contemporary processes of the racist representation of Filipino Americans, the chapter reviews how the print media, "ethnic humor," and "local literature" of Hawai'i disseminate and reinforce demeaning stereotypes of them. Some of these representations are new, such as Filipino Americans as a model minority, but others, such as their being criminally violent and sexually threatening, have been resurrected from the period prior to World War II. Finally, I discuss the efforts of Filipino American college students to contest such stereotyping by constructing a diasporic identity through a cultural production, *Pag-ibig sa Tinubuang Lupa* (Love for the Native Land).

## Racializing Filipinos

Shortly after the arrival of Filipinos in Hawai'i, the Honolulu police department began referring to them as "poke-knives" because of the alleged tendency of young men to use knives in confrontations with others (Cariaga 1935: 40). Another word used early on by the police for Filipinos was *bayao*, the kinship term for brother-in-law in all three major Philippine languages (Cebuano, Ilokano, and Tagalog), but used in a derogatory manner as later would other Filipino kinship terms, such as *manong* (older brother) and *pare* (co-godfather). It is no accident that all three of these kinship terms refer to males because the Filipino American population was predominantly adult males until the 1950s due to plantation labor recruitment that favored young men. Similarly, the stereotypes of Filipinos that initially emerged referred primarily to young males and resulted in their racist demonization by representing them as emotionally unstable and given to crime and violence.

This demonizing of Filipinos is quite evident in *Temperament and Race* (1926) in which demeaning stereotypes of Filipinos prevalent in Hawai'i were elevated to the status of psychological characteristics by the book's authors, psychologists Stanley Porteus and Marjorie Babcock.[1] *Temperament and Race* purported to be a study on "the importance of the temperamental qualities in *national* or *racial* character and to describe some attempts to measure and compare some of these traits in various races" in Hawai'i (Porteus and Babcock 1926: 19, emphasis in original). Some of the data for the book came from key informants or "judges" who provided "social ratings" of six major races in Hawai'i. They included twenty-five Whites, sixteen of whom were plantation managers, because the authors claimed "their work brought them very intimately into contact with the various racial groups." However, it might be questioned how well those Whites really knew those racial minorities, including Filipinos, Japanese, Chinese, and Puerto Ricans, and if they could converse with any of them in their native language. With regard to Filipinos, Porteus and Babcock (67) contended:

> Summing up these characteristics we may say that the Filipinos represent a fine example of a race in an adolescent stage of development. They exhibit all the signs of imbalance and temporary mal-adjustment that many adolescents show. The marks of their departure from the normal balance of maturity are to be seen in their egocentric attitude, in their rather obtrusive habits and desire for personal recognition, in their super-sensitiveness, love of display, and noisy self-expression. . . . Obviously, these defects must interfere seriously with good judgment and a balanced and sane reaction to affairs in general.

This description leads one to believe that Filipinos, although adults, are like "adolescents" in their thinking and behavior, and that and other psychological "defects" result in their "mal-adjustment" and lack of "good judgment" and "sane" responses to life situations. Elsewhere in the book, Filipinos are described as "highly emotional, impulsive and almost explosive in temperament" (64).

Porteus and Babcock (1926: 65) related supposed Filipino emotional volatility to their "crime excess" because, according to them, "crimes of violence usually due to jealousy are relatively frequent" among extroverts, as they considered Filipinos to be. Based on their analysis of data on court convictions in Hawai'i between 1910 and 1924, they maintained that Filipinos had committed 52 percent of murders, 43 percent of sex offenses, 36 percent of gambling offenses, and 28 percent of burglaries, while they constituted about 9 percent of the population during that period (66). However, instead of attributing those percentages to the predominantly young male Filipino population, Porteus and Babcock (66) contended that the "Filipino crime wave" could be accounted for primarily by their "primitive" and "explosive extrovert temperament": "Under the stress of violent anger or a sense of grave injustice he shows no tendency to reflect, so that the act of revenge often is altogether out of proportion to the offense and sometimes in cases of 'running amuck' the punishment falls on the innocent as well as the guilty."

Romanzo Adams, the leading sociologist of race relations in Hawai'i in the 1920s and 1930s, offered an alternative explanation for Filipino male involvement in crime. He maintained it was due to their being primarily between eighteen and thirty-five years of age and to most of them not having wives in Hawai'i since "trouble frequently arises between two Filipino men on account of a woman" (Adams, Livesay, and Van Winkle 1925: 35–36). A decade later in 1934, the most prevalent crimes that Filipinos (men and women) on O'ahu were charged with were gambling (46 percent of charges), (nonaggravated) assault, disorderly conduct/vagrancy, drunkenness, and sex offenses rather than murder (Cariaga 1974 [1936]: 97). Cariaga (98) argued that the "special forms" of crime among Filipinos resulted from the economic and social conditions encountered by such a young male-dominated group, particularly unemployment during the Depression. Although Filipinos were stereotypically viewed to be involved especially in sex crimes, statistics on arrests (not convictions) for sex offenses in 1934 on O'ahu denote a lower rate per one thousand males for Filipinos (4.9 arrests) compared to Puerto Ricans (18.3 arrests, highest rate) and Hawaiians (7.7 arrests), and the Filipino rate was only a little higher than for Portuguese (3.7 arrests) and Koreans (3.2 arrests) (99). Adams (cited in Cariaga 1974: 98) observed that the overall Filipino crime rate was "rather low" in relation to their total population, considering that they were a recently arrived immigrant minority.

*Temperament and Race* can be understood as being published to address a major concern, if not fear, of the dominant Whites in the 1920s, that is, labor militancy that challenged the racial hierarchy in Hawai'i. In 1924 just two years before its publication, more than nine thousand Filipino workers initiated the first territory-wide strike on the sugar plantations that lasted sixteen months (Reinecke 1996: 32–34). In 1920 more than eight thousand Filipino and Japanese laborers, representing almost 80 percent of the workforce, participated together in a strike of six plantations on O'ahu that, although unsuccessful, cost the planters $12 million in lost profits (Kotani 1985: 40).[2] The denigrating representations of Filipinos in *Temperament and Race* were intended to justify their harsh discriminatory treatment by Whites. Rather than being a comparative psychological study, the book sought to provide a supposedly scientific justification for the oppression and hostility against Filipinos (and Japanese) in retaliation for their leadership and participation in the 1920 and 1924 strikes.

Another early survey on Filipino stereotypes was conducted in 1934 by University of Hawai'i (UH) at Manoa anthropologist Felix Keesing at the start of his summer class on "The Filipino and His Cultural Trends" (Cariaga 1974: 123–124). He asked the sixty-three students in his class, who were primarily schoolteachers from different ethnic groups, to list the traits they considered to be characteristic of Filipinos. Those that had ten or more responses in descending order were: "hardworking," "emotional/excitable/temperamental," "musical," "thrifty," "low standard of living/poor food," "neatly dressed," "eager to learn," "love bright colors," "sociable and cooperative," "primitive/simple-minded/child-like," and "flashily or over-dressed." Several of these assigned traits can be considered positive (for example, neatly dressed, eager to learn, and sociable and cooperative) and very likely indicated the teachers' views of their Filipino American students rather than of Filipinos in general. Hard-working, reported by nearly 40 percent of the respondents, also can be understood as a positive attribute and was a common view of Ilokano plantation workers.

However, some of the negative characteristics given by the respondents (for example, primitive/simple-minded/child-like, emotional/excitable/temperamental) very much reflected widespread stereotypes of male Filipinos. These traits can be related to Porteus and Babcock's (1926) assertion that Filipinos were at an "adolescent stage of development" and were "highly emotional, impulsive and almost explosive in temperament." The characteristic of being flashily dressed in Keesing's survey corresponds to Porteus and Babcock's view that Filipinos have a "love of display" and their "first ambition is to have new clothes." Thus, Keesing's survey demonstrates how Porteus and Babcock's findings were based on prevalent racist stereotypes of Filipinos rather than on verifiable psychological attributes or defects they possessed. Another contemporary observer of pre–World War II Hawai'i, labor historian John Reinecke (1996: 3), provided confirmation of Keesing's results: "A great part of the population stereotyped them [Filipinos] as hotheaded, knife-wielding, overdressed, sex-hungry young men."

A 1949 study by psychologist Edgar Vinacke asked 375 UH Manoa students from seven ethnic groups divided by gender to "characterize" eight ethnic groups in Hawai'i by selecting terms from a list of traits or by adding others not on the list (1949: 268). The characteristics reported for Filipinos by 20 percent or more of male or female respondents from a majority of the seven ethnic groups were "emotional," "hot-tempered," "temperamental," "unpredictable," "ignorant (uneducated)," "flashy," "sexy," and "spendthrift" (272–273). Most of these traits were associated with Filipino men and were considered "unfavorable" by the respondents.[3] Again, the same stereotypic characteristics attributed to Filipinos in the studies by Porteus and Babcock (highly emotional, impulsive, adolescent stage of development, love of display) and by Keesing (emotional/temperamental, simple-minded/child-like, flashily dressed) are evident in Vinacke's study. In sum, through the 1940s, the racialized and gendered representations of Filipinos included being emotionally unstable, criminally inclined, ignorant, and constituting a violent "sex danger."

## Executing Filipinos

Asian American literature scholar Nerissa Balce (2006: 43) analyzes a scene in Bulosan's *America Is in the Heart* (1973 [1946]: 206–208) in which three Filipino labor organizers—including the narrator, Carlos—are kidnapped, beaten, and then tarred and feathered. She refers to this act of racial violence as a "lynching," and no doubt such extralegal violence was more extreme and more frequent on the West Coast than in Hawaiʻi. However, during the same historical period described by Bulosan, numerous Filipino men in the islands were actually hanged by the state rather than being tortured by White vigilantes. Perhaps the most severe consequence of the demonization of Filipino men through their racist stereotyping was that they were a majority of those executed in Hawaiʻi between 1900 and 1957, when capital punishment was abolished, although the last execution was in 1944. Between 1900, when Hawaiʻi formally became a U.S. territory, and 1944, of the forty-two persons executed (all by hanging), twenty-four were Filipino (predominantly young males), although they were at their highest only about one-sixth of Hawaii's population in 1930. Since Filipinos began immigrating to the islands in significant numbers during the 1910s, the first Filipino to suffer the death penalty was not until 1911; so from that year until 1944, Filipinos constituted nearly 80 percent of those executed.

The outrageously high percentage of Filipinos who were hanged by the state is not necessarily because they were killing more people than were individuals from other ethnic groups. Instead, it could have resulted because Filipinos were more likely to be charged with murder (rather than manslaughter) in the event of a homicide, were more likely to be convicted instead of being found innocent, and were more likely to be sentenced to death rather than receive a long prison term. As an indication of the eagerness of juries to convict Filipinos of murder, the jury in one trial deliberated for less than three minutes ("Filipinos Expiate Murders," *Honolulu Star-Bulletin* 1913: 8), another took only four minutes ("Vicente Kacal, Woman Slayer, Pays Penalty," *Honolulu Star-Bulletin* 1929: 2), while a third jury met for seven minutes before returning a guilty verdict ("Reyes Guilty of Murder, Is Jury Verdict," *Honolulu Advertiser* 1927: 1). In distinguishing between racism, which he maintains is "too coarse" an analytic category, and "racial stigma," race relations scholar Glenn C. Loury (2002: 88) argues that stigma involves the idea of a "withholding of the presumption of equal humanity [as] the ultimate mechanism of racism in American public life." This unwillingness to consider Filipinos as fellow human beings was a major contributing factor in their high rate of execution in Hawaiʻi. The historical experience of Filipinos with the death penalty is therefore quite similar to that of African Americans, who also were and continue to be overrepresented among those executed or on death row as a result of being racially stigmatized.

Since the annexation of Hawaiʻi, only one White person was executed, while nine Japanese and six Koreans were put to death, besides the twenty-four Filipinos (Hormann 1953: 4).[4] White killers often were able to escape the death penalty by being charged with a lesser offense than first-degree murder.

The *Hawaii Hochi*, a widely read Japanese community newspaper, reported that despite burning a Japanese plantation worker on Maui "horribly" to his death, a Haole mechanic was tried for manslaughter and subsequently acquitted (cited in Kotani 1985: 65). In 1948 a sixty-five-year-old Chinese vegetable peddler was robbed and had his throat slashed by two Haole youths who later pled guilty to first-degree robbery without ever being charged with murder (Hormann 1953: 2). Clearly, issuing the death penalty was a highly racialized practice in Hawai'i during the territorial period with non-Whites far more likely to receive it as their sentence than were Whites.[5]

As for the social background of the twenty-four Filipinos who were executed, all were males and their median age was twenty-six.[6] Their ages ranged from nineteen to fifty-four; the two oldest Filipinos (forty-three and fifty-four) were among the last to be hanged in the early 1940s, and their older age is probably related to their longer length of residence in Hawai'i compared to those put to death earlier. All of the men were very likely immigrants since the great majority of them were executed prior to the 1940s before a significantly large Hawai'i-born, adult Filipino American population had developed. Half of the men were hanged in the 1910s (twelve) with much lesser numbers in subsequent decades: 1920s (five), 1930s (three), and 1940s (four). To some extent, the large number of Filipinos put to death during their first significant decade of immigration to Hawai'i can be accounted for by the overall greater frequency of executions during the first two decades of the twentieth century. In the first decade, ten persons suffered the death penalty and were followed by sixteen in the 1910s; thus, 62 percent of the executions in Hawai'i occurred between 1900 and 1919.

The twenty-four Filipinos who were hanged were convicted of killing more than that number of persons because of three cases of multiple murder victims. With regard to the ethnicity of the victims in the twenty-four cases, they were Filipino in ten cases, including two men and eight females. Among the females, three were quite young, including a fourteen-year-old who was killed by her father ("Slayer of Daughter Is Hanged," *Honolulu Star-Bulletin* 1941). The other young Filipinas were a twelve-year-old and another described as a "girl" in the newspapers who was slain while on her way to school. The non-Filipino victims included three Japanese men and two Japanese women, the German wife of her killer and her sister, a Chinese couple, and a "navy machinist's mate" of unknown race.

It is not always possible from newspaper accounts to determine the motives for committing the murders. The cases in which the victim is a Filipina (except for the father who killed his daughter) involved a troubled relationship between a man and his wife or the object of his attention. Seven of the cases could be classified as such and are described further below. Nonetheless, in considering the possible motives of the murderers, I think it can safely be assumed that most cases of problematic relationships involving Filipino men did not result in homicide by them during the period concerned.

## Demonizing Filipinos

The Honolulu daily newspapers contributed substantially to publicizing the role of Filipinos as perpetrators in capital murder cases by highlighting their convictions and executions in their front-page headlines: "Filipinos Pay Death Penalty; Brave to Last," *(Honolulu Star-Bulletin* 1915: 1); "Filipino Youth Is Hanged for Girl's Murder," *Honolulu Star-Bulletin* 1932: 1). This practice of specifying the ethnic identity of Filipinos, not just when they were executed but also arrested and convicted of crimes, was continued by the Honolulu dailies through the 1930s. As Filipino anthropologist Roman R. Cariaga observed: "Newspapers have tended to play up their misbehavior so that the public has been constantly made conscious of the Filipino in a bad light. Whenever a serious crime is committed by a Filipino, his nationality is designated—Juan de la Cruz, a *Filipino* is charged . . ." (1937: 75, emphasis in original).

In marked contrast, such reference to ethnic identity is absent in the headlines and titles of newspaper articles about the executions of other convicted murderers, although it may be noted in the subtitle of an article or the article itself. From my review of the forty-two death penalty cases, Japanese, Koreans, Native Hawaiians, and Puerto Ricans were not identified by ethnic identity in the headlines or titles of newspaper articles about their hangings. Instead, such information might be noted in the article, as in the following piece about a Japanese convicted murderer that was simply titled, "Girl's Slayer to Be Hanged Tomorrow" (*Honolulu Star-Bulletin* 1921). By regularly referring to executed Filipinos by their ethnic identity rather than by their names in their headlines, the Honolulu newspapers made Filipinos as a group appear somehow responsible for the murders instead of the individuals who had been convicted of the crime. The journalistic practice of not indicating the ethnic identity of those executed would not be extended to Filipinos until 1940.

The press also regularly engaged in hyperbole in their accounts of capital crimes committed by Filipinos: "one of the most atrocious in the annals of the police department" ("Filipinos Expiate Murders," *Honolulu Star-Bulletin* 1913: 8); "one of the most brutal and cold-blooded murders recorded in police annals in Hawaii" ("Expiates Murder on the Gallows," *Pacific Commercial Advertiser* 1914). While it may have been the case with media descriptions of murders in general prior to World War II, crimes committed by Filipinos were vividly described by the daily newspapers: "Narcissus and Marcelo were cold-blood criminals. The former butchered his German wife and his sister-in-law . . . The latter [Marcelo] hacked to death the wife of another Filipino . . . with a cane knife" ("33 Men, 2 Women Watch Hanging of Two Filipino Slayers at Oahu Prison," *Honolulu Star-Bulletin* 1927: 1); "in Vicente Kacal's words, he had hacked Mrs. Dayaganon to death with a cane knife in a fit of jealous rage" ("Vicente Kacal, Woman Slayer, Pays Penalty," *Honolulu Star-Bulletin* 1929: 1). An especially detailed description of a "fiendish crime" appeared in a 1913 *Star-Bulletin* article ("Filipinos Expiate Murders," 1913: 8): "Each body was frightfully mutilated, the throats being cut and the bodies literally covered with wounds, believed, at the time, to have been inflicted with a blunt instrument. The breast and shoulders of the young woman, who was barely 20 years of age, were cut and gashed as though with a rough knife blade or a chisel. . . . From the brutality displayed by the murderers, the police at once evolved the theory that it was the work of Orientals." The reference to "Orientals" may very well have been to Filipinos because, during this period in Hawai'i, Japanese and Chinese were often referred to as "Asiatics." If this is the case, then the police "theory" that Filipinos were responsible for the crime is a very early manifestation of how they were being racialized as vicious and violent murderers, just seven years after the first Filipino labor recruits had arrived in the islands.

By their callous reporting, the press contributed to the racist demonization of Filipino young men as extremely cruel and violent criminals. Based on newspaper articles, cane knives and other types of knives were used in the commission of their crimes by at least twelve of the twenty-four executed Filipinos.[7] Unfortunately, the reporting of this information very likely enhanced the "poke-knife" stereotype of Filipino young males that had emerged soon after they began immigrating to Hawai'i. Cane knives were not necessarily Filipinos' weapon of choice but, as everyday work tools of plantation laborers, they were readily accessible and much easier to acquire than a handgun. Even a sympathetic and astute observer of Filipinos such as John Reinecke appears to have succumbed to their racist stereotyping in his analysis of the 1924 strike: "Everyone expected a Filipino strike to be a violent one. The stereotype of Filipinos as 'Pilipino poke knife,' with a low flash point, was widely held, and it had some justification in past experience" (1996: 35–36).

Newspaper accounts of Filipino murder cases also reinforced the widespread stereotype of Filipinos as emotionally unstable and temperamental. Filipinos sometimes were convicted of crimes of passion, such as the murder of a woman who did not return the love of a man during this period when Filipino women were especially scarce. The incident described below concerns a schoolgirl a man wanted to marry ("Filipino Youth Is Hanged for Girl's Murder," *Honolulu Star-Bulletin* 1932: 1): "Paying with his own life for that of a young girl he stabbed to death in a jealous rage, Lazaro Calibo, 23 year old Filipino, was hanged in Oahu prison today. . . . The crime for which Calibo was hanged today was the stabbing and killing of Emily Bonella at Paauhau, Hawaii. . . . The girl had refused to marry him, and . . . when she was on her way to school with her sister, Calibo laid in wait for her and killed her."[8]

In another case of unrequited love, a Filipino was executed for the murder of the mother of a young girl he desired ("Filipino Hanged for Murder Goes to Death Steadily," *Honolulu Star-Bulletin* 1917): "The convicted man who paid for the crime with his life, shot and killed the mother of Dolores at Watertown over a month ago. Dojoylongsol had been an ardent suitor for the hand of the Filipino girl, but his love was apparently not returned, for one morning the convicted man discovered her in company with another Filipino and her mother. Infuriated, the rejected lover fired, hitting and instantly killing the girl's mother." I cited above a statement by Porteus and Babcock (1926: 66) that referred to Filipinos "running amuck" as a result of "the stress of violent anger" such that sometimes "the punishment falls on the innocent as well as the guilty." What might be considered the narrow definition of running amuck (or amok) refers to indiscriminate homicidal aggression by a person in an emotionally charged state who with a weapon kills whomever he or she encounters rather than an intended victim (Spores 1988). In Hawai'i running amok was stereotypically associated with Filipinos because their counterparts in the Philippines were said to engage in such behavior, although it certainly is not limited only to Filipinos.[9] The murder of the mother described above is not an example of an amok killing since it was not indiscriminate. However, I am curious if cases of seemingly unpremeditated murder reported in the Honolulu newspapers led Porteus and Babcock and others to conclude that Filipinos, given their alleged violent anger and explosive temperament, did have a tendency to run amuck and therefore constituted an even greater homicidal threat, since they might kill anyone and not just those who had angered them for some reason.

As an indication of the emotional volatility of Filipinos, the newspapers often mentioned "jealous rage" as a precipitating factor in their commission of murder, as apparent from this article titled "Jealous Man Makes Mincemeat of Wife" (*Pacific Commercial Advertiser* 1913: 9):

> Again Paauilo has become the scene of an atrocious murder. This time a Filipino cut down his wife, of whom he was jealous. . . . The woman had left the man about a week before. He followed her up, and at two o'clock in the morning he broke into the room where she was and literally hacked her to pieces with a cane knife. . . . Doctor Taylor, who attended the woman, says that it is the worst case of butchery he ever saw. There were between seventy-five and a hundred wounds on the head and body above the waist. . . . The murderer has been apprehended by the Hamakua police.

This brief description includes all of the sensationalized elements that were common features in newspaper accounts of murders by Filipinos prior to the

1940s. It notes the "atrocious" nature of the crime, jealousy as an emotional factor, and the brutality of the attack as the "worst case of butchery" ever seen by the doctor. The article does not mention the name of the alleged perpetrator, although it does refer to him as Filipino and as the "murderer," even though he had not yet even been put on trial.

## Filipinos Contesting

There was a clear reciprocal relation between the racist demonization of Filipino men by the print media and their being grossly overrepresented among those suffering the death penalty in Hawai'i. By describing in gory detail the murders Filipinos had committed, newspaper accounts of their convictions and executions intensified dominant stereotypes of them as exceedingly violent, criminally inclined, and emotionally explosive. These malevolent representations, which also had other sources in Hawai'i, such as radio news broadcasts and word-of-mouth communication, very likely contributed to the high rate of conviction and hanging of Filipino men by seeming to justify their executions. At the same time, their numerous hangings for murder reinforced the widespread perception that Filipino males were impulsively prone to commit violent killings by legally confirming their tendency to engage in such deviant behavior and hence the danger they posed to society. Thus, the demonization of Filipino men was both cause and consequence of their constituting most of those executed in territorial Hawai'i. Certainly, these executions were not the only harmful consequence of the demonization of Filipinos. They also had to endure decades of institutional and interpersonal discrimination that severely limited their socioeconomic and political mobility, the impacts of which continue to the present. Another negative result was that during the 1930s, when their labor was no longer needed, more than nine thousand Filipinos were repatriated to the Philippines by the Hawaiian Sugar Planters' Association (Alcantara 1973: 15) as a means of ridding society of an undesirable and unemployed presence that might resort to violent crime to support themselves. Thus, there was a decline in the Filipino population of Hawai'i between 1930 and 1940 of about 10,500 persons and on the plantations of almost 17,000 workers (Lind 1980: 34, 83).

In addition to their racist demonization, other factors contributed to the high rate of hanging of Filipino men. One such factor was that they challenged the racialized economic order of Hawai'i, much to the anger and distress of the dominant Haoles. Although Filipinos were convicted of murdering only two Whites (a German wife and her sister, killed by the former's husband), their executions were directed to the larger Filipino community not to transgress the paramount racial boundary separating Whites from non-Whites. While Filipinos did not necessarily pose an immediate threat to kill Haoles or rape

Haole women, Whites were angered and troubled by their willingness to contest the racial status quo and their subjugated economic position therein through labor organizing.

Instead of ethnic identity construction, labor organizing served as the principal means for Filipinos to advance their collective economic interests prior to statehood in 1959. In addition to the 1920 and 1924 strikes, Filipino labor militancy manifested itself again in 1937 when 1,500 workers organized a strike at the Pu'unene plantation on Maui, the last major strike in Hawai'i by laborers from a single ethnic or nationality group (Beechert 1985: 226–229). Filipino labor organizing continued in the 1930s, spurred on by increasingly difficult economic conditions for them during the Depression since they comprised a majority of sugar and pineapple laborers. Filipinos started a Pineapple Workers Union on Moloka'i and organized a successful strike. In 1938 two short strikes were held on the Hamakua Coast on Hawai'i Island, and others at Kahuku Plantation on O'ahu and Kekaha Plantation on Kaua'i. It took World War II and the declaration of martial law to bring a temporary halt to such determined labor organizing efforts on the part of Filipino workers.

The demonization of Filipinos did not end with the last of their hangings in 1944. Such racist representations had other sources in Hawai'i society, and the executions themselves had a lasting impact on perceptions of Filipino Americans. In the poststatehood period, the sources of Filipino stereotyping continue to be the print media, augmented by television evening news programs, and new sources such as ethnic humor and local literature. Nonetheless, some of the same denigrating stereotypes have persisted over time due to their perpetuation by non-Filipinos. Thus, while the execution of Filipinos ended in the 1940s, their lynching by the news media and local comedians and writers continues unabated.

## Ethnic Humor or Racist Stereotyping?

Being historically an economically and politically subordinate minority, Filipino Americans have found it especially difficult to contest their stereotyping that is so pervasive and frequent that many people in Hawai'i do not consider it offensive or problematic. Nonetheless, such stereotyping is the principal problem that Filipino Americans encounter in seeking to construct and assert their ethnic identity and to advance themselves socioeconomically. One of the major contemporary sources of denigrating stereotypes of Filipino Americans in Hawai'i is joke telling about them. While in the continental United States, Filipino American comedians, such as Rex Navarrete, make fun of their behaviors and experiences in the United States, in Hawai'i it is especially non-Filipinos who target Filipino Americans as the butt of their jokes. Such joke telling about ethnic groups is referred to as "ethnic humor" or "local humor" in Hawai'i and is claimed to be one of the primary reasons that island residents get along especially well with each other because supposedly everyone laughs at such jokes, even those made at the expense of their own ethnic group. As strong advocates of the Hawai'i multicultural model, Grant and Ogawa (1993: 150) contend that ethnic joke telling is one of the major "points of commonality" among ethnic groups that historically have fostered positive ethnic relations. An editorial in the *Honolulu Advertiser* ("Island Ethnic Humor Is What Keeps Us Together" 1998) maintained that "it [ethnic humor] is the glue that holds our multi-ethnic society together; it is the lubricant that lets us touch each other daily with a minimum of friction. . . . Isle-style humor is a time-honored product of ethnic mixing, and an indication of a healthy society." However, joke telling also can serve as a way of expressing critical or even harsh comments about another ethnic group that otherwise cannot be said publicly.

Not surprisingly, since it is the source of their livelihood, local comics also have provided their own justifications for ethnic humor. In his compilation of ethnic jokes, *Frank DeLima's Joke Book*, subtitled *Having Fun with Portagees, Pakes, Buddha Heads, Buk Buks, Blallahs, Soles, Yobos, Haoles, Tidahs, Pit Bulls, and other Hawaiian Minorities*, local comedian Frank DeLima (1991: v), one of the pioneers of island comedy, presented his rationale for ethnic humor: "Here in Hawaii, we laugh at ourselves more than most people do in other places. Hawaii is a chop suey nation—Portagee [Portuguese], Pake [Chinese], Buddha Head [Japanese], Sole [Samoan], Yobo [Korean], Kanaka [Native Hawaiian], Haole [White], all mixed up. Nobody is in the majority here. We are all part of at least one minority group. Some of us are part of several minority groups. And we all laugh at ourselves."[10] While listing all of the above ethnic groups may seem inclusive, the problem with ethnic jokes is that we laugh at others who are the object of the jokes, not necessarily only at ourselves.[11] Local comics probably never consider how their jokes can hurt others since they foolishly believe everyone finds them funny, even those who are being made fun of.

The basis of the humor in ethnic jokes is common stereotypes of different ethnic groups in Hawai'i; if one is unaware of the stereotype, the joke is not likely to be very funny. With remarkable consistency (or lack of originality), local comedians represent Chinese Americans as money-hungry tightwads, Native Hawaiians as criminally inclined and physically large, Japanese Americans as knowing martial arts and having squinty eyes, Korean Americans as hot-tempered and sexually loose (young women only), Okinawan Americans as hairy and short, Portuguese Americans as loud-mouthed and not very intelligent, Samoans as violent and living in public housing, Whites as pushy and pretentious, and local people in general as also not very bright and of low-income status. But because local humor is based on ethnic stereotypes, it serves to reinforce and disseminate them at the expense of some ethnic groups that are not just being made fun of but are also being denigrated. As anthropologist Roderick Labrador (2004: 312) has argued: "Explanations and justifications of the persistence of ethnic humor view language, culture and identity as objective facts in the natural order of things rather than constructions embedded in a network of social relations and underscored by struggles of power." Stereotypes about the language, culture, and identity of an ethnic group also are constructions that reflect the unequal power relations among groups.

While the claim of many local comics that they tell jokes about all ethnic groups in Hawai'i is true, it is also the case that not all groups have the same social status or power in society. Whites, Japanese Americans, and Chinese Americans hold such high political and socioeconomic positions that jokes about them by Waikiki comedians are hardly going to affect their well-established status in society. In contrast, oppressed and therefore vulnerable ethnic minorities, such as Filipino Americans and Samoans, are far more likely to suffer harmful consequences, such as in employment and interpersonal interactions, as a result of jokes told about them, which are sometimes repeated to them in person. As an example, DeLima's jokes about "Buddha Heads" (Japanese Americans) in his joke book, videos, and CDs are primarily about Japanese nationals, including tourists, and not Japanese Americans. Local Japanese Americans know that island residents are aware of the difference between themselves and Japanese nationals and thus are not very offended by that type of joke because it is not about them and thus does not affect their ethnic identity and status and how they are perceived by non-Japanese Americans.

But DeLima is far less cautious with his jokes about Filipino Americans that are based on stereotyped notions of the supposedly strange foods they eat, their accented English, the menial jobs they perform, and the colorful clothes they wear. One of his compact discs, *Babooze*, includes a live comedy routine with the same title in which DeLima refers to "Filipino janitors arguing over a dead dog at an animal shelter" (DeLima 1995). In this one ostensibly funny line, not only are Filipino Americans represented as dog eaters, they also are stereotyped as janitors given to violence. Some of his jokes about Filipino Americans imply that they are deficient in some way or are not very intelligent and therefore reinforce other common perceptions of them, such as asking why there are no Filipino doctors, or what is a Filipino failure called (DeLima 1991: 69). Why not a joke that begins, "Did you hear the one about the Filipino American lawyer?"

DeLima (1993) resurrected the "poke-knife" stereotype of pre–World War II Filipino men in his song titled the "Purple Danube." In this parody of the "Blue Danube," the first verse refers to Filipinos wearing purple and brown, eating goat, and holding a knife to one's throat. While some may find supposed Filipino American color and food preferences to be funny, I have great difficulty finding any humor in the depiction of a Filipino American or anyone else wielding a knife at one's throat.

Another purveyor of jokes about Filipino Americans is popular local comic "Augie T" (Tulba) who says he has a Filipino father and a Portuguese mother. While his professional career as a comedian began in the late 1990s, two decades after DeLima began his, Augie's jokes about Filipino Americans include the same stereotypic references to them as wearing bright clothes, speaking English with an immigrant accent, eating dogs, and using knives. In "Crank Call: Movies" on one of his CDs (*Locally Disturbed*), he plays the role of an elderly male Filipino immigrant who calls a video rental shop to ask if they have certain martial arts videos (Tulba 2002). After becoming frustrated by the clerk's inability to understand his accented English and to locate the videos he wants, the caller angrily replies with a threat that he will come back with a knife and his dog that will bite her. The specter of the knife-wielding, violence-prone, and temperamental Filipino male from the plantations before World War II once again makes his menacing appearance but ostensibly to make one laugh.

A number of non-Filipino local comedians also disseminate jokes about Filipino Americans based on the same old stereotypes. Appearing live in a video, *Hawaii's Comedy Stars* (1997), Japanese American comic Paul Ogata does a routine about Filipino Americans eating in his words, "that weird Filipino food," in this case, *dinuguan*, a pork dish cooked with pig's blood among other ingredients. He displays his ignorance of Filipino cuisine by describing dinuguan as a "soup" and claiming that it consists of fresh pig's blood; of course, such lack of knowledge does not stop him from publicly making false assertions.

Another local comedian, Gregg "Hammer," on his CD, *Plain Brown Wrapper* (1998), sings a tune called "In Kalihi" in the heavily accented voice of a male Filipino immigrant who lives in that inner city area of Honolulu. Kalihi is a multiethnic, working-class community in which Filipino Americans, especially post-1965 immigrants, are the largest ethnic group. Rudy, the immigrant Filipino, is depicted in the song as a janitor working for $4.25 per hour at a McDonald's restaurant who is arrested for cockfighting.[12] No doubt many Filipino immigrants live in Kalihi, work at McDonald's and other fast-food restaurants, and speak with accents; however, many more live elsewhere, including middle-class suburban communities, have white-collar jobs, speak with a local accent, and have never been arrested, let alone been to a cockfight.

As apparent from the above examples, so-called "Filipino jokes" by local comics tend to be variations on prevalent stereotypes about them as eating dogs, holding menial service jobs, speaking strongly accented English, and not being very smart. To some extent, the jokes are not so much about Filipino Americans but about jokes concerning Filipino Americans insofar as they are based on other familiar jokes. Nonetheless, as jokes purportedly about Filipino American behavioral and cultural practices, they still have the harmful effect of reinforcing demeaning stereotypes. Being based on these stereotypes, jokes about Filipino Americans tend to represent them as males, often elderly immigrants, particularly in terms of the *manong* (older Filipino man) who speaks with a heavy accent and holds a menial job that Labrador (2004: 300) considers "a dominant Filipino character type" in local comedy. Indeed, such jokes are more about immigrant rather than Hawai'i-born Filipinos who constitute a majority of the Filipino American population. But by making racist jokes about Filipino immigrant language, culture, and behavior or what they imagine them to be, comedians contribute to the false notion that Filipino Americans are predominantly immigrants and therefore less local, less culturally competent, less educated, and less qualified for employment than other Hawai'i residents.

Filipino American objections to racist jokes made about them have been expressed for some time. For an article titled "Filipinos' Dilemma with Frank DeLima" that appeared in a community newspaper, the *Hawaii Filipino Chronicle*, Rex Quidilla and Dennis Galolo (1994: 4–5) interviewed Filipino American community leaders who found DeLima's "Filipino jokes" demeaning. The article was occasioned by a parody DeLima released in December 1994, "A Filipino Christmas," sung with a strong accent to "Chestnuts Roasting on an Open Fire," that substituted his lyrics, such as those referring to black dogs cooking on a fire. Filipino American business owner Eddie Flores remarked of DeLima's song (cited in Quidilla and Galolo 1994: 4): "I find it very offensive. It belittles Filipinos and looks only at their weak points. He doesn't have a Chinese or a Japanese Christmas [song]. He stereotypes Filipinos much more than other ethnicities and it's usually more heavy-handed and degrading—like we talk funny and eat dogs. He says Chinese are tight, but that's not so degrading. It implies they're rich, so what?"

It is especially ironic that the release of DeLima's song and its ample radio airplay came less than a month after Ben Cayetano was elected as the first Filipino American governor of Hawai'i and in the United States. Cayetano's election was a major breakthrough for Filipino Americans as a community that historically has viewed itself as unfairly excluded from the power and privileges enjoyed by other island ethnic groups. It indicated to many, both Filipino American and non-Filipino, that Filipino Americans finally "had made it" in Hawai'i, at least politically, in attaining the highest elective office in the state. But the fragility of Cayetano's victory as governor in enhancing the power and prestige of the Filipino American community was made painfully apparent the very next month by the release of DeLima's song.

Ethnic humor is a contemporary version of the historical practice of promulgating racist representations of Filipinos engaged in by the Honolulu daily newspapers beginning in the 1910s. Insofar as it perpetuates denigrating stereotypes of them, local comedy is a major factor that precludes Filipino Americans from asserting their own ethnic identity. Jokes about Filipino Americans are discursive acts of power against them and need to be understood as cultural representations that maintain their structural subordination in Hawai'i and derive from that subjugation. As noted by Labrador (2004: 312), ethnic humor "points to struggles over representation, in terms of which images, signs, and jokes are produced, consumed and distributed. Who makes the jokes, who is made fun of, and who laughs involves discourses of inclusion and exclusion. Jokes can effectively tell us who belongs and in the process, they construct order and hierarchy and are thus invariably linked to power." As such, ethnic humor is very much related to ethnic inequality in Hawai'i insofar as it links the cultural representations of aggrieved ethnic groups in the jokes made about them to their subordinate status and power in society.

## Representations by the News Media and Local Literature

The print media are another source of inaccurate representations of Filipino Americans in Hawai'i. Fortunately, the newspapers no longer engage in the blatant racist portrayals of Filipinos that was a regular practice of theirs before World War II. A newer stereotyped depiction of Filipino Americans by the news media is as a model minority of hardworking and struggling immigrants determined to make it in Hawai'i. Although Filipinos began immigrating to the islands in 1906, they were included in a series on "Hawaii's Newest Immigrants" by one of the Honolulu daily newspapers (Nii and Creamer 1999: A1, A8). The authors described Filipino Americans as "Struggling to adjust to a strange new homeland. Struggling to earn a living and support family here and in the Philippines. Struggling to earn the respect and power often denied them, no matter how they paid in sweat and heartbreak. . . . Their story is becoming one of determination to succeed." They then related the hardships of a "straight-A student" who graduated at the top of her 1998 class at Farrington High School in Kalihi only a year and a half after emigrating from the Philippines. While attending community college as a full-time student, she works sixty hours a week at a Waikiki convenience store and a restaurant to save money "toward her dream" of studying at a local private university to become a registered nurse (A1).

Typical of model minority stories, in seeking to emphasize Filipino American self-help initiatives through hard work, higher education, and perseverance, the authors did not question why Filipino Americans, like the student described above, have to make that kind of extraordinary effort in order to advance themselves. Are Japanese American, Chinese American, and White college students similarly required both to study and work on more than a full-time basis in order to attain socioeconomic success? The article never raised the issue of discrimination against Filipino Americans in education and employment that limits their access to the extent that even public higher education at UH Manoa is not viewed as a viable option to pursue. Instead, non-Filipinos are supposed to admire the incredible "determination to succeed" of the young woman and, by extension, other "hardworking" and "struggling" Filipino immigrants, who supposedly demonstrate through their example that Hawai'i is indeed an open and egalitarian society where anyone can realize their dreams of success, as long as they are willing to make the required individual effort and sacrifice.

Filipino Americans also were represented as a model minority in a five-part series in one of the Honolulu daily newspapers in observance of the one-hundredth anniversary of Filipino immigration to Hawai'i in 2006 ("A Toast to Success and Sacrifice," *Honolulu Star-Bulletin* 2005). The series began with the assertion that, "The story of Hawaii's Filipinos—of sacrifice and success, of families separated and reunited, of hard work and the American dream—is Hawaii's story. Their centennial is a reason for everyone to celebrate." The "success" of Filipino Americans is attributed to their "sacrifice," including family separation following immigration to Hawai'i, and "hard work" as they pursue the "American dream." The centennial is for "everyone to celebrate" because Filipino American success is an affirmation of the Hawai'i multicultural model; that is, all of Hawaii's people are fortunate to live in a society with tolerant, harmonious, and egalitarian ethnic relations such that immigrant minorities that started on the plantations can advance themselves to the very highest levels of the social status order.

The first article in the series provided vignettes of various small businesses owned and operated by Filipino immigrants in Kalihi, including restaurants, grocery stores, travel agencies, and general merchandise stores. The underlying theme of the story is of hardworking immigrants who devote long hours to their family businesses that cater to other Filipino Americans. A co-owner of a family-owned Filipino food "takeout" and grocery store is described as working "13-hour days several days a week doing everything from payroll to purchasing to dishing food into styrofoam containers behind the counter" (Barayuga 2005b). She says she also has a part-time job at a Waikiki hotel as a housekeeper and explains, "this is the way we earn our living" (cited in Barayuga 2005b). No doubt some Filipino Americans have attained a degree of socioeconomic success as small business owners. However, that success has taken a very long time to achieve compared to other ethnic groups and does not necessarily mean that the many other Filipino Americans who are not business owners have similarly succeeded in their work. While the news media may celebrate Filipino immigrant success stories, one can ask if there are other stories that could be written about Filipino American lives that depict the reality of their subordination in the islands.

The other stories in the newspaper series highlighted the assimilation and Americanization of Filipino Americans over time, again consistent with their representation as a model minority. The second article concerned an eighty-year-old Filipino immigrant woman who was "fulfilling her dream" of becoming a U.S. citizen by studying for the naturalization examination after living in Hawai'i for forty years (Vorsino 2005c). A medical doctor educated in the Philippines, whose father instilled in her a "strong work ethic" and emphasized that she and her four siblings all obtain a college education, was the subject of the third article (Bernardo 2005). The fourth segment in the series was about Filipino World War II veterans who fought in the Philippines together with American soldiers and "are hoping their sacrifices are remembered," as they continue to seek full veterans benefits from the U.S. government (Reyes 2005). The last story featured the matriarch of a family whose ancestors came to Hawai'i in 1923 and began celebrating Thanksgiving twenty years later when one of the Hawaii-born children brought home information from school on its observance (Gima 2005b). The article described the different foods that are part of their large family celebration, including Hawaiian, Japanese, and Korean dishes, which indicate how the family has become local over the generations besides intermarriage with those groups. Featuring a long-resident local Filipino family, the story is useful to counter the common notion that the Filipino American community consists predominantly of post-1965 immigrants and their offspring. Nonetheless, four of the five articles in the series were concerned with immigrants and privileged personal stories of perseverance, hard work, and devotion to education as the primary means for individual advancement rather than struggles against oppression, racism, and discrimination that restrict such progress.

Clearly, a major feature of the model minority stereotype of Filipino Americans is to represent them as immigrants, although most Filipino Americans in Hawai'i were born in the United States. The reason that they are portrayed as immigrants by the news media is because such an image of them is more consistent with their model minority representation and with certain positive stereotypes of Filipino immigrants as hardworking and willing to accept whatever jobs are available to them. The model minority stereotype also uses women to represent Filipino Americans because they are perceived more positively than Filipino American men by non-Filipinos in Hawai'i.[13] Men continue to be burdened by the racist stereotypes that originated much earlier.

Despite their model minority depiction of Filipino Americans, the news media also resurrected the pre–World War II stereotypes of Filipino men as criminally inclined, emotionally volatile, and given to violence in the so-called "amok" or "cultural" defense of Filipino American multiple-murderer Orlando Ganal in his highly publicized 1993 trial in Hawai'i (see Seto 1993: A3). In defending Ganal, a thirty-eight-year-old former delivery driver who had emigrated from the Philippines when he was seventeen, his Japanese American attorney strongly implied that Ganal had run amok when he killed five people one horrible night in 1991. According to his lawyer, the infidelity of Ganal's wife and his financial problems caused him to be under "extreme emotional distress," the legal requirement for the lesser offense of manslaughter instead of first-degree murder, the most serious of numerous charges against Ganal. However, Ganal's killings can hardly be considered running amuck since he had targeted his murder victims rather than engaged in indiscriminate homicidal behavior. Those victims included his wife's elderly parents whom he shot and killed at their home where he also wounded his estranged wife and teenage son. Perhaps believing that the lover of Ganal's wife, David Touchette, was still living with Touchette's married brother, Ganal then drove across the island to the home of the brother and his family and set it on fire, killing the brother and his two infant children and critically burning the brother's wife who was the only survivor.

Two UH Manoa professors testified in Ganal's defense and provided definitions of running amok, although neither of them had interviewed him or read his case history. One of them, who lacks any formal training in psychology, asserted that Ganal's behavior in response to his wife's extramarital affair "was a textbook case of Filipino strategy—the way Filipinos cope with stress" and that Ganal had acted culturally according to a "Filipino script" (cited in Seto 1993: A3). Such testimony by a supposed expert on Filipino culture and behavior would lead one to believe that, when confronted with stressful situations, Filipinos are not only unable to control their emotions, they also adhere to a culturally prescribed behavioral "strategy," including running amuck. The implication is that Filipinos do not respond to stress as individuals according to their own personality, life experiences, and personal circumstances but primarily as Filipinos according to a "Filipino script" of cultural practices and behavioral norms. A further implication is that Filipino immigrants, although they have lived most of their lives in the United States like Ganal had, are still susceptible to running amok since they had been raised with Filipino culture.

With daily front-page coverage, the Ganal trial was highly publicized by the Honolulu newspapers during its three-week duration, especially his amok defense. This media publicity, together with similar reporting by evening television news programs, reinforced the association of Filipino Americans with amok behavior and emotionally driven violence in general. An editorial in the *Honolulu Star-Bulletin* (1993: A10), "Ganal Case Jury Rightly Rejected 'Amok'

Defense," criticized Ganal's attorney for his "desperate defense [that] served to spread the erroneous and appalling stereotype that Filipinos are prone to run amok." The editorial correctly grasped the larger social significance of the Ganal case for Filipino Americans in Hawai'i: "In the aftermath, however, are more victims than the Ganal and Dela Cruz [Ganal's in-laws] families. The Filipino [American] community has been set back in its efforts to quash stereotypes that haunt its elders and shackle its younger generation." Unfortunately, Filipino Americans continue to encounter numerous setbacks in their ongoing efforts to rid themselves of degrading stereotypes (some of them originating in a previous era) from the larger society, including the news media.

One of the more significant negative consequences of the racist stereotyping of Filipino Americans in Hawai'i is the tendency among some young people to feel "ashamed" of their ethnic identity and consequently often to disavow it. In a very representative narrative, a University of Hawai'i male student described his experiences as a local Filipino in high school (cited in Bumanglag 1996): "I was ashamed of being Filipino because most of the kids at school teased Filipinos about eating *bagoong*, *balut*, and black dog.[14] They also teased the immigrant Filipinos about their thick accent and the bright colored clothes they wore. They were considered the weirdest group in school. This is why I did not want to associate with the Filipino immigrants in school." The behaviors about which Filipino American students are harassed, such as eating dog and speaking with an accent, are the very same ones about which DeLima and other local comedians make jokes. During the course of my teaching at UH Manoa since 1989, students also have told me or written in their papers about feeling ashamed of their parents because they were immigrants. Certainly, not all Filipino Americans grow up being ashamed of their ethnic identity, but it is such a common experience among them that, even if they did not feel that way, they knew of others who did.

Feelings of shame about their ethnic identity result in the claims of some Filipino Americans to have Spanish ancestry as noted in Chapter 2, although they may not be able to trace descent to a specific Spanish ancestor. A local Filipino college student remarked about her experience in high school: "I was ashamed to be Filipino because of the negative things the other students said about the immigrants. When people asked what ethnicity I was, I would say that I am Spanish and Japanese" (cited in Bumanglag 1996). Disavowal of being Filipino also occurs through assertions of being "local" or Hawaiian (Revilla 1996: 9). Another Hawai'i-born Filipino college student wrote in a paper about why and how he dissociated himself from his ethnic identity (K. A. 2006):

> I am not necessarily ashamed of being Filipino, nor am I particularly proud of it. . . . In one of my [high school] classes I overheard the

> phrase "Filipino Pride." It struck me as peculiar; why would anyone be proud of that? . . . In high school I wanted to be black. After all, black people could sing better, dance better, and play basketball better than whites, Hawaiians and most certainly Filipinos. The nonsense continued into my first year of college. Before leaving [for the continental United States], I decided to give myself an exotic Hawaiian name to exaggerate my Hawai'i-ness. What better time to reinvent myself? From that point on, I decided to be Kaleo from Hawai'i, who was twenty-five percent Hawaiian.

This tendency to dissociate themselves from their ethnic identity among some young people, particularly local Filipinos, makes it that much more problematic for Filipino Americans to construct a collective identity when some group members are unwilling to claim it.

This unfortunate phenomenon of Filipino Americans disclaiming their ethnic identity was raised in an op-ed essay, "The Vanishing Filipinos," by *Honolulu-Star Bulletin* cartoonist Corky Trinidad (2005). His essay was published in December 2005 at the beginning of the yearlong celebration of the one-hundredth anniversary of Filipino immigration to Hawai'i. Trinidad asked:

> Where have all the Filipinos gone? The mystery of the vanished Filipinos bugged me for years . . . It turned out that Filipinos born in Hawaii, as soon as they reached the age of reason, and the Filipinos migrating from the Philippines, as soon as they left the airport, became Chinese-Spanish or . . . Chinese-American-Irish or some such combination. I have seen even friends change their names or the pronunciation of their names to make them sound more haole . . . they have added more blood to their lines, thinking it would make them a "better" class of Filipinos.

Included with his essay was a cartoon that Trinidad had drawn for a commemorative book published in 1981 for the 75th anniversary of Filipino immigration to Hawai'i that appears in a chapter on "Overcoming Stereotypes: Directions for Change" (Teodoro 1981: 57). In the cartoon, a young Filipino American woman is asked "Are you Filipino?" and responds, "Oh no. I'm Chinese-Spanish-Portuguese-Irish-Welsh-Mexican-Dutch-Scottish-Korean-Japanese-Hawaiian . . . but my parents are." In short, twenty-five years later, the same problem of disavowal of being Filipino American persists.

In seeking to understand this social problem of some young Filipino Americans being ashamed of or disclaiming their ethnic identity, there is a need to avoid blaming the victim, that is, the young people themselves. The explanation of this problem is found in the larger society of Hawai'i and how it has denigrated their identity to the extent that Filipino Americans wish to distance themselves from their own ethnic group and identity. As noted above, Filipino Americans are and have been represented in especially degrading ways in Hawai'i, so the blame for their feelings of shame ultimately lies with the racist stereotyping of them, not with the victims of that racism.

Attending college at UH Manoa appears to result in many Filipino American students losing their sense of shame and instead developing positive feelings of pride about their identity. Ironically, this is because there generally is a much lower proportion of Filipino American students at Manoa than at their high schools (where they might have been the largest group of students), which leads them to develop a stronger awareness of being Filipino and a desire to affiliate with other Filipino American students. A UH Manoa female student commented on the experiences she shared with other local Filipino students (Badua 2001):

> In high school many [students] shunned their Filipino heritage. Many did not learn or stopped talking their parents' native tongue, many made fun of the different types of foods and beliefs. Many local Filipinos ridiculed immigrant Filipinos. Many did not take part in any Filipino functions or events. But in college it is a completely different story. Local Filipino students embrace everything and anything Filipino. They are proud of being Filipino, taking as many courses they can that have anything to do with the Philippines like taking Ilokano or Tagalog languages, Filipino literature, history, and culture. They take part in student organizations like Timpuyog (Ilokano) and Katipunan (Tagalog).

This student's statement indicates the importance of providing Filipino American and other ethnic minority students the opportunity to learn about their cultures, histories, literatures, and languages in college, since such courses are generally not available in high school. However, most Filipino American high school graduates do not attend college, so some of them may not overcome their feelings of shame about being Filipino unless they have some other significant personal experience that can lead them to develop pride in their ethnic identity.

## *Local Literature: Back to the Plantation*

Lois-Ann Yamanaka has attained notoriety in Hawai'i for the ways that some of the characters in her books perpetuate historical racist stereotypes of Filipino men. One of these stereotypes is of Filipino males as sexual predators that resulted from their much larger number than Filipino women in Hawaiʻi. This demonic image is evident in the warning issued by a Japanese language newspaper, *Maui Shinbun*, to its readers during the Filipino strike in 1937 (cited in Jung 2006: 102, translated by the HSPA): "Filipinos in this strike are very peaceful and orderly. . . . But we can not tell what they may do. The best and safest thing is not to go near them, and have nothing to do with them. After sunset, every woman and girl should never go out of the house without a male guardian."

Yamanaka's collection of poems, *Saturday Night at the Pahala Theatre* (1993: 15–16), written in pidgin English, begins with a poem titled "Kala Gave Me Anykine Advice Especially About Filipinos When I Moved to Pahala." With its verbal warning from Kala about an elderly Filipino man who cuts off the vagina of girls with a cane knife, the poem resurrects the stereotype prevalent before World War II of sexually dangerous Filipino men in the plantation camps noted above. As a result of such word-of-mouth storytelling over the decades, the old Filipino man has been unable to rid himself of the demonized image of the young Filipino man of pre–World War II Hawaiʻi as given to sexual violence, including with a cane knife. Whether in literature or comedy, Filipino Americans seem unable to escape having a cane knife thrust into their hands long after almost all of the plantations have been shut down. The same poem also includes another warning from Kala about a young Filipino American, Felix, who Kala says has raped two of their classmates. Felix, along with other young Filipino American males, has inherited the historical stereotype of young Filipino plantation men as sexual predators, indicative of the great difficulty that Filipino Americans still face in unburdening themselves of the stigmatized stereotypes applied to them.[15]

Following the publication of *Saturday Night at the Pahala Theatre,* the Filipino American community expressed its strong objections of the book's denigrating representations of Filipino men in a community newspaper, *The Fil-Am Courier*. In an article titled "Killing Us Softly with These Words," Bennette Evangelista (1994) included the views of Filipino Americans who maintained that Yamanaka's book perpetuates racist stereotypes of Filipino men. This article is highly significant because it constitutes a very early protest by the Filipino American community about how they saw themselves being depicted in Yamanaka's work, well before the controversy over her later novel, *Blu's Hanging*. Focusing on the importance of asserting their objections, Evangelista (1994: 6) contended: "Inasmuch as artists or writers have a right to free expression, we too have a right to express our outrage and anger. . . . To keep silent means we agree." However, the response to these legitimate complaints of Filipino Americans, particularly from representatives of the politically powerful ethnic groups including Whites, Japanese Americans, and Chinese Americans, was further racism directed against them. English literature professor

Candace Fujikane (1997, 1998), who has written several insightful articles on Yamanaka's writings, has noted how Filipino Americans were told by academics and writers from the dominant ethnic groups that if they found Yamanaka's work to be racist, then they do not know how to read literature, which is clearly a racist statement (Fujikane 2000: 168).[16] As Fujikane observed: "The refocusing of the discussion not on the possibility of different readings of the poem but on the inability of local Filipinos to 'read' literature points to the ways that literary criticism continues to be used to divert attention away from substantive issues like racism in order to maintain existing relations of power." Insofar as racism is based on unequal power relations, including the power to represent others in demeaning ways, such inequality was very evident in the restricted access of Filipino Americans to the mainstream media in order to have their objections reach a larger audience. Instead, their concerns were disseminated in limited-circulation community newspapers such as the *Fil-Am Courier* and the *Hawai'i Herald*, a Japanese American paper.

Filipino American protests against their stigmatized portrayals in *Saturday Night at the Pahala Theatre* appeared to have no effect on Yamanaka because her later novel, *Blu's Hanging* (1997), generated even greater complaints from Filipino Americans, not only in Hawai'i but also across the nation. They were particularly outraged with the Filipino American character Uncle Paulo who is depicted as a sexual predator of his preteen-aged nieces and rapist of the eight-year-old Japanese American boy, Blu. In an especially troubling scene, after being asked by his sister to watch her four adolescent daughters while she goes to work, Uncle Paulo instead has sex with one of them, nine-year-old Blendie, as described by Blu (Yamanaka 1997: 173–174). Instead of being a singularly despicable character, anyone familiar with the historical and contemporary representations in Hawai'i of Filipino American men as sexually threatening can easily recognize them manifested in Uncle Paulo. In her comprehensive article on the *Blu's Hanging* controversy, Fujikane (2000: 176) addressed the common argument made in defense of the novel that, rather than reinforcing the above stereotype, *Blu's Hanging* contests it. She observed: "The novel does not challenge racist representations of Filipino male sexual violence; instead, Uncle Paulo's actions confirm them." Fujikane's analysis of the controversy extended to a discussion of institutional racism against Filipino Americans in Hawai'i that was manifested in their continued stereotyping in *Blu's Hanging* and in the criticisms of them because of their protests against how they were being represented in the book.

During the 1998 Association for Asian American Studies (AAAS) national conference in Honolulu, the AAAS fiction award to *Blu's Hanging* was rescinded by a vote of the assembled members. About a year later, an advertisement for *Honolulu Weekly,* featuring a photograph of Yamanaka, appeared in that free alternative newspaper (see Fujikane 2000: 184). With Yamanaka dressed in black and a hangman's noose hovering in front of her, the photo was captioned: "THINK FREE. SPEAK FREE. BE FREE. LOIS-ANN YAMANAKA, WRITER." I find this portrayal of Yamanaka as the victim of a lynching implicitly by Filipino American and other critics of her writings as especially ironic given the considerable number of Filipino men hanged by the state during the period prior to World War II. This was when they were demonized as violent and sexually dangerous criminals, historical stereotypes that Yamanaka revived with the Filipino American characters in her books. Furthermore, the photo implies that she is the target of attempts to censor her, not by the state that did execute Filipinos, but perhaps by the Filipino American community that obviously lacks that power. The real lynching victims in the controversy about Yamanaka's writings—that is, Filipino Americans—were portrayed as not intelligent enough to read her books and as foolish enough to try to censor an internationally acclaimed author. In this ongoing process of diversion and obfuscation, the institutional racism against Filipino Americans is allowed to continue.

## Constructing a Diasporic Identity

In his article, "Performing Identity: The Public Presentation of Culture and Ethnicity among Filipinos in Hawai'i," Labrador (2002) raises several important issues regarding Filipino American ethnic identity.[17] He analyzes a theatrical cultural production, *Pag-ibig sa Tinubuang Lupa* (Love for the Native Land) by Filipino American students at UH Manoa, which was performed to celebrate the centennial anniversary of Philippine independence from Spain in 1998. Some of the issues concerning Filipino American identity discussed by Labrador are the difference between "immigrant" and "local" Filipino identities, pride as opposed to shame in being Filipino American, the collective effort to construct a Filipino American identity, and the diasporic identity expressed by young Filipino Americans. Since these are arguably the most significant issues pertaining to Filipino American ethnic identity in Hawai'i, I discuss Labrador's article at some length and present some arguments of my own regarding these issues.

*Pag-ibig sa Tinubuang Lupa* was organized by Katipunan, an association of students studying Filipino, the national language of the Philippines, and Philippine literature at UH Manoa (Labrador 2002: 294). A majority of the association's members are first-, 1.5-, or second-generation Filipinos and thus are part of the post-1965 Filipino American community rather than being third- or fourth-generation descendants of the earlier plantation labor recruits. In its format and content of songs and drama, *Pag-ibig sa Tinubuang Lupa* is somewhat similar to the Pilipino Cultural Night (PCN) productions annually performed by Filipino American college students in the continental

United States. Gonzalves (1995: 134) contends that one of the principal elements of a PCN performance is a "narrative within the show as a vehicle for historicizing the Filipino American experience." However, perhaps because it celebrated a historical event in the Philippines, *Pag-ibig sa Tinubuang Lupa* was centered on Philippine rather than Filipino American history and did not even mention Filipino Americans in Hawai'i or the continental United States.[18] Thus, *Pag-ibig sa Tinubuang Lupa* expressed a Filipino rather than a Filipino American identity for its performers and to its audience that consisted largely of Filipino Americans.

Labrador (2002: 289) notes the important distinction in Hawai'i between local (Hawai'i-born) and immigrant (Philippine-born) Filipino ethnic identities that is a major reason why there is "no unified 'Filipino' identity." For local Filipinos, their identity expresses their belonging to the multiethnic Hawai'i society, while immigrant Filipinos claim a "nationalistic and diasporic notion of ethnic identity, one that represents and indexes membership in the Philippine nation-state and a 'Filipino' transnational community" (289). As Labrador explains: "The adjective—immigrant [or] Local . . . attached to 'Filipino' indexes specific identities and triggers a chain of cultural associations, its social manifestations a type of identity-play in different cultural fields" (289). Regarding these "cultural associations," a young Hawai'i-born Filipino American male reflected "On Growing Up Local Filipino" (Quidilla 1997: 10): "My parents hoped to instill a set of [Filipino] values, but I nevertheless grew up shaped by my friends, school and, of course, the media. Local Filipinos are faced with different and occasionally divergent cultural perspectives. . . . As a local-born Filipino, I have had to withstand the barrage of comments from people who make fun of the Filipino accent and insist that eating a dog is one bark away from cannibalism." This concern with being perceived and treated as an immigrant Filipino because of the pervasiveness of disparaging stereotypes of them results in the "identity-play" of Hawai'i-born Filipinos that emphasizes their local background, for example, by speaking pidgin English and disclaiming any knowledge of a Philippine language, although they probably grew up hearing their immigrant parents speak one at home.

The division between local and immigrant Filipinos began to emerge in the early 1970s shortly after post-1965 immigrants began arriving in significant numbers. Among young people, it was evident in frequent violent conflicts between representatives of these two groups of Filipino Americans (Okamura 1983). In school, when not teasing or otherwise harassing immigrant Filipinos, local Filipinos sought to avoid any social or cultural association with them. The same local Filipino quoted above recalled his experiences in high school, including feelings of shame about being Filipino (Quidilla 1997: 10):

> Ashamed, I resigned myself to believing that my continued acceptance was contingent on not displaying any of the weirdness and peculiarities of my culture. I didn't want people to think I had anything in common with those immigrant kids who were out of the mainstream and instead attended that foreign kid [English as a second language] class. They were "dogeaters," all right, displaced Third World types who spoke with that ridiculous accent.

Unfortunately, many Hawai'i-born Filipinos internalized the stigmatized stereotypes of Filipino immigrants and blamed them, instead of non-Filipinos, for their prevalence in society.[19] As a result, beyond the social and cultural manifestations of their distinct ethnic identities, local and immigrant Filipinos constitute somewhat distinct communities with Filipino immigrants much more likely to be involved as leaders and participants in institutions, organizations, and events (such as *Pag-ibig sa Tinubuang Lupa)* associated with the Filipino American community in Hawai'i. In contrast, local Filipinos may seek to avoid such involvement because of its association with Filipino immigrants and demeaning stereotypes of them.

As for ethnic identity formation, Labrador (2002: 297) contends that through *Pag-ibig sa Tinubuang Lupa*, the participating "students construct and perform their own definitions of themselves and, in turn, they can become what and who they (re)present." In contrast to the shame they have been made to feel, the students construct an ethnic identity for themselves that asserts their pride in being Filipino (299):

> The loud, passionate, and repeated declarations of "Ako ay Pilipino" and "Pilipino Ako" ("I am Filipino") during the performance are fervent proclamations of self which reclaim and affirm racial/ethnic and cultural pride. They announce that being Filipino is something to be proud of and not a source of shame. . . . For these students, to take pride in being Filipino means to recognize their marginal and minority status and to take steps in the direction of subverting the existing systems and structures of power. In this way, the cultural representation can be seen as a project that strategically essentializes "Filipino" as part of efforts to develop solidarity and political mobilization in order to challenge the prevailing social order and hierarchy.

It is significant that the students are viewed as seeking to "reclaim" and not only to "affirm" their pride in their ethnic identity because this pride was taken away from them through the historical denigrating stereotyping of Filipinos in Hawai'i. The simple and, for some, courageous act of claiming to be Filipino (rather than "Filipino-Spanish" or "Filipino-Hawaiian") is a necessary first step in individual and collective consciousness raising toward organizing and mobilizing Filipino Americans to contest their continuing subordination in Hawai'i. However, this larger structural context of unequal relations with more powerful and privileged ethnic groups is where the construction of Filipino American identity becomes problematic given their relative lack of political and economic power and thus their continuing vulnerability to being culturally defined and represented by others, including comedians, journalists, academics, and novelists.

Regarding diasporic identities, Labrador (2002: 298) cites my work on the global Filipino diaspora, particularly my argument that Filipinos in diaspora express diasporic identities through their transnational social, economic, and political relations with the Philippine homeland (Okamura 1998b). He productively adds to the overly structural emphasis in my notion of diasporic identity a cultural dimension that is evident in *Pag-ibig sa Tinubuang Lupa.* Labrador (2002: 298) contends that this cultural production demonstrates that "the stories that people tell also prove to be important resources for the constitution of diasporic identities" and that *Pag-ibig sa Tinubuang Lupa* serves as a site "where the articulation of historical events and struggles (which represent the Philippine nation-state) enables the construction of affiliations and sentiments of national belonging for dispersed Filipinos." The diasporic identity of young Filipino Americans thus asserts their attachment and belonging to the Philippines as their "homeland" rather than to the " 'Local' Hawai'i community" (299). Asian American studies scholar Yen Le Espiritu (2003: 214) has made remarkably similar observations of Filipinos in the continental United States:

> The practice of symbolic transnationalism is perhaps most poignant among U.S.-born Filipinos, many of whom look on the Philippines with "utopian longing"—in part out of their deep dissatisfaction with their marginalized place in the United States. . . . [G]iven their desire to be more "authentically" tied to the Filipino culture, many young Filipinos have internalized a cultural definition of "Filipinoness" that is tied to "homeland" traditions and represented by a fixed profile of shared traits such as language and folk songs.

A diasporic identity can be a significant source of cultural meaning for young Filipino Americans, especially immigrants, in an unequal Hawai'i that at times does not seem to welcome and appreciate their presence, except as lowly paid service workers in the tourist industry. As I have written elsewhere, rather than merely assimilating to U.S. society: "Filipino Americans can be viewed more significantly as subjects engaged in a larger process of constructing and articulating their distinct diasporic identity because of the racist subordination and exclusion they encounter in society" (Okamura 1998b: 10). However, insofar as a diasporic identity articulates an immigrant rather than a local identity for Filipino Americans in Hawai'i, it does have certain social costs in making them more vulnerable to denigrating stereotypes. While second-generation Filipino Americans, and not only immigrants, can assert a diasporic identity, most Filipinos born and raised in Hawai'i are more likely to claim a local identity that expresses their attachment to the islands and their peoples and cultures. For them, Hawai'i is their home where they have their strongest sense of affiliation and belonging.

Besides racist stereotyping, the contrasting local and diasporic (or immigrant) identities might seem to be another factor that contributes to the predicament the Filipino American community faces in constructing a common ethnic identity that can serve as a basis for their collective pursuit of economic and political advancement. However, the social, cultural, and political reality of Filipino Americans in Hawai'i is that local and diasporic identities are indicative of clear divisions and relatively distinct communities within their ethnic group. Nonetheless, Filipino Americans have demonstrated they can come together as a community to pursue shared goals, as in the election campaigns of Ben Cayetano for governor of Hawai'i in 1994 and 1998 and in the campaigns of other Filipino American candidates. Community organization and unity also were evident in the effort to establish the Filipino Community Center that opened in 2001 and has become a symbol of considerable community pride and achievement.

## Conclusion

This chapter has reviewed nearly a one-hundred-year period of misrepresenting Filipino Americans through racist stereotypes and other denigrating images applied to them. It is especially troubling how some of the earliest stereotypes that depicted Filipinos as highly emotional, prone to violence, and criminally inclined have persisted for most of the past century. Certainly, newer and seemingly more positive images have emerged during this period, such as their being a model minority, as the Filipino American community has changed its composition and status. At the same time, new sources of cultural representation have developed, such as ethnic humor and local literature, that have resurrected old stereotypes of Filipino Americans and created new ones.

Thus, I have demonstrated how Filipino Americans have been and continue to be under constant bombardment by racist representations of them from varied sources in Hawai'i, including the news media, academia, and popular culture. The cumulative result of these historical and contemporary processes is that the ethnic identity of Filipino Americans is being ascribed to them by non-Filipinos due to their power and desire to misrepresent others.

What it means to be Filipino American has been appropriated and given false meanings by non-Filipinos for their own political, economic, and social purposes without regard to their impact on Filipino Americans. These essentially lies being told or written about them and their culture and behaviors are so offensive that some Filipino Americans have been made to feel ashamed of who they are and do not wish to claim their own ethnic identity. Whether by local journalists, local writers, or local comedians, racist representations of Filipino Americans continue to limit their full and equal participation in society, particularly in employment and education. Insofar as stigmatized stereotypes both reflect and contribute to their oppressed social status, the Filipino American case demonstrates how ethnicity can be viewed as both cultural representation and structural principle.

The misrepresentation of Filipino Americans makes it that much more difficult for them to employ ethnic identity construction as a means to foster their collective economic and political interests because they first have to counter the denigrating stereotypes that dominate their public perception in Hawai'i. To be sure, there are other means, such as electoral politics, that Filipino Americans could resort to in order to advance themselves. However, achieving such political power has been a long historical process for them, although considerable gains were made at the state and county levels in the early 2000s. Ethnic identity formation can be used in conjunction with electoral politics; for example, mobilizing support for a Filipino American candidate for office among Filipino Americans by emphasizing their shared ethnic identity and common concerns. However, in Hawai'i, candidates must not appear too closely tied to their own ethnic community since a backlash against them might develop from other ethnic groups. Historically, another important means employed by Filipinos to foster their economic and political interests was labor organizing since most of them could not vote. In this case again, asserting a common ethnic or national identity played a significant role insofar as labor unions, such as the Filipino Labor Union, and strikes were organized by single ethnic/national groups until 1945 when all plantation workers were united in "one big union" by the International Longshoremen's and Warehousemen's Union.

Samoans are another politically and economically subjugated minority in Hawai'i that similarly is subject to racist stereotyping by the news media and ethnic humor. Thus, much like Filipino Americans, they have not been able to articulate their own view of their ethnic identity and use it to advance their economic and political concerns in society. However, other ethnic groups, such as Korean Americans, are subject to harsh stereotyping but have been able to construct a distinct ethnic identity for themselves, or at least their 1.5 generation. This may indicate the complexity of the problem for Filipino Americans in having substantially large immigrant and local segments with diverse ethnic identities of their own. The challenge for Filipino Americans is to create a common ethnic identity that both immigrant and local Filipinos can share and embrace. As in the Korean American case, this collective identity may emerge initially from a particular segment of the Filipino American community that is more concerned with the continuing impact of racism and discrimination against them, such as college-educated young people, rather than from the community at large.

# 8
# Conclusion

In spring 2007, as I finalized the manuscript of this book, three highly publicized ethnicity-related incidents occurred in Hawaiʻi, two of which were extremely violent. These ethnic altercations captured the attention of Hawaiʻi residents because their violent and abusive nature represented such a stark challenge to the prevalent view of cordial and tolerant relationships between individuals from different ethnic groups.

In February, a real-life Hawaiʻi version of the race-related car encounters depicted in the Academy Award–winning film *Crash* took place in the parking lot of a shopping center in Waikele in west Oʻahu. According to newspaper accounts of this incident (Boylan and Pang 2007: A1; Hench 2007: B4; Platte 2007: B3), an SUV (sport-utility vehicle) driven by a twenty-six-year-old White male Iraq war veteran accidentally struck a parked car while entering a parking stall. A sixteen-year-old male, described as "extremely angry" according to a police affidavit, exited the parked car and began kicking the doors of the SUV while yelling "fucking Haoles" at its occupants, who also included the soldier's twenty-three-year-old wife, also White, and their three-year-old child. As events unfolded, the young male was shortly joined by his forty-five-year-old father who had been in an ice cream shop when the accident occurred, the soldier and his wife left their SUV, and a violent encounter ensued among the four people. The police arrested the father and son for beating the soldier and his wife to the extent that they both lost consciousness, had their noses broken, and suffered concussions. Given his youth, the son's case was referred to Family Court, and he subsequently pled guilty to assault and was sentenced to a year in a juvenile detention facility. The father was charged with two counts of second-degree assault in the case, and in September 2007 he pled guilty to one count of second-degree assault and one count of third-degree assault. While he and his son were not identified as Native Hawaiian in newspaper and television news accounts of the incident, they do have a recognizable Hawaiian last name. The reporting of this information resulted in the perception by the public that they are Native Hawaiian, as evidenced by a comment to a reporter published by the press: "You know that Hawaiians like to settle disputes by fighting" (cited in Platte 2007: B3).

Another violent encounter involving a White victim occurred in April 2007 at a beach park in Nanakuli on the leeward coast of O'ahu (Park 2007). Christopher Reuther was a thirty-four-year-old photography editor from North Carolina who arrived in Honolulu on April 22 to visit the University of Hawai'i Law School, one of four law schools to which he had been accepted. Before the day was over, he was reportedly punched in the neck causing a severe brain hemorrhage that left him clinically dead two days later. After arriving in Honolulu, Reuther, who was said to have a zeal for the natural environment, drove a rental car to attend a lu'au and later went to the beach park to camp for the night. Shortly before midnight, he was taking photos, one of his other "passions" in life, when he had a fatal encounter with a twenty-one-year-old local male from Nanakuli, who reportedly became upset with Reuther's picture taking and delivered the lethal blow to his neck. His alleged assailant was charged with reckless manslaughter in his killing.

In yet another incident in May 2007, a popular radio talk show personality, Larry Price, was interviewing a state senator, Gary Hooser, on his morning program to discuss the work of the state Senate during the recently concluded legislative session (Au 2007: A6).[1] At one point during the interview, Price, who is Native Hawaiian, said to Hooser, who is White, "You keep using the word 'honest,' senator. Where you from?" After Hooser answered that he was from Kapa'a, Kaua'i, Price asked him, "Yeah, where were you were born and raised?" Hooser responded that he was born in California and graduated from one of the public high schools on O'ahu. Price then asked him, "You got blue eyes?" Hooser laughed and said he does, and replied, "Does that matter?" Price responded somewhat testily, "Yes, to us it does. Because when local people hear somebody from the mainland talk about how honest everything is, that means that something's wrong."

As apparent from his questions and comments to Hooser, Price was invoking the race-based original meaning of local that referred to non-White people born and raised in Hawai'i and that categorically excluded Haoles, even those born in the islands. His question about "blue eyes" was a racial reference intended to deny Hooser being considered local, despite his having lived well more than half of his life in Hawai'i. Price then went on to affirm the boundary between "local people" and those from the "mainland" and used the issue of honesty further to divide the two groups. While some letters sent to the Honolulu daily newspapers defended Price, most of them were highly critical of his comments and referred to them as "racial slurs." Some letter writers compared Price's statements to that of then recently fired radio talk show host Don Imus and his racist and sexist comment about the Rutgers University women's basketball team being "nappy-headed hos," and they called for Price to be fired by the radio station that employs him.

While those events were occurring in Hawai'i, Seung-Hui Cho engaged in his murderous rampage at Virginia Tech University, shooting to death thirty-two students and faculty on April 16, 2007. Since Cho was non-White, I was not surprised at all when a "public affairs editor" for one of the Honolulu daily newspapers responded in a commentary to media reports of Cho's mass killing by invoking the Hawai'i multicultural model (see Burris 2007: A31). He contended that "Hawai'i may have a little extra to teach the rest of the nation in dealing with this tragedy; a lesson it can teach because of our unique cultural and ethnic heritage." His point was not that such a horrific massacre could not happen in the islands but that, while news stories about Cho never failed to note that he was a "Korean immigrant," people from Hawai'i "know . . . that individuals speak for themselves and not as representatives of any larger cultural groups" (A31). Burris concluded: "Hawai'i is far from perfect. But we have learned as well as anyone to judge people and their successes and failures not on their ethnic background, but on their qualities as a human being and unique individual." In other words, while island residents "have an ability to stereotype" others based on their ethnicity (not that they actually do), we have learned to go beyond "superficial stereotypes," and this is a lesson we can "teach the rest of the nation" given our "unique" experience in managing cultural diversity. I sincerely doubt that the Haoles involved in the altercations described above, and very likely other Haoles who live in the islands, would agree that Hawai'i provides a model on how to get along with others of differing ethnicity.

The three incidents noted above may not seem to relate directly to the topic of this book, that is, ethnic inequality in Hawai'i, especially since they concern cases of extremely violent assault or verbal harassment in which the victims are all Haole. However, those encounters indicate deep and persisting fissures in ethnic relations and the widening gap between the dominant and subjugated ethnic groups in Hawai'i society. Rather than view the above altercations as isolated and random occurrences between individuals without regard to their ethnicity, at least the first two of them should be understood as constituting desperate expressions of protest against continuing conditions of institutionalized inequality directed to some of those considered responsible for maintaining that inequality.

As I argue in this book, the principal problem in ethnic relations in Hawai'i is persisting inequality. Unfortunately, it is not viewed as a major societal issue by the news media, most government, business, and community leaders, and perhaps a majority of Hawaii's people as is evident from the general indifference to the persistence of pronounced disparities in socioeconomic status among ethnic groups. Given this lack of concern, it seems as though ethnic inequality has come to be accepted as a general condition of social life in an unequal Hawai'i, and any disadvantages or inequities suffered by ethnic minority groups or individuals ultimately are their responsibility to overcome. Nonetheless, ethnic inequality demands the attention of Hawaii's people and race and ethnic relations scholars.

## Discussion of Findings

The previous chapters clearly establish the institutionalized nature of ethnic inequality in Hawai'i that contradicts the multicultural model view of the islands as a site of egalitarian, harmonious, and tolerant ethnic relations. To the contrary, ethnic relations in Hawai'i have been shown to be highly unequal, and ethnic stratification is very much a dominant feature of those relations. The life chances of Samoan, Native Hawaiian, and Filipino American youth differ substantially from those of their Japanese American, Chinese American, and White counterparts in terms of the quality and level of education they will attain, the kinds of jobs they will hold, and how much income and wealth they will receive during the course of their respective lives, which also will differ significantly in length and quality. Ethnic groups hold differential socioeconomic status in island society, and those relative positions have not changed much since the 1970s, indicative of how ethnic inequality, rather than equality of opportunity, is becoming further entrenched in Hawai'i.

In this section, I draw together the major findings and generalizations from the previous chapters toward an overall analysis of the maintenance of ethnic inequality in Hawai'i. This analysis is guided by the argument presented in Chapter 1 that ethnicity is situated at the intersection of ethnic identity and social structure where ethnic difference frames inequality. Chapters 3 and 4 analyze Hawaii's social structure in terms of socioeconomic and educational inequality among its ethnic groups, while Chapters 5 to 7 are concerned with ethnic identity construction, including the strategic use of ethnic identity to contest inequality. I also argue that ethnicity can be viewed as both structural principle and cultural representation; thus, Chapters 3 and 4 address primarily the structural dimension of ethnicity, and Chapters 5 to 7 focus on its cultural aspect.

Considering ethnicity as both cultural representation and structural principle provided a framework for analyzing the maintenance of ethnic inequality in Hawai'i. As a cultural representation, ethnic identity is both asserted by groups and assigned to them by other groups. In the latter case, stereotypes as assigned ethnic identities represent minorities with stigmatized images that can contribute to their subordinate status in society. As discussed in Chapter 7, Filipino Americans have found their ethnic identity overwhelmed by denigrating stereotypes ascribed to them through ethnic humor, the news media, and local literature such that constructing an identity that could be employed to contest their subservient position has been extremely difficult. In contrast, some groups, such as Native Hawaiians and Korean Americans, have used identity construction to represent themselves culturally as a collective means to advance their political and economic concerns and interests and thereby to challenge their subjugated status in society. Other more dominant groups, such as Japanese Americans, do not have to engage in ethnic identity formation to foster their collective interests because of their already established political power and financial resources. In addition, insofar as the Hawai'i multicultural model portrays ethnic relations as distinguished by their equality, harmony, and openness, it also needs to be recognized as a widely accepted cultural representation that contributes to the perpetuation of ethnic inequality. By obscuring the substantial power and status differences among ethnic groups and the racism and discrimination against subordinate groups, the model serves to sustain the ethnic hierarchy of Hawai'i.

As for ethnicity as a structural principle, Chapters 3 and 4 demonstrate how it regulates highly unequal access to occupational, income, and educational status among ethnic groups and thereby maintains the ethnic stratification order. Chapter 3 made evident that ethnicity is the dominant structural principle of the stratification system because the ethnic stratification order has not changed very much since 1970. Ethnic groups continue to hold the same relative positions, with the exception of Japanese Americans who joined Whites and Chinese Americans as one of the socioeconomically privileged groups by 1990. The socioeconomic status system was shown to be highly "racialized" insofar as ethnic groups are subject to differential racialization that results in the unequal distribution of education, income, and employment among them. Given that ethnicity is the primary organizing principle of the stratification order, ethnic difference frames or demarcates inequality in Hawai'i. Class is of secondary importance to ethnicity in regulating socioeconomic status allocation; otherwise, class difference would frame inequality, and classes, rather than ethnic groups, would comprise the significant constituent units of the stratification system. Nonetheless, as structural principles of status distribution in Hawai'i, ethnicity and class tend to reinforce more than counteract each other such that the ethnic hierarchy and class hierarchy of ranked groups tend to correspond with one another. Japanese Americans, Chinese Americans, and Whites dominate the middle and upper-middle classes, while Filipino Americans, Samoans, and Native Hawaiians comprise a substantial majority of the working class. While all of the ethnic groups, except for Samoans, are significantly represented in the middle class, more Filipino Americans and Native Hawaiians hold working-class rather than middle-class status. Except for Korean Americans and African Americans, smaller ethnic minorities, such as other Pacific Islanders, Vietnamese Americans, and Puerto Ricans, also are predominantly working class.

In Chapter 4, public education at both the K–12 and university levels is shown to constitute a site of institutionalized discrimination rather than equal opportunity and social mobility for ethnic minority groups. Discriminatory policies and practices include particularly the long-term underfunding of K–12 education by the state government that has far more detrimental consequences for minorities, such as Native Hawaiians, Filipino Americans, and Samoans, since they comprise a majority of public school students, than for the socioeconomically advantaged ethnic groups. In the University of Hawai'i system, what was already considerable minority underrepresentation has increased even more since the late 1990s due to huge tuition hikes and recruitment initiatives directed to students on the continental United States in order to compensate for declining state funding. Insofar as higher education provides the technical skills and qualifications, especially a college degree, necessary for gaining entry to the more financially rewarding and higher-status professional, managerial, and other white-collar employment, it serves to limit the occupational and income mobility of ethnic minorities, much to the benefit of the dominant ethnic groups.

As the dominant regulating principle of the social stratification order, ethnicity works to the considerable advantage of the privileged ethnic groups—that is, Chinese Americans, Japanese Americans, and Whites—in facilitating their greater access to socioeconomic rewards and benefits, including an affluent lifestyle, financially lucrative jobs, and college education for themselves and their children. At the same time, ethnicity as a structural principle unfairly restricts access and opportunities for the subordinate minorities—including Native Hawaiians, Samoans, Filipino Americans, and other immigrant minorities—and thereby maintains them in their subjugated position in low-paying service and other blue-collar jobs that preclude their socioeconomic mobility. But beyond the workings of ethnicity as an organizing principle of Hawai'i society, ethnic inequality persists because the social stratification system is controlled primarily by members of the dominant ethnic groups who occupy positions of power or influence through which they can establish policies or make decisions that foster the interests of their own ethnic groups to a greater extent than those of ethnic minorities or the larger society. Nonetheless, the social status order is relatively open in providing avenues for socioeconomic advancement for a limited number of individuals from ethnic minority groups; however, such opportunities are not widely available to the groups themselves, ensuring the continuation of ethnic inequality.

Chapter 5 discusses how ethnic identity formation can serve as a means for politically or economically disadvantaged groups to disrupt the intersection of ethnic identity and social structure and thereby advance their concerns and interests. This process is made most evident in the case of Native Hawaiians who have constructed a collective identity for themselves as the indigenous people of Hawai'i or *kanaka maoli* as a critical component of the sovereignty movement that began to emerge in the 1970s. This identity and status differentiate them from ethnic groups who are all historically immigrants to the islands; thus, Native Hawaiians maintain that they are not another aggrieved ethnic minority like Samoans or Filipino Americans. Given their ancestral origins in Hawai'i prior to Western contact, Native Hawaiians emphasize that they have native rights and entitlements that immigrant groups cannot assert, especially to self-determination, land, and other natural resources. By articulating their identity and status as an indigenous people with unique claims, Native Hawaiians are challenging the dominant view of Hawai'i as a multicultural society consisting of ethnic groups that all share equal rights and opportunities. Most significantly, they are contesting the highly unequal political and economic structure of Hawai'i society in which they are a subjugated and, some would say, colonized people in their own homeland.

Korean Americans, particularly the 1.5 generation, are discussed as an ethnic minority that seeks socioeconomic advancement by constructing an identity for themselves as well-educated, articulate, and community-oriented members of Hawai'i society. Although somewhat of a model minority image, this cultural representation of themselves is intended to challenge the prevalent stereotypes of Korean Americans as money-hungry, short-tempered, and sexually promiscuous (young women) immigrants and the relegation of a sizable proportion of them to service and sales work in the tourist industry. Compared to Filipino Americans, Korean Americans are another ethnic minority with a large segment of post-1965 immigrants employed as service workers and also subject to racist stereotypes, but they have had greater success in attaining socioeconomic mobility, especially through higher education. This difference in social status between Filipino Americans and Korean Americans can be partially accounted for by the much higher socioeconomic status attained by the descendants of Korean plantation laborers compared to that of the progeny of the Filipino plantation generation.

Another example of identity formation is provided by Okinawan Americans or *Uchinanchu*, who construct their distinct ethnic identity primarily to differentiate themselves as a community from Japanese Americans, although (and because) as individuals they can, and many do, claim to be Japanese

American. Given the porous group boundaries between Okinawan Americans and Japanese Americans, the Okinawan American community is especially concerned with boundary maintenance, that is, distinguishing itself structurally and culturally from Japanese Americans. In terms of the former, Okinawan American identity is asserted by having their own community center, community festival, and federated community organization to represent themselves and their concerns separately from Japanese Americans. Culturally, given the loss of their language, traditional religion, and other beliefs and practices, Okinawan Americans have focused on Okinawan classical and folk music and dance as the principal representation of "Okinawan culture" in Hawai'i. Many of them also express their cultural distinctiveness from Japanese Americans by expressing their ethnic identity as Uchinanchu, using a term from the language of their ancestral homeland rather than from Japanese or English.

The case of Filipino Americans underscores how ethnic identity intersects with social structure in ways that reinforce each other and maintain ethnic inequality in Hawai'i, particularly the subjugation of ethnic minorities. This intersection is quite similar to the notion of "causal feedback loops" involving "race-influenced processes of social cognition" and "race-constrained social interactions" that "perpetuate racial inequality" among African Americans as described by Loury (2002: 160). Denigrating stereotypes of Filipino Americans that greatly influence their cognition as culturally inept immigrants with limited English, educational, and employment skills and qualifications dominate their ethnic identity and thus constrain them in their subservient position in the social stratification order. At the same time, that subordinate status as lowly paid service and other blue-collar workers contributes to the tendency of local comedians, writers, journalists, academics, and the general public to perceive and stereotype them in especially demeaning ways. Consequently, Filipino Americans have encountered severe obstacles in employing ethnic identity construction as a strategic means to advance themselves socioeconomically and politically and to contest their unequal status in Hawai'i.

Samoans are another ethnic minority in Hawai'i for whom the intersection of ethnic identity and social structure supports each other and thereby their subjugation in society. They also are plagued with extremely degrading stereotypes that portray them as violent, uneducated, welfare-dependent, and criminally inclined. As assigned identities, these stereotypes contribute to their very low socioeconomic position by restricting their educational and employment opportunities. Like Filipino Americans, the oppressed status of Samoans, in turn, leads to the greater tendency for disparaging representations of them to be produced and disseminated by the news media, ethnic humor, and the general public. Their small population makes it that much more problematic for Samoans to challenge their subjugated status and racist stereotyping through ethnic identity formation.

In contrast to these disadvantaged ethnic minorities, the intersection of ethnic identity and social structure for Japanese Americans maintains them in their privileged social status. They have such dominant political and economic positions in Hawai'i that they need not concern themselves as a community with their ethnic identity as perceived by other groups, although individual Japanese Americans certainly may have such concerns. The same is generally the case for Whites and Chinese Americans, who together with Japanese Americans comprise the socioeconomically and politically advantaged groups in Hawai'i. Even though these ethnic groups are also subject to demeaning stereotypes like Filipino Americans and Samoans, their superior position is sufficiently established that such representations do not significantly affect their social status or ethnic identity. Japanese Americans, Whites, and Chinese Americans can literally laugh off jokes made about them by local comedians because they do not have serious detrimental consequences for them. Ethnic humor and other forms of stereotyping certainly do not limit their opportunities for socioeconomic advancement.

As discussed in Chapter 3, their greater wealth enables many Japanese American, Chinese American, and White families to provide private education from kindergarten for their children and thereby avoid the deficiencies, inferior quality, and other problems of the chronically underfunded public school system. Their children consequently have much greater access to a college education, either in Hawai'i or in the continental United States, compared to ethnic minority students that significantly increases their chances for well-paying professional, managerial, or other high-status occupations. Through the greater income, wealth, and other economic resources they control, Japanese American, White, and Chinese American families are able to reproduce themselves socioeconomically in the same or higher status through their children, thus maintaining ethnic inequality from one generation to the next. Besides their dominant social status, these ethnic groups also share the same affluent neighborhoods, expensive private schools for their children, interpersonal social networks, and intermarriage with one another, which also contribute to the perpetuation of their collective power and privilege in Hawai'i. In addition, Whites, Chinese Americans, and Japanese Americans share control of the major institutions of society, such as education, the economy, law, and government, and thereby are able to maintain ethnic inequality for their collective benefit and advantage. Unless these dominant groups are either willing or are somehow urged to provide greater opportunities to subordinate minorities, the highly unequal ethnic status quo in the islands is not likely to change much in the near future.

Unfortunately, the cumulative result of the cultural and structural processes reviewed above is that Hawai'i is increasingly becoming a society divided between, on the one hand, Whites, Japanese Americans, and Chinese

Americans and, on the other, Filipino Americans, Native Hawaiians, Samoans, and smaller ethnic minorities such as other Pacific Islanders, Southeast Asians, and Puerto Ricans. The prospects for collective socioeconomic mobility for disadvantaged ethnic minorities in the next twenty years are not very promising given the two principal factors (besides ethnicity as an organizing principle and cultural representation) that sustain ethnic inequality: (1) Hawaii's continued overdependence on tourism, and (2) a lack of commitment to eliminating institutional discrimination in education and employment (see below). In short, ethnic inequality will persist unless major changes occur in island ethnic relations that provide significant opportunities for ethnic minorities to advance and empower themselves.

## Fostering Ethnic Equality

In discussions of overcoming racial inequality in the United States, a recommendation often advanced is to develop "interethnic antiracist coalitions" as the organizational and ideological basis for attaining that goal (see Lipsitz 1998: 232). Historically in Hawai'i, such alliances among Chinese Americans, Filipino Americans, Native Hawaiians, Japanese Americans, and Portuguese Americans were successful in the "interracial working class" labor movement (Jung 2006) led by the International Longshoremen's and Warehousemen's Union in the late 1930s and 1940s, and in the rise to power of the Democratic Party in the 1950s. In addition to these economic and political movements that created new opportunities for advancement for the working class, Hawai'i experienced an economic boom during the 1960s following statehood. Tourism replaced sugar as the major industry, and the economy underwent an overall expansion and diversification as many more and new types of jobs were created, especially in retail trade and services related to tourism (Lind 1980: 79). Besides tourism, increased military spending during the Vietnam War was another major factor in the robust economy of the 1960s.

Of the three largest groups that were part of the multiracial working class of the 1950s, that is, Japanese Americans, Native Hawaiians, and Filipino Americans, the former were able to take advantage of the new economic opportunities and advance themselves into the middle class to a much greater extent than did the other two groups. Japanese American social mobility was facilitated by the several thousand *nisei* (second generation) World War II veterans who were able to attend college through the GI Bill. They and other nisei subsequently gained access to professional, managerial, and other white-collar employment as positions in those fields became increasingly available, although many other nisei men continued to hold blue-collar jobs, particularly as skilled craft workers. In the 1970s and 1980s, many *sansei* (third generation) baby boomers went to college, even though in most cases their parents had not, and obtained professional and technical work. The sansei continued the progressive upward mobility of Japanese Americans into the highest levels of the socioeconomic status order where they joined Whites and Chinese Americans. The latter group already had entered the middle class by World War II and continued their socioeconomic ascent in the subsequent decades, eventually surpassing Haoles in median income and educational attainment.

Japanese American economic mobility was fostered by their growing political power since the 1950s as they emerged as a plurality of territorial and state legislators already by that decade. By the 1970s, Japanese Americans would be elected to the major political offices, including governor, lieutenant governor, U.S. senator, U.S. representative, and county mayor, all as Democrats, the dominant political party in Hawai'i since the 1950s. Democratic governors appointed Japanese Americans as the largest group of directors of state government departments. Especially as legislators, Japanese Americans were in a position to enact laws and appropriate funds that could promote social equality, social justice, and economic reform, as they had done previously during the 1950s and 1960s. However, in the 1970s and 1980s Japanese American state legislators, and the Democratic Party in general, became much more centrist in political orientation, as observed by Kotani (1985: 162):

> By the eighties, mainstream AJA [Americans of Japanese Ancestry] Democrats enthusiastically supported corporate tax breaks, an increase in the excise tax rate, and changes in the progressive workers' compensation law. Where rebellious Nisei Democrats of the fifties had insisted on greater funding for social services and public education, established Nisei politicians now readily accepted cutbacks in government welfare programs and stagnation in the budget for Hawaii's public schools and university system.

This change in political and social values significantly restricted access to employment and education among Native Hawaiians and Filipino Americans. Furthermore, Kotani (1985: 161–162) contended that the Democratic Party itself, and not just its Japanese American leaders, "seemed to have replaced the Republican Party as the 'Establishment' in the Islands," and thus "the drive for social reform faltered." The so-called "Democratic Revolution" was over by the late 1970s.

As a result, Filipino Americans and Native Hawaiians were left behind as Japanese Americans moved up the social status hierarchy. While certainly many families in both groups have attained middle-class status, most Native Hawaiian and Filipino American families continue to belong to the working class. In the case of Filipino Americans, the relatively small number of women who immigrated to Hawai'i during their period of plantation labor recruitment that ended in 1946 substantially limited the size of their second generation that otherwise would have led their social mobility in the postwar period. After the 1965 Immigration Act was passed, many families were joined by their relatives from the Philippines who also went to work on the plantations or obtained similarly low-paying jobs in the tourist industry. As the plantations began to close in the 1970s, and tourism expanded its dominance in the economy, increasing numbers of Filipino immigrants gained employment as service workers in tourism where they remain as the largest group of employees. However, given its primarily low-mobility service and sales jobs, tourism does not provide viable avenues for Filipino American socioeconomic advancement. As discussed above, other factors that have precluded Filipino Americans from becoming "the next group to make it" in Hawai'i include the public education system not serving as a means for their upward mobility due to discriminatory policies and practices that have kept them very much underrepresented in the UH system and as college graduates in general.

Native Hawaiians have been particularly disadvantaged by the state of Hawai'i not fulfilling its trust obligations to them according to the Admission Act by which Hawai'i became a state in 1959. According to the act, the state is legally obligated to use the proceeds from the ceded lands trust established at that time for five purposes, one of which is "the betterment of the condition of Native Hawaiians." When the Office of Hawaiian Affairs (OHA) was created in 1978, 20 percent of the annual revenues from the ceded lands trust was to be used to fund its programs and services, but the state has resisted coming to an agreement with OHA on how much the agency is owed and on which revenues it is entitled to. Like Filipino Americans, Native Hawaiians have not found the University of Hawai'i system to provide them with a means for their upward mobility, and they are even more underrepresented. As a group also substantially employed in tourism, Hawaii's overdependence on that industry has limited Native Hawaiian employment in other more financially rewarding fields. As noted above, Native Hawaiians attribute their relative lack of socioeconomic advancement to discrimination in employment by Japanese Americans as they gained in political and economic power in the two decades following statehood.

Consequently, half a century later, significant class differences prevail among the groups that constituted the multiracial working class of the 1950s, although they are not necessarily a barrier in establishing interethnic coalitions among at least some of those groups, such as in electoral politics. Thus, one could somewhat facilely suggest that eliminating ethnic inequality in Hawai'i can be achieved through an interethnic and intersectoral alliance among ethnic groups, labor unions, the Democratic Party, and certain community-based advocacy organizations. However, advocating coalition building as a means to foster ethnic equality still leaves unanswered the important question of exactly how such partnerships are to be developed and maintained. As Lipsitz (1998: 232) has observed, "Aggrieved groups will not magically unite simply because they are separately oppressed." The aforementioned ethnic groups and organizations have differing and sometimes opposed political and economic concerns and appear willing to set aside those differences only when it serves their particular interests, such as during elections every two years. Thus, while I can appreciate the larger political and economic significance of interethnic coalitions, I also understand the difficulty in creating and sustaining them toward resolving a long-term entrenched problem such as ethnic inequality.

The "Discussion of Findings" section indicates that the likelihood of establishing ethnic equality in Hawai'i in the near future does not appear very promising. Instead, ethnic inequality based on socioeconomic status is very much institutionalized as a fundamental condition of island society and has been for decades. While ethnic equality has not (and arguably has never) been attained, considerable social mobility has occurred among some ethnic groups that started life in Hawai'i at the very bottom as plantation laborers, such as Japanese Americans, Chinese Americans, and Korean Americans. How, then, can at least socioeconomic mobility be provided for other ethnic groups that have not achieved the same middle-class status of the aforementioned groups? An obvious first step would be to eliminate or at least mitigate the cultural and structural barriers against ethnic minority advancement.

As noted above, the most salient cultural barrier that restricts ethnic minorities are denigrating stereotypes and other representations about them produced and disseminated by local comedians, the news media, and the general populace. Ethnic humor needs to be recognized as a racist practice that has no place in a multiethnic society that supposedly places great value on tolerance, respect, and the aloha spirit. While it is not very likely that local comics and disc jockeys will stop making racist jokes about Hawaii's ethnic groups and their cultures and behaviors, the general public need not repeat such jokes to their friends, fellow employees, and schoolmates. Such word-of-mouth transmission is a major means by which the demeaning stereotypes at the base of local humor infect island society. The print and broadcast news media need to produce more feature stories and information in general on the accomplishments and contributions of ethnic minority group members to counter the prevalence of degrading representations about them. Another significant cultural obstacle against ethnic minorities is the widespread belief in the tenets of the Hawai'i multicultural model that represent ethnic relations as unproblematic, if not exemplary. Rather than continuing to promulgate its false premises of equality of opportunity and aloha for all, more of Hawaii's people, especially academics, need to underscore the deficiencies and fallacies of the model in explaining the scope and nature of ethnic relations in the islands.

I have noted above the limited avenues for socioeconomic advancement for ethnic minorities because of Hawaii's economy being dominated by the tourist industry. Thus, as a necessary condition, upward social mobility requires an economy with a labor market that can foster income growth and occupational advancement. However, the local economy continues to be mired in tourism with its low-wage, low-security, and low-mobility jobs that do not comprise viable means for ethnic minority groups to advance socioeconomically. The obvious need to diversify the economy by creating jobs other than primarily in service and sales work and by making it less based on tourism has long been recognized; however, state government support for such initiatives has not been sufficient and sustained to result in substantial changes in the economy. A major reason for the relative lack of such support is the state government's reliance on the fundamentally unreliable tourist industry for tax revenues with which to appropriate funds for developing economic alternatives to tourism. A first step toward such economic diversification would be the development of knowledge-intensive industries instead of the labor-intensive tourist industry. As one of the most underused economic resources in the state, the University of Hawaiʻi can be provided with greater government funding to develop such industries or to train more professional workers critically needed in the islands. These workers who directly serve Hawaii's people include teachers and nurses who already are faced with significant shortages in their ranks that will only expand with the ongoing retirement of baby boomers among them.

Besides diversification of the economy, another necessary condition for fostering socioeconomic mobility for Hawaii's ethnic minorities is reducing, if not eliminating, institutional discrimination as another major structural barrier. In *The Anatomy of Racial Inequality*, Loury (2002: 93) contends that racial stigma should replace racial discrimination from "its current prominent place" in the discourse on racial inequality in American society. He maintains that "[d]iscrimination is about how people are treated; stigma is about who, at the deepest cognitive level, they are understood to be" (167); therefore, these two concepts lead to "radically distinct intellectual and political programs" to address the problem of racial inequality. According to Loury (168), a focus on discrimination results in a "search for harmful or malicious actions . . . using the law and moral suasion to curtail or modify those actions," while a concern with stigma leads one to seek for "insidious habits of thought, selective patterns of social intercourse, biased processes of social cognition, and defective public deliberations" when endeavoring to diminish racial inequality. While one can fully agree with Loury (168) that "deeper and more far-reaching structural reform" is required than the typical legal action and moral arguments against racial discrimination, his greater emphasis on racial stigma yields to a focus on "the ways in which race-mediated social meanings are constructed." While there are laws in place that prohibit racial discrimination through "harmful or malicious actions," it is far more difficult, at least for the moment, to sanction or eliminate "insidious habits of thought," "biased processes of social cognition," and "defective public deliberations," however racist they may be, because they may not be illegal. A primary focus on eliminating racial discrimination, rather than racial stigma, seems to be a more direct and productive course of political action toward alleviating racial inequality in society.

In a formally democratic society such as Hawai'i, it should be the responsibility of those ethnic groups that wield political and economic power to initiate actions that would lessen the pernicious effects of discrimination and racism. Those groups should take the lead in revising, or prohibiting if necessary, policies and practices that continue to disadvantage ethnic minorities in obtaining equal access to employment, education, and other social services and benefits. While some practices and policies may not legally discriminate against ethnic minorities, nonetheless, if they result in unequal treatment of them, then they should be changed or replaced in order to reduce their unfair consequences. A notable example of such a practice is the long-term underfunding of the Department of Education that has had equally long-term detrimental outcomes for ethnic minorities, as evidenced by their persisting subjugated status in Hawai'i. Clearly, substantially increased public funds need to be appropriated to the public schools, rather than the private tourist industry, so that they can provide at least an "adequate" education to their majority clientele of ethnic minority students. While, admittedly, such funding is only possible if the state legislature has sufficient resources, public education needs to be given greater policy priority by state government leaders and legislators so that ethnic minority students are at least provided with equal educational opportunity. One means that the general public, including members of ethnic minorities, can take to foster greater funding of the public school system is to support candidates for the state legislature and Board of Education who advocate that position.

It might be argued that discrimination by race or ethnicity already is formally banned by federal and state civil rights laws; however, such prohibition is effective only if the laws are enforced. The same can be said of affirmative action and equal employment opportunity policies of the state of Hawai'i that are meaningful only if they are being actively implemented. Can it legitimately be contended that the highly unequal distribution of occupational, income, and educational status among ethnic groups in Hawai'i is the cumulative result of several decades of policies, programs, and laws that ensure equal employment and educational opportunity, nondiscrimination, and affirmative action?

In this section, I focus on tourism and discrimination as key economic and political arenas that require major changes in order to foster ethnic equality in Hawai'i. At first glance, tourism and institutional discrimination may not appear comparable at all; the former is an economic activity, while the latter is a social practice, albeit with economic consequences. However, tourism and discrimination are very much interrelated and interdependent in Hawai'i insofar as the tourist industry directly benefits from the various forms of institutional discrimination against ethnic minorities (and women) that channel a steady supply of workers to its hotels, restaurants, shops, and golf courses, especially Asian and Pacific Islander immigrants. If more Filipino Americans, Native Hawaiians, Samoans, and other Pacific Islanders could earn college degrees that would enable them to compete for professional and other white-collar occupations, the tourist industry might find itself with a labor shortage or would have to pay higher wages to keep its workers.

Admittedly, both diversifying the economy away from tourism and reducing institutional discrimination are much easier to advocate than to accomplish. Since tourism and institutional discrimination are such fundamental features of Hawai'i society, substantive changes in both areas will require a lengthy period of time, at least a generation, to be achieved. In addition, both arenas are highly resistant to change since they are allowed to continue by government and business leaders as well as by the average Hawai'i resident, albeit more in the case of tourism than discrimination. They both are also difficult to reduce because any significant positive changes—that is, developing alternative industries to tourism or ensuring fair and equal treatment—will result in a redistribution of economic and political power and resources between the dominant and subordinate ethnic groups, especially in the case of institutional discrimination. Nonetheless, the effort to advance ethnic equality, or at least socioeconomic mobility, must be made in order to ensure the continuity of the quality of social and cultural life valued by Hawaii's people, rather than to descend into the race-based conflict and hostility that are starkly evident among racial groups in the continental United States.

As I noted in the introduction, more than forty years ago in his highly regarded social history, *Hawaii Pono*, Lawrence Fuchs (1961: 449) lauded Hawai'i for exemplifying the "nation's revolutionary message of equality of opportunity for all, regardless of background, color, or religion." He described this as "the promise of Hawaii . . . that peoples of different races and creeds can live together . . . in harmony and democracy." Hawai'i needs to realize that promise of equal opportunity for its own people, not just to individuals but much more importantly to its constituent indigenous and ethnic groups. Far too many of Hawaii's people have been and continue to be denied equality of opportunity, let alone equality of result, because of their ethnicity. The promise of Hawai'i should be that ethnic and racial inequality will no longer be tolerated. Unfortunately, in the larger national context of expanding racialization of American life, neoconservative racial politics, and anti-affirmative action and anti-immigrant sentiments and actions, that promise still represents a revolutionary message for the nation.

# Notes

**CHAPTER 1**

1. A revised version of my testimony was subsequently published in the *Honolulu Advertiser* as a commentary on May 25, 2005 on p. A16.

2. This lack of questioning can be contrasted with the lengthy grilling by several Regents of then interim UH Manoa chancellor Denise Konan when she discussed her decision against establishing a University Affiliated Research Center (UARC) at Manoa at a Board of Regents hearing on January 20, 2006. In November 2004, the board had given its approval for proceeding with negotiations toward signing a contract with the U.S. Navy for a UARC.

3. I thank Michael Omi for drawing my attention to the applicability of Oliver and Shapiro's arguments to the case of ethnic inequality in Hawai'i.

4. The exceptions to this generalization would be ethnic groups with significant post-1965 immigrant segments, such as Filipino Americans and Korean Americans.

5. African Americans may be considered an exception to this generalization.

6. My article, "The Illusion of Paradise: Privileging Multiculturalism in Hawai'i," was written in 1996; in this section, therefore, I discuss publications on multiculturalism that have been published since then.

7. Another example by journalists of the representation of Hawai'i as a model of multiculturalism is evident in the welcome message on the Web site for the18th Annual National Convention of the Asian American Journalists Association held in Honolulu in June 2006 (Asian American Journalists Association 2006): "Welcome to a place where diversity works, where Asian American and Pacific Islander men as well as women anchor the news on television . . . Hawai'i is the most ethnically diverse

state in the nation . . . Diversity is as much a part of Hawai'i as surfing, hula, poi and rice. Our food, culture and traditions blend East, West and Polynesia like no other place in the world."

8. Hall (2000: 210) has noted six different types of multiculturalism in the literature: conservative, liberal, pluralist, commercial, corporate, and critical. Perhaps questioning the usefulness of distinguishing those and other multiculturalisms, he ends his brief discussion of them with "And so on."

9. The late Glen Grant taught an American studies course called "Multiculturalism: Is Hawai'i the Answer?" in the early 2000s at UH Manoa.

10. Besides ethno-racial bloc, another term in *Postethnic America* that Hollinger introduced in place of race and ethnic group is "communities of descent." This term is even less satisfactory than ethno-racial bloc since, as historian Henry Yu (2003) has noted for Asian Americans, "There is no evidence . . . that at any time historically people have considered themselves 'Asian American' because of a pan-Asian sense of shared descent."

11. Similarly, Melissa Nobles (2005: 82) contends that the "myth of Latin American multiracialism," like the myth of Latin American "racial democracy, functions as an ideology" that obscures persisting racial injustice and thus hinders economic, political, and social change.

12. Even in Asian American studies, major works on race relations have not included Hawai'i in their discussion, for example, *The State of Asian Pacific America: Transforming Race Relations* (Ong 2000); *Race, Rights, and the Asian American Experience* (Ancheta 2003); and *Yellow: Race in America beyond Black and White* (Wu 2002). Nakano Glenn's *Unequal Freedom, How Race and Gender Shaped American Citizenship and Labor* (2002), which has a chapter on "Japanese and Haoles in Hawaii," is a notable exception, although it is a historical work.

## CHAPTER 2

1. The U.S. census data in this section are from "Race and Hispanic Origin, by Counties: 2000," table 1.32, from the online version of *The State of Hawaii Data Book 2002* (Hawai'i Department of Business and Economic Development and Tourism 2003b), http://www.hawaii.gov/dbedt/.

2. In computing the percentage of the state population represented by an ethnic group, I used the figure for a group "alone or in combination with one or more other races." This procedure means that the total percentage for all ethnic groups exceeds 100 percent because the figure for a group alone or in combination is based on responses rather than individuals. For example, a person who reported being White and Native Hawaiian for his or her race provided two responses. The total number of responses was about 1.57 million for Hawai'i in the 2000 census.

3. The University of Hawai'i still uses "Other Caucasian" as an ethnic category for student enrollment. Together with Portuguese Americans and "Middle Easterners," they comprise the larger "Caucasian" ethnic group.

4. *Uchinanchu* is the term in *Hoogen* (the language spoken by the people of Okinawa) for Okinawans living abroad, including in the United States, Peru, Argentina, and Brazil where their largest overseas community is located.

5. This figure is from the Hawai'i Health Surveillance Program sample survey of Hawai'i residents conducted by the state Department of Health in 1992. It may very well

be an overestimation since in 1930 Romanzo Adams estimated the "pure" Native Hawaiian population at 12,856 (Lind 1980: 28).

6. The lasting contribution of those Spanish labor recruits is the Hawaiian word *paniolo* (from *Español*) for cowboy, since Spaniards were among the first cowboys in Hawai'i.

7. Those unions, particularly of couples from the American continent and Japan, represented about 40 percent of the marriages registered in Hawai'i during the study period.

8. The percentages are from "Profile of Selected Social Characteristics: 2000," table DP-2, from Summary File 4 of the 2000 census for Hawai'i, http://factfinder.census.gov/servlet/QTTable? and http://factfinder.census.gov/servlet/Dataset/MainsetPageServl.

**CHAPTER 3**

1. The four racial groups are African American, Asian American, Native American and Alaska Native, and White. Unlike most social scientists, the U.S. Census Bureau considers Latinos to be an ethnic group whose members belong to different races. For the 2000 census, the bureau also created a new racial category of Native Hawaiian and Other Pacific Islander.

2. The data in this section on occupational status are from "Sex by Occupation for the Employed Civilian Population 16 Years and Over," table PCT86, Summary File 4 of the 2000 U.S. Census, http://factfinder.census.gov/servlet/DatasetMainPageServlet?.

3. Evidence that this might be the case is the far greater number of employed Chinese Americans (72,300) in the 2000 census compared to the 1990 census (36,300), although the higher figure also could be due to persons of White and Chinese descent or of Japanese and Chinese descent indicating such in the 2000 census. At any rate, the doubling of the working population of Chinese Americans cannot be accounted for by demographic processes.

4. The data in this section on family and individual income are from "Median Family Income in 1999 (Dollars)," table PCT113, http://factfinder.census.gov/servlet/DatasetMainPageServlet? and "Median Income in 1999 (Dollars) by Sex by Work Experience in 1999 for the Population 15 Years and Over with Income," table PCT133, http://factfinder.census.gov/servlet/DatasetMainPageServlet?. Both tables are from Summary File 4 of the 2000 U.S. census.

I fully agree with Oliver and Shapiro (2006) that wealth, as opposed to income, is a much more significant indicator of socioeconomic inequality, especially among racial and ethnic groups. However, lack of sufficient data on wealth accumulation in Hawai'i, except for home ownership, resulted in my use of income data.

5. The lower income status of Chinese American women also could be due to the inclusion of Native Hawaiian women who also claimed to be Chinese.

6. In 2004, the median annual wage of $29,300 in Hawai'i was slightly above the national median of $28,800 (Schaefers 2005: A6).

7. I follow Omi and Winant's definition of racialization as "the extension of racial meaning to a previously racially unclassified relationship, social practice or group" (1986: 64).

8. I am not claiming that Chinese Americans, Whites, and Japanese Americans who occupy positions of power always make decisions that benefit members of their own ethnic group, only that they sometimes do. Certainly, they have more opportunities to make those decisions compared to members of the subordinate ethnic minorities.

9. A study on "Quality of Life in Hawai'i" by the University of Hawai'i Center on the Family (2005) reported findings that indirectly support my argument of a widening socioeconomic gap between the privileged and disadvantaged ethnic groups since the 1970s. Citing a report, *Pulling Apart: A State-by-State Analysis of Income Trends* (Bernstein et al. 2002), the study stated that in the late 1990s, the average income of the poorest 20 percent of Hawai'i families was $16,540, while the average income of the richest 20 percent was almost ten times greater at $159,420. Furthermore, between the late 1970s and the late 1990s, the inflation-adjusted change in earnings of the poorest 20 percent of island families was only $620 or a 3.9 percent increase, while the comparable income change for the richest 20 percent was $47,630 or nearly a 43 percent gain. During the same time period, the average income of the middle 20 percent of Hawai'i families increased by just $6,970 to $58,020. Bernstein et al. (2002) contended that "Since the late 1970s, income inequality has increased in Hawaii. The economic growth of the 1980s and the 1990s was not shared evenly among the poor, the rich, and the middle class."

10. While I stated earlier that African Americans and Korean Americans hold an intermediate position in the ethnic stratification order, both groups have relatively small populations.

11. The data in this section are from the online version of the *State of Hawai'i Data Book 2004*, http://www.hawaii.gov/dbedt/info/economic/databook/db2004/. The data, particularly from tables 7.03, 7.23, 7.29, 12.10, and 13.05, pertain primarily to 2004 when Hawaii's economic recovery already had begun.

12. The second-largest contributor to the gross state product is military spending at $3.2 billion.

13. While the slumping economy was viewed as a societal problem that required the appointment of a special government task force to propose possible solutions, ethnic inequality in Hawai'i is not similarly seen as serious or problematic enough to necessitate government intervention for its alleviation.

14. One of the public high schools—that, not coincidentally, has a substantial majority of Filipino American and Samoan students—has an "Academy of Hospitality and Tourism" for channeling high school graduates into dead-end tourism jobs instead of college.

15. In a typical evaluation, in 2000 the Corporation for Enterprise Development, a nonprofit organization based in Washington, DC, gave the state economy grades of an F and two Ds in its annual nationwide survey, "Development Report Card for the States," which evaluates a state's potential for economic growth (Ruel 2005 A1). Hawai'i received an F in "business vitality" and was awarded Ds for development capacity and for economic performance.

## CHAPTER 4

1. Like Hawaii's population, many, if not most, of those students are of multiracial or multiethnic descent.

2. As a result of the Reinventing Education Act passed in 2004, beginning in the 2006–2007 school year, a school's budget is to be determined by a "weighted student formula" that allocates funds based on the characteristics of its students rather than on their total number (Essoyan 2005: A3). More funds will go to schools that have students who cost more to educate, such as English for second language learners and those who are

socioeconomically disadvantaged. The act also provides for school principals to have control over at least 70 percent of their school's budget.

3. For 2004–2007, the No Child Left Behind Act requires that 28 percent of Hawai'i public school students be proficient in mathematics and 44 percent in reading.

4. Another study by the National Center for Policy Analysis found that Honolulu's average annual public schoolteacher salary ($45,467) in 2003–2004 was the lowest in fifty U.S. metropolitan areas when adjusted for the high cost of living and probably would remain in that position despite pay raises in 2005 and 2006 (Martin 2005c: A1). Honolulu's average teacher salary actually ranked twenty-sixth in the nation, but the state's high cost of living reduced that figure to $27,048 using a cost-of-living formula that factors in the local cost of housing, groceries, and other expenditures.

5. In 2004 the state legislature appropriated $100 million for repair and maintenance work in the public schools, although not necessarily for high-priority projects requested by the DOE.

6. While the new budgeting process under the Reinventing Education Act appears to provide for more equitable treatment of ethnic minority students at the school level, it remains to be seen if that will actually be the case.

7. For other social issues, the survey respondents were less willing to contribute more in tax payments. When asked if they would pay more in taxes if they believed the state "government has developed a good solution" to address Native Hawaiian concerns, only 10 percent expressed their willingness to pay significantly more, while a majority (52 percent) stated they were unwilling to pay any more, and another third (34 percent) indicated they would pay a little more.

8. In 2004 the State Ethics Commission found the Office of the Governor had violated state ethics provisions because it had provided state funds and the time of state employees to work for the CARE organization.

9. After more than two weeks of repeated requests from the *Honolulu Star-Bulletin* to make the poll data public, the Lingle administration finally agreed, one day after being informed by the newspaper that it was writing an article about the governor's efforts not to release the survey results (Perez 2004: A1).

10. Other problems mentioned by respondents included overcrowded classrooms (4 percent), discipline problems (4 percent), lack of academic standards (4 percent), and lack of parental involvement (3 percent). A catchall category of "other" for responses that did not fit into eighteen general areas was assigned 25 percent of the answers (Perez 2004: A11).

11. Other issues that received a significant percentage of responses included "eliminating drugs, violence and weapons from schools" (14 percent), "reducing the bureaucracy" (12 percent), "restoring discipline in the classroom" (10 percent), and "reducing class size" (10 percent).

12. In her January 2006 State of the State address, the governor proposed using $300 million of the surplus funds for "tax relief" for Hawai'i residents, no doubt thinking ahead of its benefits for her reelection campaign later in the year.

13. There are several small private universities in Hawai'i that charge much higher tuition than the UH institutions and that do not offer the full range of degree programs available at UH Manoa, especially at the graduate level. These private institutions include Hawaii Pacific University (8,000 students), Chaminade University (1,100), and Brigham Young University at Hawaii (2,400). I focus my discussion on the University of Hawai'i because it is a publicly supported institution and has a much greater enrollment.

14. In its student enrollment reports, the Institutional Research Office of the University of Hawai'i has an ethnic category of "Caucasian" that includes separate subcategories for "Middle Easterner," "Portuguese," and "Other Caucasian." The latter is a term used historically in Hawai'i for Whites; thus, I cite the figures for Other Caucasian when referring to Whites.

15. The University of Hawai'i Board of Regents has a very similar "Policy on "Nondiscrimination and Affirmative Action" for the UH system.

16. Only 10 percent of UH Manoa students in the study graduated within the "traditional" four-year period. Reasons for this low average include part-time work, changing majors, and unavailability of courses.

17. The 1990 U.S. census reported findings somewhat similar to 2000 for bachelor's degree or higher educational attainment among persons twenty-five years and older in Hawai'i: White (31 percent), Chinese American (30 percent), Japanese American (25 percent), Korean American (19 percent), African American (15 percent), Filipino American (12 percent), Native Hawaiian (9 percent), and Samoan (5 percent) (U.S. Bureau of the Census 1993). The median figure for Hawai'i was 23 percent. Thus, Japanese Americans, Korean Americans, Filipino Americans, and Native Hawaiians increased their respective percentages between 1990 and 2000, but the relative positions of groups are virtually the same as in 2000, especially in relation to the Hawai'i median.

## CHAPTER 5

1. The late historian Yuji Ichioka is often credited with creating the term "Asian American" in 1968 when the Asian American Political Alliance was organized at the University of California, Berkeley.

2. In general, Smith (1985: 497) maintains that race and ethnic relations "scholars [need] to tackle the conditions and structures of authority and power that together provide the framework, bases, content and dynamic elements of all interracial and interethnic contexts."

3. I express my *mahalo* (thanks) to Kawika Tengan for reading an earlier draft of this section and discussing his very useful comments with me.

4. I agree with Eva Marie Garroutte (2003: 137) who discusses the notion of tradition in relation to Native American peoples: " '[T]radition' does not equate to some petrified pattern of life: to what The People have always, unchangingly done. American Indian communities have found so many and such varied solutions to the problems of survival that individuals living in different historic periods might have difficulty even recognizing their ancestors."

5. Another term in Hawaiian used to represent their native status in Hawai'i is *kanaka o'iwi*, literally "people of the bone."

6. I thank Michael Omi for bringing Eva Marie Garroutte's work to my attention.

7. Generally, a birth certificate that indicates the ancestry of one's parents suffices.

8. In 1997 Rice, perhaps with Goemans's legal services, filed two federal lawsuits against Kamehameha's admissons policy for violating civil rights laws and tax laws. He later withdrew those suits because he lacked sufficient funds to pursue them at the same time as his suit against the Office of Hawaiian Affairs (OHA) (Okamura 2002: 142).

9. Indicative of how easily some non-Hawaiians claim to be Native Hawaiian, Santos remarked upon the resolution of her and her son's lawsuit, "We're very proud that we are Hawaiians," although they are not (cited in Daysog 2003b).

10. In 2002 Goemans submitted several complaints to the Bush administration concerning a $400 million federal loan to provide fiber-optic lines to 20,000 Native Hawaiians living on Hawaiian Home Lands administered by the state Department of Hawaiian Home Lands (DHHL), a four-hundred-home DHHL project he claimed violated the U.S. Fair Housing Act, and the federal tax-exempt status of the Kamehameha Schools (Dunford 2004: A8).

11. The suit was filed in 2002 by William Burgess, the attorney in previous suits against Native Hawaiian rights following the Rice decision. Burgess and his wife, Sandra, who is Hawaiian, are leaders of the "Aloha for All" group that seeks to eliminate state agencies for Native Hawaiians. On their Web site (http://aloha4all.org), they contend: "Hawaii's gift to the world is the Aloha spirit embodied daily in the beautiful people of many races living here in relative harmony. . . . It is not in keeping with the spirit of Aloha for the government to give one racial group land or money or special privileges or preferences from which all other racial groups in Hawaii are excluded."

12. The protests were held to mark the one-hundredth anniversary of the overthrow of the Hawaiian monarchy.

13. According to a U.S. Department of Education spokesperson, the investigation was put on temporary hold because of several then pending court cases involving Native Hawaiians (Gima 2005a: A6).

14. The information that follows is from Mary Yu Danico's two publications on 1.5-generation Korean Americans in Hawai'i (2002, 2004). I thank her for reading and commenting on a draft of this section.

15. The cartoon drawings that accompanied the article are of adult males and children but not adult females.

16. Again invoking a humorous perspective on local culture and identity, the cover of the magazine has a cartoonish caricature of a dumbfounded Dobelle perusing a book with the same title as the article in a parody of the familiar yellow-and-black-covered books on various technical subjects "for Dummies."

17. The "Grinds: The foods we love" category is evident in the business tip to "Come hungry" because "In Hawaii, the only thing that bonds people faster than the 'What high school you went?' routine is food. Local people love food."

18. Shops at Ala Moana Center that can be found at many other shopping malls across America include Abercrombie & Fitch, Banana Republic, Disney Store, Gucci, Louis Vuitton, Neiman Marcus, Polo Ralph Lauren, and Williams-Sonoma.

19. Very small numbers in the sample were from other ethnic groups, including White, African American, and Vietnamese American, or said they represented various combinations of ethnic groups such as Chinese and White.

20. The aloha spirit can be defined as a cultural norm that emphasizes relating to others in a caring and considerate manner.

21. Although not a major racial group in Hawai'i in terms of population, African Americans are another group that historically has not been viewed as local.

**CHAPTER 6**

1. Another reason advanced for Hirono's defeat is that many Japanese Americans, not attracted to her candidacy, did not vote for her, but neither did they vote for Lingle. Evidence to support this thesis is the relatively low voter turnout in precincts with a

majority of Japanese American residents, such as Pearl City and Manoa. Also, Lingle won the 2002 election with several thousand fewer votes than she had when she lost in 1998.

2. When Ariyoshi left office in 1986, he remarked that he would very likely be the last Japanese American elected governor for a long while. While I do not know the reasons for his prediction, which still is correct, I am sure he was very aware of the anti-Japanese backlash in the larger society to which he had contributed by serving three four-year terms. The state legislature subsequently passed a bill limiting the governor to two consecutive terms in office.

3. Odo and Yim (1993: 228) introduced the notion of Japanese Americans acting defensively "by circling the wagons."

4. I thank Michael Omi for raising this question, which resulted in my thinking about how local identity and culture have decentered Whiteness in Hawai'i.

5. The thirteen kachikan are *koko* (filial piety), *on* (debt of gratitude), *gaman* (quiet endurance), *ganbari* (persistence), *shikata ga nai* (acceptance with resignation), *kansha* (gratitude), *chugi* (loyalty), *sekinin* (responsibility), *haji* (shame), *hokori* (pride), *meiyo* (honor), *giri* (sense of duty), and *gisei* (sacrifice) (Japanese Cultural Center of Hawai'i 2001).

6. Uesugi supposedly was upset with a possible change in his work assignment.

7. Hagino (1977: 23) explained: "Palaka is a cloth that has a fascinating, weaving pattern of lines and colors. Its criss-cross pattern represents the interlocking strength of all our peoples to make one people and one culture. United, we can meet any challenge."

8. Waters (1990: 147) maintained that the other major factor in the persistence of symbolic ethnicity is that it meets a need that Americans have for community on the one hand, and for individuality on the other.

9. Chinese introduced the practice of lighting firecrackers on New Year's Day, but on the first day of the Chinese New Year. Japanese Americans (and other ethnic groups) adopted the custom and observe it on January 1, a much more significant holiday for them. Japanese American families traditionally eat ozoni together on the morning of New Year's Day, as families also do in Japan. It is not consumed at any other time during the year.

10. I conclude that the mother's friend is Haole based on textual evidence, such as his unfamiliarity with pidgin English.

11. Since I was aware that my class lectures might influence the students' responses, I conducted the survey in the third week of the course.

12. There were twenty-nine non-yonsei Japanese—including students from Japan or Japanese Americans who did not provide information on their generational status—who participated in the survey. Fifty-six non-Japanese students also completed the survey form but answered different questions.

13. The other response categories that were mentioned much less frequently included "means being both Japanese and American," "doesn't mean that much," and "means being more American."

14. Bon or obon dances are held at Buddhist temples throughout the islands during the summer and are popular community events among Japanese Americans, most of whom attend not to dance but to eat the variety of foods that are offered for sale. According to traditional Japanese belief, bon dances are held to welcome back the spirits of deceased ancestors.

15. The other response categories that were mentioned less frequently included being "both Japanese and American" and consumption of Japanese food.

16. Given their long-term presence in Hawai'i, privileged socioeconomic status, and substantial intermarriage with other ethnic groups, Chinese Americans in Hawai'i—but not those in the continental United States because of their majority immigrant population—are very likely another ethnic group that expresses its ethnic identity symbolically.

17. While Okinawan Americans can claim to be Japanese American, and many do, I will make a distinction between these two ethnic groups.

18. According to sociologist Joyce Chinen (2006), the change in name of the association was intended so that it would be more inclusive—that is, less descent-based and more community-based—because many of the most active members of Okinawan American organizations are Japanese American or from other ethnic groups. I thank her for providing me with this information, for reading a draft of this section on Uchinanchu identity, and for her comments and discussions.

19. Growing up in Hawai'i in the 1950s and early 1960s, two of my best friends were Okinawan American, but I did not know this until I was in my mid-twenties when one of them mentioned it to me. Another reason for my lack of knowledge of my friends' ethnicity is because my parents never said anything disparaging about Okinawan Americans.

20. I am not certain why Japanese Americans generally do not have the same kind of kinship ties with relatives in Japan that many Okinawan Americans continue to have, even though Japanese continued to immigrate to Hawai'i during the same period as Okinawans until 1924.

21. Diasporic identity and connections have been described among second-generation Filipino Americans in California by Espiritu (1994) and Strobel (1996).

22. The discussion that follows is based on information from Arakaki (2002).

23. The most recent Worldwide Uchinanchu Festivals were held in Okinawa in 2006 and Honolulu in 2003.

24. Sports leagues, such as a volleyball league sponsored by the Hawaii United Okinawa Association (HUOA), have nothing to do with Okinawan or Okinawan American culture, but do provide a means for regularly interacting with other Okinawan Americans. Such interactions, which otherwise might not occur on a daily basis except with relatives, can result in greater awareness and maintenance of their ethnic identity.

## CHAPTER 7

1. The then new social sciences building at UH Manoa was initially named for Stanley Porteus in 1976, presumably in recognition of his academic achievements. However, after protests by students and faculty in the late 1990s that emphasized the racist nature of Porteus's publications, the UH Board of Regents rescinded the naming of the building for him. It is now called Saunders Hall in memory of Allan and Marion Saunders.

2. Most of the blame for this strike was placed upon Japanese workers who were depicted by the Honolulu press and the planters as seeking to take over Hawai'i through the strike for the Japanese Empire (Okamura 2000: 131). Porteus and Babcock's (1926: 52) description of Japanese was clearly intended as a criticism of their labor organizing efforts rather than as a psychological analysis of their temperament: "collectively they are intensely race-conscious, ready to combine for any purposes of group advancement, aggressive and rather untrustworthy when self-interest is in question."

3. Nearly forty years after Vinacke's study, Trudy Ann Narikiyo (1987) replicated his research for her master's thesis in psychology. She also used UH Manoa students as her

respondents and the same methodology of having them characterize various ethnic groups in Hawai'i by selecting terms from a list of traits or by adding others not on the list. Narikiyo (1987: 22–23) found that non-Filipinos assigned the following characteristics to Filipino Americans: "flashy," "lower class," "uneducated," "talkative," and "religious," all of which except the latter can be considered negative to varying degrees. Most of these traits are associated primarily with Filipino immigrants rather than with Hawai'i-born Filipinos and are an indication of how Filipino Americans are generally perceived based on stereotypes that originate with immigrant Filipinos. Narikiyo's findings also demonstrate the persistence of several demeaning stereotypes of Filipino Americans (flashy, uneducated, talkative) over a forty-year period since Vinacke's study and thus the great difficulty of changing others' misperceptions of them.

4. Hormann (1953: 4) stated that three Native Hawaiians were hanged since the annexation of Hawai'i in 1898, but I have been able to find references only to two of them: Kapea on April 11, 1898 and Solomon Mahoe on August 5, 1937. However, another Native Hawaiian, named Noa, was hanged on December 13, 1897 before annexation. Hormann also noted the prevalent view in the 1950s, held by Native Hawaiians as well as non-Hawaiians according to him, that none of the former could be executed because of the "political pressure" they could exert to prevent it from occurring. This political influence was very likely based on the alliance between Haoles and some Native Hawaiians in maintaining Republican control of the territory.

5. Many island residents familiar with the territorial period cite the Massie-Kahahawai case of 1931–1932 as a prime example of how Haoles were literally able to get away with murder. Lieutenant Thomas Massie, together with two navy sailors and his mother-in-law, were convicted of manslaughter in the shooting and beating death of Joe Kahahawai, a young Native Hawaiian (Stannard 2005). Kahahawai was one of five "local" youths accused in 1931 of raping Thalia Massie, the twenty-year-old wife of Lieutenant Massie, but the jury in their trial was deadlocked, and a mistrial was declared (Rosa 2000). A few months later, Massie and his accomplices kidnapped, beat, and finally shot Kahahawai to death. After tremendous pressure was applied on the territorial governor Lawrence Judd to pardon them, including by more than one hundred members of the U.S. House of Representatives, he commuted their sentence from ten years of hard labor to one hour in custody (Kotani 1985: 72).

6. The information in this paragraph is from the "Before the Needles" Web site that has a table on "Hawaii Executions," http://users.bestweb.net/~rg/execution/hawaii.htm.

7. Of the fifteen cases for which I have been able to determine the weapon, if any, that was used, a knife was employed in twelve murders, including a cane knife (machete) in four cases. A gun was used in two crimes and a pair of scissors in another.

8. Historian Dawn Mabalon (2003: 258) cites a 1929 case in Vallejo, California in which a thirty-six-year-old Filipino killed a fourteen-year-old girl and then himself after she declined his advances. She added, "Intense jealousies over women fueled fistfights and stabbings among Filipinos."

9. The term "amok" is Malay in origin, and amok behavior was historically reported in Malaysia. Over time it has come to refer generically to incidents of "violent homicidal aggression" by an individual using a weapon. While he did not refer to it as running amok, Bulosan (1973: 176) described an incident in Seattle that could be considered such: "The Filipino had gone completely crazy. He was running up and down the sidewalk with a long knife, stabbing everyone in his way. . . . He had killed eight and wounded sixteen before the policemen caught him."

10. Local comedian Augie T provides a similar justification for ethnic humor: "On the mainland, you can't do ethnic jokes, people get all offended . . . But us local people, we live on an island, we real open, we share everything. . . . And that's the beauty of Hawai'i. We can laugh at ourselves" (cited in Labrador 2004: 309).

11. In an interview with a Filipino American community newspaper, the *Hawai'i Filipino Chronicle*, DeLima contended that ethnic humor promotes closer ethnic relations, if not world peace: "For me, when people can laugh at themselves, the world will be a much better place to live. . . . If you learn to laugh at them ['idiosyncrasies' of different ethnic groups], then there won't be any walls built between the different ethnic groups" (cited in Quidilla and Galolo 1994: 4). Unfortunately, under the influence of the Hawai'i multicultural model, many, if not most, island residents, including academics, journalists, and the general public, actually believe this absurd argument to be true.

12. Hammer's other CD, *Caught in the Act* (1996), includes three routines that have Filipino immigrant characters who speak in heavily accented English and are portrayed as not very bright insofar as they are easily confused by others.

13. Yet another gendered model minority representation of Filipino Americans by the news media is evident in a special series in commemoration of the centennial of Filipino immigration to Hawai'i by the *Honolulu Advertiser* (Toth 2006: A1). Titled "Filipinos in Hawai'i 100 Years, Far from Sakada [plantation labor recruit] Roots," the first article nonetheless featured a front-page photo of an immigrant Filipino woman at work as a "guest services agent" at a large Waikiki hotel. The caption of the picture stated, "She has a degree in economics, but hopes to get a nursing degree and work as a registered nurse. 'It's higher pay,' she said." The photo and caption depict Filipino Americans as hardworking and persevering immigrants who, even with a college degree, still seek to advance themselves through further education.

14. *Balut* is duck embryo boiled in the shell.

15. While Felix is not specifically identified as Filipino American in the poem, Candace Fujikane (1997: 54) contends that he is based on textual evidence.

16. I resigned my position as a member of the board of the Association for Asian American Studies in 1998 in protest against a similar statement made by a board member in an e-mail message sent to the board, this time in reference to Filipino American inability to read and teach *Blu's Hanging*.

17. The article is based on a chapter in Labrador's doctoral dissertation in anthropology, "Constructing 'Home' and 'Homeland': Identity-Making among Filipinos in Hawai'i" (2003), from the University of California, Los Angeles.

18. This Philippine focus is evident from the five parts of the "historical narrative" of the presentation that consisted of: the Spanish colonial period; American colonial rule; the "questioning" of Philippine national identity during the 1960s and 1970s; martial law under former Philippine dictator Ferdinand Marcos; and the post-Marcos period (Labrador 2002: 295–296).

19. Espiritu (2003: 183, emphasis added) quotes a Filipino immigrant who astutely realized that he was being blamed for the feelings of shame held by American-born Filipinos while in high school in San Diego: "To my surprise, I offended many Filipinos because I was an 'FOB'—'fresh off the boat.' I was ridiculed because my accent reminded them of their parents. *It was their shame coming out at my expense.* I was a reminder of the image they hate, part of themselves. The overt racism from the Filipino Americans broke my heart."

**CHAPTER 8**

1. Price and his cohost, Michael W. Perry, who is White, have the highest-rated radio program in Hawai'i. The following week, after Price apologized on air to Hooser for his comments, Perry responded: "You're crazy, you don't have to apologize. I am the blue-eyed member of this morning team. This was not about racism; it was about hypocrisy" (cited in Au 2007: A6). Perry maintained that the interview with Hooser was more concerned with the "dysfunctional state Senate" than with race.

# References


Adams, Romanzo C. 1933. *The Peoples of Hawaii.* Honolulu: American Council, Institute of Pacific Relations.

———. 1936. Race Relations in Hawaii (A Summary Statement). *Social Process in Hawaii* 2:56.

———. 1937. *Interracial Marriage in Hawaii.* New York: Macmillan.

Adams, Romanzo C., T. M. Livesay, and E. H. Van Winkle. 1925. *The Peoples of Hawaii: A Statistical Study.* Honolulu: Institute of Pacific Relations.

"AJA of the Year, Bob Watada." 2003. *Hawai'i Herald,* December 19, p. A6.

"Akaka Bill Faces Crucial Vote." 2006. *Honolulu Star-Bulletin,* June 7.

Alba, Richard D. 1985. *Italian Americans: Into the Twilight of Ethnicity.* Englewood Cliffs, NJ: Prentice-Hall.

———. 1990. *Ethnic Identity: The Transformation of White America.* New Haven: Yale University Press.

Alcantara, Ruben R. 1973. The Filipino Community in Waialua. PhD dissertation (American Studies), University of Hawai'i.

Altonn, Helen. 1999. "Years of Neglect Cripple UH-Manoa." *Honolulu Star-Bulletin,* April 22, pp. A1, A8.

Ancheta, Angelo N. 2003. *Race, Rights, and the Asian American Experience.* New Brunswick, NJ: Rutgers University Press.

Antone, Rod. 2002. "Murder Victim's Family Pleads for Information." *Honolulu Star-Bulletin,* February 27, pp. A1, A9.

Apgar, Sally. 2005a. "Con: Diverse Groups Fight 'American Apartheid.'" *Honolulu Star-Bulletin,* July 18, p. A6.

———. 2005b. "Activists Fear Ripple Effect for Hawaiian Issues." *Honolulu Star-Bulletin,* August 3, p. A7.

———. 2005c. "Appeals Court Lets Group Challenge State Funding of OHA." *Honolulu Star-Bulletin*, August 31, pp. A1, A6.

———. 2006. "Court Will Rehear School Case." *Honolulu Star-Bulletin*, February 23.

Arakaki, Makoto. 2002. Hawai'i *Uchinanchu* and Okinawa: *Uchinanchu* Spirit and the Formation of a Transnational Identity. In *Okinawa Diaspora*, ed. Ronald Y. Nakasone. Honolulu: University of Hawai'i Press.

Asian American Journalists Association. 2006. http://www.aaja.org/programs/convention06/.

Au, Laurie. 2007. "KSSK's Sincerity Questioned." *Honolulu Star-Bulletin*, May 8, p. A6.

Badua, Anna Belle. 2001. Filipino Identity: Being Ashamed. Paper submitted for Ethnic Studies 301 (Ethnic Identity), University of Hawai'i, fall.

Bakalian, Amy P. 1993. *Armenian Americans: From Being to Feeling Armenian*. New Brunswick, NJ: Transaction Publishers.

Balce, Nerissa S. 2006. Filipino Bodies, Lynching, and the Language of Empire. In *Positively No Filipinos Allowed*, eds. A. T. Tiongson, Jr., E. V. Gutierrez, and R. V. Gutierrez, pp. 43–60. Philadelphia: Temple University Press.

Banton, Michael. 1980. Ethnic Groups and the Theory of Rational Choice. In *Sociological Theories: Race and Colonialism*, pp. 475–499. Paris: United Nations Educational, Scientific and Cultural Organization (UNESCO).

———. 1998. *Racial Theories*. New York: Cambridge University Press.

Barayuga, Debra. 2005a. "Kamehameha Will Fight Ruling." *Honolulu Star-Bulletin*, August 3, pp. A1, A7.

———. 2005b. "Community." *Honolulu Star-Bulletin*, November 20.

———. 2006. "Kamehameha Rejoices over Ruling." *Honolulu Star-Bulletin*, December 6.

Barrett, Greg, and Beverly Creamer. 1996. "Chasing Dreams, Choosing Exile." *Honolulu Advertiser*, June 16, pp. A1–A2.

Beechert, Edward D. 1985. *Working in Hawaii: A Labor History*. Honolulu: University of Hawai'i Press.

Before the Needles. n.d. Hawaii Executions (table), http://users.bestweb.net/~rg/execution/hawaii.htm.

Bernardo, Rosemarie. 2005a. "HSTA Lauds New Two-Year Contract." *Honolulu Star-Bulletin*, April 25, pp. A1, A6.

———. 2005b. "Caring." *Honolulu Star-Bulletin*, November 22.

Bernstein, J., H. Boushey, E. McNichol, and R. Zahradnik. 2002. *Pulling Apart: A State-by-State Analysis of Income Trends*. Washington, DC: Center on Budget and Policy Priorities.

Blaisdell, Kekuni. 1989. "Historical and Cultural Aspects of Native Hawaiian Health." *Social Process in Hawai'i* 32:1–21.

Borreca, Richard. 2005. "OHA Poll Shows Strong Community Support of Akaka Bill." *Honolulu Star-Bulletin*, August 23.

Boylan, Peter, and Gordon Pang. 2007. "Hate Crime Not Ruled Out in Waikele Assault." *Honolulu Advertiser*, February 27.

Brannon, Johnny. 2005a. "Democrats Control Most School-Repair Money, Critics Say." *Honolulu Advertiser*, June 5, p. A7.

———. 2005b. "Politicians Pick Which Schools to Fix, Not DOE." *Honolulu Advertiser*, June 5, pp. A1, A6.

Brubaker, Rogers. 2004. *Ethnicity without Groups*. Cambridge: Harvard University Press.

Bulosan, Carlos. 1973 [1946]. *America Is in the Heart*. Seattle: University of Washington Press.

Bumanglag, Brenda. 1996. Filipino Identity in Hawai'i. Paper submitted for Ethnic Studies 333 (Filipinos in Hawai'i), University of Hawai'i, fall.

Burris, Jerry. 2007. "Killer's Korean Ancestry Has No Real Relevance." *Honolulu Advertiser*, April 22, p. A31.

Cariaga, Roman R. 1935. "Filipinos in Honolulu." *Social Science* 10:39–46.

———. 1937. *The Filipinos in Hawaii: Economic and Social Conditions, 1906–1936*. Honolulu: Filipino Public Relations Bureau.

———. 1974 [1936]. The Filipinos in Hawaii: A Study of Their Social and Economic Conditions. Master's thesis (Anthropology), University of Hawai'i.

Cataluna, Lee. 2002. "You Know You're a Malihini Starting to Turn Local When . . ." *Honolulu Advertiser*, May 5, p. A25.

Cerulo, Karen A. 1997. "Identity Construction: New Issues, New Directions." *Annual Reviews in Sociology* 23:385–409.

Chinen, Joyce. 2006. Personal communication, May 8.

Choo, David. 2004. "Local Style for Lolos." *Hawaii Business*, September, pp. 24–26, 29.

Chuh, Kandice. 2003. *Imagine Otherwise: On Asian Americanist Critique*. Durham, NC: Duke University Press.

Cornell, Stephen, and Donald Hartmann. 1998. *Ethnicity and Race, Making Identities in a Changing World*. Thousand Oaks, CA: Pine Forge Press.

Cox, Oliver C. 1948. *Caste, Class and Race: A Study in Social Dynamics*. Garden City, NY: Doubleday.

Creamer, Beverly. 2005. " 'Easy to Get Lost' at Biggest Public School." *Honolulu Advertiser*, October 9, pp. A1, A7.

———. 2006. "At Graduation Time, Dropouts Left Behind." *Honolulu Advertiser*, May 28, pp. A1, A10–A11.

Danico, Mary Y. 2002. Internalized Stereotypes and Shame: The Struggles of 1.5 Generation Korean Americans in Hawai'i. In *Contemporary Asian American Communities: Intersections and Divergences*, eds. Linda Vo and Rick Bonus, pp. 147–160. Philadelphia: Temple University Press.

———. 2004. *The 1.5 Generation: Becoming Korean American in Hawai'i*. Honolulu: University of Hawai'i Press.

———. 2005. 1.5 Generation Korean American Identity. Lecture, Ethnic Studies 301, University of Hawai'i, August 9.

Da Silva, Alexandre. 2007. "Suits Challenge Legality of Hawaiian Programs." *Honolulu Star-Bulletin*, May 15, p. A6.

Daysog, Rick. 2003a. "Company Settles Political Donation Complaint." *Honolulu Star-Bulletin*, May 2, p. A3.

———. 2003b. "School Lets Non-Hawaiian Stay." *Honolulu Star-Bulletin*, November 29, http://starbulletin.com/2003/11/29/news/story3.html.

———. 2003c. "Kauai Student's Lineage at Center of Controversy." *Honolulu Star-Bulletin*, December 23, http://starbulletin.com/2003/12/23/news/story7.html.

DeLima, Frank. 1991. *Frank DeLima's Joke Book*. Honolulu: Bess Press.

———. 1993. *DeLima's Jurassic Classics*. Audiocassette, Pocholinga Productions.

———. 1995. *Babooze*. Sound disc, Pocholinga Productions.

DePledge, Derrick. 2005. "Help Sought in Finding Teachers." *Honolulu Advertiser*, January 22, p. B5.

DePledge, Derrick, and Beverly Creamer. 2004. "Dobelle Flunked 'Locals 101.'" *Honolulu Advertiser*, June 20.

DePledge, Derrick, and Treena Shapiro. 2006. "State Legislators Close Out 'A Great Year.'" *Honolulu Advertiser*, May 5.

Dirlik, Arif. 1996. The Global in the Local. In *Global/Local: Cultural Production and the Transnational Imaginary*, eds. Rob Wilson and Wimal Dissanayake. Durham, NC: Duke University Press.

Donnelly, Christine. 1996. "Report Flunks Hawaii on School Funding." *Honolulu Star-Bulletin*, April 4, pp. A1, A6.

Dunford, Bruce. 2004. "Tuition Waiver at UH Probed." *Honolulu Star-Bulletin*, March 17, pp. A1, A8.

Dyson, Michael E. 2004. The Liberal Theory of Race. In *The Michael Eric Dyson Reader*, pp. 37–45. New York: Basic Civitas Books.

Edles, Laura D. 2004. "Rethinking 'Race,' 'Ethnicity' and 'Culture': Is Hawai'i the 'Model Minority' State?" *Ethnic and Racial Studies* 27(1):37–68.

Equal Employment Opportunity and Affirmative Action Office. n.d. UHM Tenured and Tenure Track Faculty, Change from 1983–1994 (table).

Espiritu, Yen L. 1992. *Asian American Panethnicity: Bridging Institutions and Identities.* Philadelphia: Temple University Press.

———. 1994. "The Intersection of Race, Ethnicity and Class: The Multiple Identities of Second-Generation Filipinos." *Identities* 1(2–3):249–273.

———. 2003. *Homebound: Filipino American Lives across Cultures, Communities, and Countries.* Berkeley: University of California Press.

Espiritu, Yen L., and Michael Omi. 2000. "Who Are You Calling Asian?" Shifting Identity Claims, Racial Classifications, and the Census. In *The State of Asian Pacific America: Transforming Race Relations,* ed. Paul M. Ong, pp. 43–101. Los Angeles: LEAP Asian Pacific American Public Policy Institute and UCLA Asian American Studies Center.

Essoyan, Susan. 2005. "Overhaul in School Spending Is Met by Debate." *Honolulu Star-Bulletin,* January 14.

Evangelista, Bennette. 1994. "Killing Us Softly with These Words." *Fil-Am Courier*, March, p. 6.

"Expiates Murder on the Gallows." 1914. *Pacific Commercial Advertiser*, April 8.

"Filipino Hanged for Murder Goes to Death Steadily." 1917. *Honolulu Star-Bulletin*, November 16.

"Filipino Youth Is Hanged for Girl's Murder." 1932. *Honolulu Star-Bulletin*, July 28, p. 1.

"Filipinos Expiate Murders." 1913. *Honolulu Star-Bulletin*, July 8, p. 8.

"Filipinos Pay Death Penalty; Brave to Last." 1915. *Honolulu Star-Bulletin*, October 5, pp. 1–2.

First Worldwide Uchinanchu Conference Booklet Committee. 2003. *First Worldwide Uchinanchu Conference: Sharing Uchinanchu Aloha.* Honolulu: the Committee.

Franco, Robert W. 1987. Samoans in Hawaii: A Demographic Profile. Population Institute, East-West Center, Honolulu, HI.

Fu, Xuanning, and Tim B. Heaton. 1997. *Interracial Marriage in Hawaii, 1983–1994.* Lewiston, NY: Edwin Mellen Press.

Fuchs, Lawrence. 1961. *Hawaii Pono: A Social History.* New York: Harcourt, Brace & World.

Fujikane, Candace. 1997. "Reimagining Development and the Local in Lois-Ann Yamanaka's *Saturday Night at the Pahala Theatre.*" In *Women in Hawai'i: Sites, Identities, Voices*, eds. Joyce N. Chinen et al. *Social Process in Hawai'i* 38:40–61.

———. 1998. "*Blu's Hanging* and the Responsibilities Faced by Local Readers and Writers." *Hawai'i Herald*, January 16, pp. A9–A11.

———. 2000. "Sweeping Racism under the Rug of 'Censorship': The Controversy over Lois-Ann Yamanaka's *Blu's Hanging.*" *Amerasia Journal* 26(2):158–194.

"Ganal Case Jury Rightly Rejected 'Amok' Defense." 1993. *Honolulu Star-Bulletin*, April 9, p. A10.

Gans, Herbert. 1979. "Symbolic Ethnicity: The Future of Ethnic Groups and Cultures in America." *Ethnic and Racial Studies* 2(1):1–20.

———. 1992. "Comment: Ethnic Invention and Acculturation: A Bumpy-Line Approach." *Journal of American Ethnic History* (fall):42–52.

Garroutte, Eva M. 2003. *Real Indians: Identity and the Survival of Native America.* Berkeley: University of California Press.

Gima, Craig. 2004. "State Population Increased at the 10th-Fastest Pace in the Nation." *Honolulu Star-Bulletin*, April 9, p. A3.

———. 2005a. "UH Officials Say Hawaiian Waivers Will Continue." *Honolulu Star-Bulletin*, August 3, p. A6.

———. 2005b. "Giving Thanks." *Honolulu Star-Bulletin*, November 24.

———. 2007. "UH-Manoa and Hilo Breaking Caps on Enrollment." *Honolulu Star-Bulletin*, June 7, p. A1.

"Girl's Slayer to Be Hanged Tomorrow." 1921. *Honolulu Star-Bulletin*, June 2.

Glazer, Nathan and Daniel P. Moynihan. 1970. *Beyond the Melting Pot.* Cambridge, MA: MIT Press.

Glenn, Evelyn N. 2002. *Unequal Freedom: How Race and Gender Shaped American Citizenship and Labor.* Cambridge: Harvard University Press.

Godvin, Tara. 2005. "UH Raises Forecast for State Economy." *Honolulu Advertiser*, June 3.

Gonzalves, Theodore. 1995. "The Show Must Go On: Production Notes on the Pilipino Cultural Night." *Critical Mass: A Journal of Asian American Cultural Criticism* 2(2):129–144.

Gordon, Milton M. 1964. *Assimilation in American Life: The Role of Race, Religion, and National Origins.* New York: Oxford University Press.

Grant, Glen, and Dennis Ogawa. 1993. "Living Proof: Is Hawai'i the Answer?" In *Interminority Affairs in the U.S.: Pluralism at the Crossroads*, ed. Peter I. Rose. *Annals of the American Academy of Political and Social Science* 530:137–154.

Griffin, John. 2004. "Hawai'i's Ethnic Rainbow." *Honolulu Advertiser*, March 14, pp. B1, B4.

Haas, Michael. 1998. Conclusion. In *Multicultural Hawai'i: The Fabric of a Multiethnic Society*, ed. M. Haas, pp. 285–306. New York: Garland Publishing.

Hagino, David. 1977. Palaka Power. Unpublished paper.

Hall, Stuart. 2000. Conclusion: The Multi-cultural Question. In *Un/Settled Multiculturalisms: Diasporas, Entanglements, Transruptions*, ed. Barnor Hesse. London: Zed Books.

Hammer, Gregg. 1996. *Caught in the Act.* Sound disc, Quiet Storm Records.

———. 1998. *Plain Brown Wrapper.* Sound disc, Neos Productions.

Hawai'i Department of Business and Economic Development and Tourism. 1993. *The State of Hawai'i Data Book 1992*. Table 1.27, Ethnic Stock by Military Status: 1992. Honolulu: the Department.

———. 1997. *The State of Hawai'i Data Book 1996*. Table 1.27, Ethnic Stock by Military Status: 1996. Honolulu: the Department.

———. 2001. *The State of Hawai'i Data Book 2000*. Table 1.32, Ethnic Stock by Counties: 2000, Honolulu: the Department. http://www.hawaii.gov/dbedt/.

———. 2002. *The State of Hawai'i Data Book 2001*. Table 1.35, Ancestry: 2000, Honolulu: the Department. http://www.hawaii.gov/dbedt/.

———. 2003a. *The State of Hawai'i Data Book 2002*. Table 1.03, Population by Military Status for Counties and Islands, State of Hawaii: 2000, Honolulu: the Department. http://www.hawaii.gov/dbedt.

———. 2003b. *The State of Hawai'i Data Book 2002*. Table 1.32, Race and Hispanic Origin by Counties: 2000, Honolulu: the Department. http://www.hawaii.gov/dbedt/.

———. 2004. *The State of Hawai'i Data Book 2003*, Honolulu: the Department. http://www.hawaii.gov/dbedt/.

———. 2005. *The State of Hawai'i Data Book 2004*. Table 1.35, Ranking of Races: 2000; Table 1.58, Immigrants Admitted, by Country of Birth: 1999 to 2003, Honolulu: the Department. http://www.hawaii.gov/dbedt/.

Hawaii Department of Planning and Economic Development. 1976. Hawaii's Immigrants. Statistical Report No. 132.

"Hawaii Jobless Rate Drops to 2.4 Percent." 2006. *Honolulu Star-Bulletin*, March 11, p. C1.

*Hawaii Revised Statutes*. 1993. Honolulu: State of Hawai'i.

*Hawaii's Comedy Stars*. 1997. Videocassette, Quiet Storm Records.

"Hawaii's Economy Dead Last in 1990s." 2001. *Honolulu Star-Bulletin*, June 4, pp. A1, A12.

Hayashi, Brandon J. 2002. "Are Traditional Values Relevant?" *Hawai'i Herald*, April 5, pp. A8–A9.

Hench, Virginia E. 2007. " 'Hate': Two Families Violently Collide." *Honolulu Advertiser*, April 1, pp. B1, B4.

Henry, Jacques M., and Carl L. Bankston. 1999. "Louisiana Cajun Ethnicity: Symbolic or Structural?" *Sociological Spectrum* 19:223–248.

Higa, Masanori. 1981. Okinawa in Hawaii. In *Uchinanchu: A History of Okinawans in Hawaii*, pp. 37–47. Honolulu: Ethnic Studies Oral History Project, University of Hawai'i and United Okinawan Association of Hawaii.

Hitz, Randy. 2006. "Five Steps to Improve Schools." *Honolulu Advertiser*, February 5, pp. B1, B4.

Hollinger, David A. 2000. *Postethnic America: Beyond Multiculturalism*, 10th anniversary edition. New York: Basic Books.

Hormann, Bernhard L. 1952. Race Relations in Hawaii. In *Thrum's Hawaiian Annual*. Honolulu: *Honolulu Star-Bulletin*.

———. 1953. "The Significance of the Wilder or Majors-Palakiko Case: A Study in Public Opinion." *Social Process in Hawaii* 17:1–13.

Hurley, Timothy. 2003. "Census Releases Migration Figures." *Honolulu Advertiser*, September 17, pp. A25, A31.

Inglis, Christine. 1996. *Multiculturalism: New Policy Responses to Diversity*. Most: UNESCO.

Institutional Research Office. 1991. Fall Enrollment Report, University of Hawai'i, Fall 1991. Honolulu: University of Hawai'i.

———. 1994. Fall Enrollment Report, University of Hawai'i, Fall 1994. Honolulu: University of Hawai'i.

———. 1995a. Fall Enrollment Report, University of Hawai'i, Fall 1995. Honolulu: University of Hawai'i.

———. 1995b. Fall Enrollment Report, University of Hawai'i at Manoa, Fall 1995. Honolulu: University of Hawai'i.

———. 1998. Fall Enrollment Report, University of Hawai'i, Fall 1998. Honolulu: University of Hawai'i. http://www.hawaii.edu/iro/maps.htm.

———. 1999. Fall Enrollment Report, University of Hawai'i, Fall 1999. Honolulu: University of Hawai'i. http://www.hawaii.edu/iro/maps.htm.

———. 2001a. Fall Enrollment Report, University of Hawai'i, Fall 2001. Honolulu: University of Hawai'i. http://www.hawaii.edu/iro/maps.htm.

———. 2001b. Fall Enrollment Report, University of Hawai'i at Manoa, Fall 2001. Honolulu: University of Hawai'i. http://www.hawaii.edu/iro/maps.htm.

———. 2002. Fall Enrollment Report, University of Hawai'i at Manoa, Fall 2002. Honolulu: University of Hawai'i. http://www.hawaii.edu/iro/maps.htm.

———. 2003. Fall 2003 Preliminary Classified First-Time Freshmen Highlights. Honolulu: University of Hawai'i. http://www.hawaii.edu/iro/maps.htm.

———. 2004a. Faculty and Staff Report, University of Hawai'i, Fall 2003. Honolulu: University of Hawai'i. http://www.hawaii.edu/iro/maps.htm.

———. 2004b. Graduation and Retention Rates, Peer and Benchmark Group Comparisons, University of Hawai'i at Manoa, Fall 1990 to Fall 2001 Cohorts as of 2002. Honolulu: University of Hawai'i. http://www.hawaii.edu/iro/maps.htm.

———. 2006a. Fall Enrollment Report, University of Hawai'i, Fall 2005. Honolulu: University of Hawai'i. http://www.hawaii.edu/iro/maps.htm.

———. 2006b. Fall Enrollment Report, University of Hawai'i at Manoa, Fall 2005. Honolulu: University of Hawai'i. http://www.hawaii.edu/iro/maps.htm.

———. 2006c. High School Background of First-Time Students, University of Hawai'i, Fall 2005. Honolulu: University of Hawai'i. http://www.hawaii.edu/iro/maps.htm.

Ishikawa, Juri. 2006. Yonsei Japanese American Women in Hawai'i: Multiple Perspectives on Ethnic Identity, Generation, and Gender. Master's thesis (American Studies), University of Hawai'i.

"Island Ethnic Humor Is What Keeps Us Together." 1998. *Honolulu Advertiser*.

"Isle Economy Is Rated Worst." 1992. *Honolulu Star-Bulletin*, September 16, p. D1.

Japanese Cultural Center of Hawai'i. 2001. *Kachikan (Values)*. Honolulu: the Center.

"Jealous Man Makes Mincemeat of Wife." 1913. *Pacific Commercial Advertiser*, July 16, p. 9.

Jung, Moon Kie. 2006. *Reworking Race: The Making of Hawaii's Interracial Labor Movement*. New York: Columbia University Press.

K. A. 2006. Paper submitted for Ethnic Studies 301 (Ethnic Identity), University of Hawai'i, fall.

Kakesako, Gregg K. 2000a. "Isle People: On the Move, More Feminine, More Gray." *Honolulu Star-Bulletin*, March 7, pp. A1, A8.

———. 2000b. "Study Ranks Hawaii's Schools 47th in Nation." *Honolulu Star-Bulletin*, April 14, p. A1.

Kanahele, George. 1982. "The New Hawaiians." *Social Process in Hawaii* 29:21–31.

Kaneshiro, Norman. 2002. "Uchinanchu Identity in Hawai'i." In *The Japanese American Contemporary Experience in Hawai'i*, ed. J. Y. Okamura, *Social Process in Hawai'i*, pp. 75–94.

Kivisto, Peter. 1989. The Attenuated Ethnicity of Contemporary Finnish Americans. In *The Ethnic Enigma: The Salience of Ethnicity for European Origin Groups*, ed. P. Kivisto, pp. 67–88. Philadelphia: Balch Institute Press.

Kotani, Roland. 1985. *The Japanese in Hawaii: A Century of Struggle*. Honolulu: Hawaii Hochi.

Kuper, Leo, and M. G. Smith (eds.). 1969. *Pluralism in Africa*. Berkeley: University of California Press.

Kwon, Bill. 1998. "Pak's Victory Celebration Touches Seoul." *Honolulu Star-Bulletin*, May 19, p. D1.

Labrador, Roderick. N. 2002. "Performing Identity: The Public Presentation of Culture and Ethnicity among Filipinos in Hawai'i." *Cultural Values* 6(3):287–307.

———. 2003. Constructing "Home" and "Homeland": Identity-Making among Filipinos in Hawai'i. PhD dissertation (Anthropology), University of California, Los Angeles.

———. 2004. " 'We Can Laugh at Ourselves': Hawai'i Ethnic Humor, Local Identity and the Myth of Multiculturalism." *Pragmatics* 14(2/3):291–316.

Lai, Eric, and Dennis Arguelles (eds.). 2003. *The New Face of Asian Pacific America*. San Francisco: AsianWeek.

Leong, Lavonne. 1999. "Isles Lose Many of the 'Best and Brightest.' " *Honolulu Star-Bulletin*, March 24, pp. A1, A8.

Lind, Andrew W. 1955. *Race Relations in World Perspective*. Honolulu: University of Hawai'i Press.

———. 1969. *Hawaii: The Last of the Magic Isles*. London: Oxford University Press.

———. 1980. *Hawaii's People*. Honolulu: University of Hawai'i Press.

Lipsitz, George. 1998. *The Possessive Investment in Whiteness*. Philadelphia: Temple University Press.

Loury, Glenn C. 2002. *The Anatomy of Racial Inequality*. Cambridge: Harvard University Press.

Lowe, Lisa. 1991. "Heterogeneity, Hybridity, Multiplicity: Marking Asian American Differences." *Diaspora* 1(1):24–44.

———. 1996. *Immigrant Acts: On Asian American Cultural Politics*. Durham, NC: Duke University Press.

Lynch, Russ. 1996. "Isle Economy Weakest in Nation." *Honolulu Star-Bulletin*, March 12, p. D1.

Mabalon, Dawn B. 2003. Writing Angeles Monrayo into the Pages of Pinay History. In A. Monrayo, *Tomorrow's Memories: A Diary, 1924–1928*, pp. 247–280. Honolulu: University of Hawai'i Press.

Mak, James. 2004. *Tourism and the Economy*. Honolulu: University of Hawai'i Press.

Martin, Dan. 2005a. "Study Urges $278M Boost in School Funds." *Honolulu Star-Bulletin*, January 26, pp. A1, A9.

———. 2005b. "Hawaii Schools Rated Worst." *Honolulu Star-Bulletin*, March 29, pp. A1, A6.

———. 2005c. "Isle Teacher Pay at Bottom in Survey of 50 U.S. Areas." *Honolulu Star-Bulletin*, September 16, pp. A1, A9.

———. 2005d. "Public Schools Want $453M of Surplus." *Honolulu Star-Bulletin*, September 28, pp. A1, A6.

———. 2005e. "Language Barrier." *Honolulu Star-Bulletin*, October 9, pp. A1, A12.

———. 2006. "Isle Private School Costs to Continue Steep Rise." *Honolulu Star-Bulletin*, February 26, p. A1.

Matsuoka, Jon K. 1999. Cited in "State Population Undergoing Transformation." *Honolulu Star-Bulletin*, June 1, p. A6.

Matsuoka, Jon K., Cathleen Lum, and Sonja Ome. 1998. Brain Drain or Cultural Drain? The Waning of Hawaii's Local Populace. School of Social Work, University of Hawai'i.

Miyazaki, Hirokazu. 1994. Sansei Radicals: Identity and Strategy of Japanese American Student Activists in Hawaii. In *New Visions in Asian American Studies: Diversity, Community, Power*, eds. Franklin Ng et al. Pullman: Washington State University Press.

Murayama, Milton. 1988 [1968]. *All I Asking for Is My Body*. Honolulu: University of Hawai'i Press.

Nagel, Joanne. 1994. "Constructing Ethnicity: Creating and Recreating Ethnic Identity and Culture." *Social Problems* 41:152–176.

Nakata, Bob. 1999. "The Struggles of the Waiahole-Waikane Community Association." *Social Process in Hawai'i* 39:60–73.

Narikiyo, Trudy A. 1987. Ethnic Stereotypes in Hawaii: Persistence and Change over Time. Master's thesis (Psychology), University of Hawai'i.

National Center for Public Policy and Higher Education. 2004. *Measuring Up: The National Report Card on Higher Education*. http://www.highereducation.org.

Nii, Esme, and Beverly Creamer. 1999. "Silent Struggle Yields First Fruits of Labor." *Honolulu Advertiser*, October 10, pp. A1, A8.

Nobles, Melissa. 2005. "The Myth of Latin American Multiracialism." *Daedalus* (Winter):82–87.

Nordyke, Eleanor. 1989. *The Peopling of Hawaii*. Honolulu: University of Hawai'i Press.

Odo, Franklin, and Susan Yim. 1993. Ethnicity. In *The Price of Paradise*, ed. Randy W. Roth, vol. II, pp. 225–229. Honolulu: Mutual Publishing.

Office of Institutional Research and Analysis. 1985. Management Information, Part 1. Honolulu: University of Hawai'i.

Office of the Governor, State of Hawai'i. 1977. Population Growth Policies and Strategies: A Public Opinion Survey.

Office of the Superintendent/Planning and Evaluation Office. 2004. The Superintendent's Fourteenth Annual Report on School Performance and Improvement in Hawai'i, 2003. Honolulu: Hawai'i State Department of Education.

Ohnuma, Keiko. 2002. "Local *Haole*—A Contradiction in Terms? The Dilemma of Being White, Born and Raised in Hawai'i." *Cultural Values* 6(3):273–285.

Okamura, Jonathan Y. 1980. "Local Culture and Society in Hawaii." *Amerasia Journal* 7(2):119–137.

———. 1982. Ethnicity and Ethnic Relations in Hawaii. In *Ethnicity and Interpersonal Interaction in Pluralistic Societies: A Cross-Cultural Study*, ed. David Y. H. Wu, pp. 213–235. Singapore: Maruzen Asia.

———. 1983. Immigrant and Local Filipino Perceptions of Ethnic Conflict. In *Culture, Ethnicity and Identity: Current Issues in Research*, ed. William C. McCready, pp. 241–263. New York: Academic Press.

———. 1990. Ethnicity and Stratification in Hawaii. *Operation Manong Resource Papers*, no. 1. Operation Manong Program, University of Hawai'i.

———. 1994. "Why There Are No Asian Americans in Hawai'i: The Continuing Significance of Local Identity." *Social Process in Hawai'i* 35:161–178.

———. 1998a. The Illusion of Paradise: Privileging Multiculturalism in Hawai'i. In *Making Majorities: Constituting the Nation in Japan, Korea, China, Malaysia, Fiji, Turkey, and the United States*, ed. Dru C. Gladney, pp. 264–284. Stanford: Stanford University Press.

———. 1998b. *Imagining the Filipino American Diaspora: Transnational Relations, Identities and Communities*. New York: Garland Publishing.

———. 1998c. Social Stratification. In *Multicultural Hawai'i: The Fabric of a Multiethnic Society*, ed. Michael Haas. New York: Garland Publishing.

———. 2000. "Race Relations in Hawai'i during World War II: The Noninternment of Japanese Americans." In *Whose Vision? Asian Settler Colonialism in Hawai'i*, eds. C. Fujikane and J. Y. Okamura. *Amerasia Journal* 26(2):117–141.

———. 2002. "Baseball and Beauty Queens: The Political Context of Ethnic Boundary Making in the Japanese American Community in Hawai'i." *Social Process in Hawai'i* 41:122–146.

———. 2003. "Asian American Studies in the Age of Transnationalism: Diaspora, Race, Community." *Amerasia Journal* 29(2):171–193.

———. 2005. "Minorities Hurt Most by Tuition Increases." *Honolulu Advertiser*, May 25, p. A16.

Okinawan Centennial Celebration Committee. 2000. *To Our Issei . . . Our Heartfelt Gratitude*. Honolulu: the Committee.

Oliver, Melvin, and Thomas Shapiro. 2006. *Black Wealth/White Wealth: A New Perspective on Racial Inequality*, 10th anniversary edition. New York: Routledge.

Omandam, Pat. 2001. "Maui Leads Neighbor Isles' Double-Digit Population Boom." *Honolulu Star-Bulletin*, March 20.

Omi, Michael. 1994. Out of the Melting Pot and into the Fire: Race Relations Policy. In *The State of Asian Pacific America: Economic Diversity, Issues and Policies*, ed. Paul M. Ong, pp. 199–214. Los Angeles: LEAP Asian Pacific American Public Policy Institute and UCLA Asian American Studies Center.

Omi, Michael, and Howard Winant. 1986. *Racial Formation in the United States: From the 1960s to the 1980s*. New York: Routledge.

———. 1994. *Racial Formation in the United States: From the 1960s to the 1990s*. New York: Routledge.

Ong, Paul M. (ed.). 2000. *The State of Asian Pacific America: Transforming Race Relations*. Los Angeles: LEAP Asian Pacific American Public Policy Institute and UCLA Asian American Studies Center.

Pang, Gordon. 2005. "From Korea to Ke'eaumoku." *Honolulu Advertiser*, October 16, pp. A1, A6, A7.

Park, Gene. 2007. "Law Student Accepted to UH Is Killed." *Honolulu Star-Bulletin*, May 4.

Perez, Rob. 1999. "Local E. Coast Students Lament Isle Job Market." *Honolulu Star-Bulletin*, May 3, pp. A1, A6.

———. 2004. "Lingle's Poll Finally Released in Full." *Honolulu Star-Bulletin*, April 25, pp. A1, A11.

Platte, Mark. 2007. "Waikele Story Is One Where No One Wins." *Honolulu Advertiser*, April 1, p. B3.

*The Politics of Plate Lunch*. 1997. Videocassette, Japanese American National Museum.
Porteus, Stanley, and Marjorie Babcock. 1926. *Temperament and Race*. Boston: R. G. Badger.
Pratt, Richard C. 2000. *Hawai'i Politics and Government: An American State in a Pacific World*. Lincoln: University of Nebraska Press.
Quidilla, Rex. 1997. "On Growing Up Local Filipino." *Hawaii Filipino Chronicle*, November 1, p. 10.
Quidilla, Rex, and Dennis Galolo. 1994. "Filipinos' Dilemma with Frank DeLima." *Hawaii Filipino Chronicle*, December 16, pp. 4–5.
Reinecke, John E. 1996. *The Filipino Piecemeal Sugar Strike of 1924–1925*. Honolulu: University of Hawai'i Press.
Revilla, Linda. 1996. Filipino Americans: Issues for Identity in Hawai'i. In *Pagdiriwang 1996: Legacy and Vision of Hawaii's Filipino Americans*, eds. J. Y. Okamura and R. N. Labrador, pp. 9–12. Honolulu: Center for Southeast Asian Studies.
Reyes, B. J. 2005a. "Anatomy of the Akaka Bill." *Honolulu Star-Bulletin*, July 17, p. A12.
———. 2005b. "Patriotism." *Honolulu Star-Bulletin*, November 23.
"Reyes Guilty of Murder, Is Jury Verdict." 1927. *Honolulu Advertiser*, March 29, p. 1.
Rokicki, Jaroslaw. 1995. "Euro-American Ethnicity and Polish Americans." *History of European Ideas* 20(1–3):627–636.
Rosa, John P. 2000. "Local Story: The Massie Case Narrative and the Cultural Production of Local Identity in Hawai'i." *Amerasia Journal* 26(2):93–115.
Ruel, Tim. 2005. "State Gets Low Marks Again for Economic Development." *Honolulu Star-Bulletin*, October 17, p. A1, A6.
S. A. 2002. Paper submitted for Ethnic Studies 301 (Ethnic Identity), fall.
Schaefers, Allison. 2005. "Average Hawaii Paycheck Ranks 19th." *Honolulu Star-Bulletin*, August 6, pp. A1, A6.
———. 2006. "Final 2005 Visitor Tallies Confirm Milestones." *Honolulu Star-Bulletin*, January 30, pp. C1, C3.
Segal, Dave. 2005. "Isle Unemployment Rate Falls to Lowest in 14 Years." *Honolulu Star-Bulletin*, June 18.
Seto, Benjamin. 1993. "Professors Call Amok a Killing Frenzy." *Honolulu Star-Bulletin*, April 2, p. A3.
"77% Would Pay to Aid Schools." 2003. *Honolulu Advertiser*, February 9, p. A6.
Shapiro, Treena, and Beverly Creamer. 2005. "66% of Isle Schools Miss No Child Goals." *Honolulu Advertiser*, August 9, pp. A1, A14.
Shapiro, Treena, and Jan TenBruggencate. 2005. "Schools Await Fixes: $525M and Growing." *Honolulu Advertiser*, December 12, pp. A1, A2.
"Slayer of Daughter Is Hanged." 1941. *Honolulu Star-Bulletin*, September 19.
Smith, M. G. 1965a. *The Plural Society in the British West Indies*. Berkeley: University of California Press.
———. 1965b. *Stratification in Grenada*. Berkeley: University of California Press.
———. 1975. Race and Stratification in the Caribbean. In *Corporations and Society*, pp. 271–345. Chicago: Aldine Publishing Co.
———. 1982. "Ethnicity and Ethnic Groups in America: The View from Harvard." *Ethnic and Racial Studies* 5(1):1–21.
———. 1984. *Culture, Race and Class in the Commonwealth Caribbean*. Mona, Jamaica: Department of Extra-Mural Studies, University of the West Indies.

———. 1985. "Race and Ethnic Relations as Matters of Rational Choice." *Ethnic and Racial Studies* 8(4):484–499.

"Special Report." 1993. *Honolulu Star-Bulletin*, p. A6.

Spores, John C. 1988. *Running Amok: An Historical Inquiry*. Athens: Ohio University Center for International Studies, Center for Southeast Asian Studies.

Stannard, David. 2005. *Honor Killing: How the Infamous "Massie Affair" Transformed Hawai'i*. New York: Viking.

Strobel, Leny M. 1996. "'Born-Again Filipino': Filipino American Identity and Asian Panethnicity." *Amerasia Journal* 22(2):31–53.

Takahata, Carrie. 1998. Making Yonsei. In *Growing Up Local: An Anthology of Poetry and Prose from Hawai'i*. Honolulu: Bamboo Ridge Press.

Takaki, Ronald. 1993. *A Different Mirror: A History of Multicultural America*. Boston: Little, Brown and Company.

———. 1998. "Look to Hawaii for Answers on Race." *AsianWeek*, July 16, p. 5.

"Teacher Pay Ranks 20th in the Nation." 2004. *Honolulu Star-Bulletin*, May 28, p. A3.

Teodoro, Luis. 1981. *Out of This Struggle*. Honolulu: University Press of Hawaii for Filipino 75th Anniversary Commemoration Commission.

Thernstrom, Stephan, Ann Orlov, and Oscar Handlin (eds.). 1980. *Harvard Encyclopedia of American Ethnic Groups*. Cambridge: Harvard University Press.

"33 Men, 2 Women Watch Hanging of Two Filipino Slayers at Oahu Prison." 1927. *Honolulu Star-Bulletin*, May 27, p. 1.

"A Toast to Success and Sacrifice." 2005. *Honolulu Star-Bulletin*, November 20.

Toth, Catherine E. 2006. "Economic, Political Challenges Lie Ahead." *Honolulu Advertiser*, June 21, pp. A1–A2.

Trask, Haunani-Kay. 1984. "Hawaiians, American Colonization, and the Quest for Independence." *Social Process in Hawaii* 31:101–136.

———. 2000. "Settlers of Color and 'Immigrant' Hegemony: 'Locals' in Hawai'i." In *Whose Vision? Asian Settler Colonialism in Hawai'i*, eds. C. Fujikane and J. Y. Okamura. *Amerasia Journal* 26(2):1–24.

Trinidad, Corky. 2005. "The Vanishing Filipinos." *Honolulu Star-Bulletin*, December 11.

Tulba, Augie. 2002. *Locally Disturbed*. Sound disc, KDE Records.

Ueunten, Wesley. 1989. The Maintenance of the Okinawan Ethnic Community in Hawaii. Master's thesis (Sociology), University of Hawai'i.

University of Hawai'i. 2002. University of Hawai'i System Strategic Plan: Entering the University's Second Century, 2002–2010.

University of Hawai'i at Manoa. 2002. University of Hawai'i at Manoa Strategic Plan: Defining Our Destiny, 2002–2010.

———. 2004. UH Manoa Equal Opportunity/Affirmative Action Policy Statement. http://www.hawaii.edu/myuh/manoa/fall2004/notices/equal_opportunity.htm.

University of Hawai'i Center on the Family. 2005. Quality of Life in Hawai'i.

U.S. Bureau of the Census. 1993. *Social and Economic Characteristics, Hawaii*. Washington, DC: U.S. Government Printing Office.

———. 2003. Summary File 4 of the 2000 U.S. Census. http://factfinder.census.gov/servlet/DatasetMainPageServlet?

"Vicente Kacal, Woman Slayer, Pays Penalty." 1929. *Honolulu Star-Bulletin*, March 2, p. 1.

Vinacke, William E. 1949. "Stereotyping among National-Racial Groups in Hawaii: A Study in Ethnocentrism." *Journal of Social Psychology* 30:265–291.

Vorsino, Mary. 2005a. "UH Tuition Might Rise by 123%." *Honolulu Star-Bulletin*, January 22, p. A1.

———. 2005b. " 'This Ruling Is Disgusting.' " *Honolulu Star-Bulletin*, August 7, p. A1.

———. 2005c. "Citizenship." *Honolulu Star-Bulletin*, November 21.

Waters, Mary C. 1990. *Ethnic Options: Choosing Identities in America*. Berkeley: University of California Press.

Wieviorka, Michel. 1998. "Is Multiculturalism the Solution?" *Ethnic and Racial Studies* 21(5):881–910.

Winant, Howard. 2001. *The World Is a Ghetto: Race and Democracy since World War II*. New York: Basic Books.

———. 2004. *The New Politics of Race*. Minneapolis: University of Minnesota Press.

Wist, Benjamin. 1940. *A Century of Public Education in Hawaii*. Honolulu: Hawaii Educational Review.

Wu, Frank. 2002. *Yellow: Race in America beyond Black and White*. New York: Basic Books.

Yamamoto, Eric K. 1974. From "Japanee" to Local: Community Change and the Redefinition of Sansei Identity in Hawaii. Thesis (Liberal Studies), University of Hawai'i.

———. 1999. *Interracial Justice: Conflict and Reconciliation in Post–Civil Rights America*. New York: New York University Press.

Yamanaka, Lois-Ann. 1993. *Saturday Night at the Pahala Theatre*. Honolulu: Bamboo Ridge Press.

———. 1997. *Blu's Hanging*. New York: Farrar, Straus, Giroux.

Yim, Susan. 1992a. "Hawaii's Ethnic Rainbow: Shining Colors, Side by Side." *Sunday Star-Bulletin & Advertiser*, January 5, pp. B1, B3.

———. 1992b. "Growing Up 'Hapa': Interracial Marriage, Chop Suey Society." *Sunday Star-Bulletin & Advertiser*, January 5, p. B3.

"You Know You're Local if . . ." 1996. *Honolulu Advertiser*, August 4, pp. D1, D3.

Youn, Jacy L. 2004. "How to Do Business Local Style." *Hawaii Business*, September, pp. 27–28.

Yu, Henry. 2001. *Thinking Orientals: Migration, Contact, and Exoticism in Modern America*. New York: Oxford University Press.

———. 2003. "Tiger Woods Is Not the End of History: Or, Why Sex across the Color Line Won't Save Us All." *American Historical Review*, vol. 108, issue 5. http://www.historycooperative.org.

Zenner, Walter P. 1985. Jewishness in America: Ascription and Choice. In *Ethnicity and Race in the U.S.A.: Toward the Twenty First Century*, ed. Richard D. Alba, pp. 117–133. London: Routledge and Kegan Paul.

Zhou, Min. 2004. "Are Asian Americans Becoming 'White'?" *Context* 3(1):29–37.

# Index

*Other books in the* Asian American History and Culture *series*

Teresa Williams-León and Cynthia Nakashima, eds., *The Sum of Our Parts: Mixed-Heritage Asian Americans*

Tung Pok Chin with Winifred C. Chin, *Paper Son: One Man's Story*

Amy Ling, ed., *Yellow Light: The Flowering of Asian American Arts*

Rick Bonus, *Locating Filipino Americans: Ethnicity and the Cultural Politics of Space*

Darrell Y. Hamamoto and Sandra Liu, eds., *Countervisions: Asian American Film Criticism*

Martin F. Manalansan, IV, ed., *Cultural Compass: Ethnographic Explorations of Asian America*

Ko-lin Chin, *Smuggled Chinese: Clandestine Immigration to the United States*

Evelyn Hu-DeHart, ed., *Across the Pacific: Asian Americans and Globalization*

Soo-Young Chin, *Doing What Had to Be Done: The Life Narrative of Dora Yum Kim*

Robert G. Lee, *Orientals: Asian Americans in Popular Culture*

David L. Eng and Alice Y. Hom, eds., *Q & A: Queer in Asian America*

K. Scott Wong and Sucheng Chan, eds., *Claiming America: Constructing Chinese American Identities during the Exclusion Era*

Lavina Dhingra Shankar and Rajini Srikanth, eds., *A Part, Yet Apart: South Asians in Asian America*

Jere Takahashi, *Nisei/Sansei: Shifting Japanese American Identities and Politics*

Velina Hasu Houston, ed., *But Still, Like Air, I'll Rise: New Asian American Plays*

Josephine Lee, *Performing Asian America: Race and Ethnicity on the Contemporary Stage*

Deepika Bahri and Mary Vasudeva, eds., *Between the Lines: South Asians and Postcoloniality*

E. San Juan, Jr., *The Philippine Temptation: Dialectics of Philippines-U.S. Literary Relations*

Carlos Bulosan and E. San Juan, Jr., ed., *The Cry and the Dedication*

Carlos Bulosan and E. San Juan, Jr., ed., *On Becoming Filipino: Selected Writings of Carlos Bulosan*

Vicente L. Rafael, ed., *Discrepant Histories: Translocal Essays on Filipino Cultures*

Yen Le Espiritu, *Filipino American Lives*

Paul Ong, Edna Bonacich, and Lucie Cheng, eds., *The New Asian Immigration in Los Angeles and Global Restructuring*

Chris Friday, *Organizing Asian American Labor: The Pacific Coast Canned-Salmon Industry, 1870–1942*

Sucheng Chan, ed., *Hmong Means Free: Life in Laos and America*

Timothy P. Fong, *The First Suburban Chinatown: The Remarking of Monterey Park, California*

William Wei, *The Asian American Movement*

Yen Le Espiritu, *Asian American Panethnicity*

Velina Hasu Houston, ed., *The Politics of Life*

Renqiu Yu, *To Save China, To Save Ourselves: The Chinese Hand Laundry Alliance of New York*

Shirley Geok-lin Lim and Amy Ling, eds., *Reading the Literatures of Asian America*

Karen Isaksen Leonard, *Making Ethnic Choices: California's Punjabi Mexican Americans*

Gary Y. Okihiro, *Cane Fires: The Anti-Japanese Movement in Hawaii, 1865–1945*

Sucheng Chan, *Entry Denied: Exclusion and the Chinese Community in America, 1882–1943*

**Jonathan Y. Okamura** is an Associate Professor in the Department of Ethnic Studies at the University of Hawaiʻi at Manoa. A social anthropologist, he is the author of *Imagining the Filipino American Diaspora: Transnational Relations, Identities, and Communities.*